THE LIGHTIN(

SETTING THE FLAMES OF ENCHANTMENT

BY

CHRISTOPHER PENCZAK

Book Two of the Magickal Craft Series

**COPPER
CAULDRON**
PUBLISHING

Credits

Editing: Connie Blankenship, Tina Whittle

Proofreading: Sara Bosma, Leeon Pezok, Kathy Pezok, Lindsey Piech

Cover Design and Photography: Rory McCracken

Interior Photography: Amanda Keith and T.J. Vancil

Layout & Publishing: Steve Kenson

For more information visit:
www.christopherpenczak.com
www.coppercauldronpublishing.com

ISBN 978-1-940755-13-7, First Printing

Printed in the U.S.A.

Acknowledgements

Special thanks to Steve and Adam for all their love and support in all things. To my Nunnie, Jennie D'Angelo, for letting me light votives at church. Thank you to my father, Ron, for supporting me in all things. Thank you to my first mentors in the Craft, teaching me candle magick and encouraging me to share it with others. A very special thanks to the following practitioners who have shared their thoughts and techniques on candle magick with me, in person and through their writing: Laurie Cabot, Judika Illes, Dorothy Morrison, Catherine Yronwode, Lady Rhea Rivera, Matthew Venus of Spiritus Arcanum, Glen Velez, Matthew Sawicki of Witch & Famous, Joe & Doug from Otherworld Apothecary, Stephanie Taylor Grimassi of Raven's Loft, and a very special thank you to Amanda Keith and T.J. Vancil of 3 Crows Conjure.

FIAT LVX

Other Books by Christopher Penczak

City Magick (Samuel Weiser, 2001, 2nd Edition 2012)
Spirit Allies (Samuel Weiser, 2002)
The Inner Temple of Witchcraft (Llewellyn Publications, 2002)
Gay Witchcraft (Samuel Weiser, 2003)
The Outer Temple of Witchcraft (Llewellyn Publications, 2004)
The Witch's Shield (book with CD) (Llewellyn Publications 2004)
Magick of Reiki (Llewellyn Publications 2004)
Sons of the Goddess (Llewellyn Publications 2005)
The Temple of Shamanic Witchcraft (Llewellyn Publications 2005)
Instant Magick (Llewellyn Publications 2005)
The Mystic Foundation (Llewellyn Publications 2006)
Ascension Magick (Llewellyn Publications 2007)
The Temple of High Witchcraft (Llewellyn Publications 2007)
The Living Temple of Witchcraft Volume I (Llewellyn Publications 2008)
The Living Temple of Witchcraft Volume II (Llewellyn Publications 2009)
The Witch's Coin (Llwellyn Publications 2009)
The Three Rays of Witchcraft (Copper Cauldron Publishing 2010)
The Plant Spirit Familiar (Copper Cauldron Publishing 2011)
The Witch's Heart (Llewellyn Publications 2011)
The Gates of Witchcraft (Copper Cauldron Publishing 2012)
Buddha, Christ, and Merlin (Copper Cauldron Publishing 2012)
The Feast of the Morrighan (Copper Cauldron Publishing 2012)
The Mighty Dead (Copper Cauldron Publishing 2013)
The Phosphorous Grove (Copper Cauldron Publishing, Limited Edition Hardcover
    2013, Softcover 2017)
Foundations of the Temple (Copper Cauldron Publishing 2014)
The Casting of Spells (Copper Cauldron Publishing 2016)
The Witch's Hut (Copper Cauldron Publishing 2020)

Books with Christopher Penczak

Laurie Cabot's Book of Spells and Enchantments by Laurie Cabot
    with Penny Cabot and Christopher Penczak (Copper Cauldron Publishing 2014)
Laurie Cabot's Book of Shadows by Laurie Cabot
    with Penny Cabot and Christopher Penczak (Copper Cauldron Publishing 2015)
Laurie Cabot's Book of Visions by Laurie Cabot
    with Penny Cabot and Christopher Penczak (Copper Cauldron Publishing 2019)

Anthologies

The Green Lovers (editor, Copper Cauldron Publishing 2012)
Ancestors of the Craft (editor, Copper Cauldron Publishing 2012)
The Waters and Fires of Avalon (editor, Copper Cauldron Publishing 2013)

Audio Recordings by Christopher Penczak

The Inner Temple of Witchcraft CD Companion (Llewellyn Publications, 2002)
The Outer Temple of Witchcraft CD Companion (Llewellyn Publications, 2004)
The Temple of Shamanic Witchcraft CD Companion (Llewellyn Publications 2005)
The Temple of High Witchcraft CD Companion (Llewellyn Publications 2007)
The Living Temple of Witchcraft Volume I CD Companion (Llewellyn Publications 2008)
The Living Temple of Witchcraft Volume II CD Companion (Llewellyn Publications 2009)

TABLE OF CONTENTS

INTRODUCTION

I remember my grandmother taking me to St. Anne's Church, by bus, along with a shopping trip to the corner store for candy, and the Woolworth's Department Store to look at the toys. We always went to the church first. In the church, she didn't take me to Mass. Nunnie—as I called her—didn't seem to care much for the Mass or the priests, but she loved the church. She didn't seem too concerned about services and sacraments. To the right of the entrance, there was a little alcove to a saint. I'm not sure if it was St. Anne herself, or some form of the Virgin Mary, but I remember it was the figure of a woman in the center of the alcove, looking down upon us lovingly. And there would be rows of red and blue glass votive holders in a cast-iron rack, most with a burning candle illuminating the colored glass. Nunnie would drop money into the slot at the top of the locked wooden box, grab a little white candle, look at the statue deeply, mumble something under her breath and place the candle in the glass container. She would then light it with a long match from one of the other candles. One day she even let me do it, putting more money in the locked box and holding my hand as I held the long match. I didn't realize what I was doing, but it was fun and magickal and a feeling I would never forget, even if the details get fuzzy. And of course it was followed by candy and toys, so the whole trip was a wonderful adventure. She didn't drive, and was the only member of the family who got around town by bus because she didn't want to rely on anyone any more than necessary.

Since that time, I realized that my adventures in St. Anne's Church was my first introduction to candle magick. While under the guise of an ostensibly Catholic ritual, I was coming to it again from Witchcraft perspective, and the essence of the magick was basically the same. We both start by having an intention and lighting the candle with that intention in mind, while also petitioning the divine for aid in the matter. The colors, light, and atmosphere all play a role, even though both settings are different. My altar with ritual tools and Goddess and God statue are not that different in function to the church alcove. Regardless of theological belief, the technology of the magick was the same, and in this series of books on Magickal Craft, we are less concerned about the belief and religion, and far more about the practice, the spiritual technology, and how it works, so you can adapt it to work best for you and your life.

Since my days as a Catholic school boy and my early days as a Witch casting candle spells so often because they worked incredibly well, I've grown to love and respect this powerful form of magick. It's simple but in no way should its simplicity diminish its power or responsibility. Extending my study of candle, lamp, and flame magick across different cultures, it helps me appreciate how so many seemingly simple things bond us together in the human experience. While we have different formats, magick is magick. Magick belongs to no one person or culture.

As a Tarot reader, I offer spells and rituals to clients who struggle with the outcome of an unfavorable reading. As a Witch, rather than a fatalistic form of psychic, I think the reading can be changed with magick. One of the most effective and popular methods to help such people change their situation has been candle magick. The universality, despite religion or lack thereof, helps people tap into their own magickal power.

One of my favorite stories involving a tarot client is a woman who wanted a reading to know exactly when her house was going to sell. My answer, much to her anger and disappointment, was "not anytime soon." She told me it was on the market for the last three years with no serious offers. The market was booming. Neighbors were selling their similar places. Hers would just not move, even reducing the price several times. I asked her about the energy of the home, if there had been any violence or a murder there, or in any way haunted. She said no, and I didn't feel that was the case intuitively based on the reading. We talked about spiritual work she could do, or we could do together, to sell the house. Though she buried a statue of St. Joseph upside down in the front yard, as a good Catholic would, she's still had no luck. When I got more esoteric in my magickal suggestions, she freaked out, stating it was against her religion. So instead, I urged her towards candle magick. She thought that was Catholic enough for her, as they light candles in church, so she used it. With a large green candle for money, and a paper with her realistic price of selling the home written on it folded under the candleholder, she found the house under contract for her asking price three days after the candle burned out. Three years of frustrations were resolved in three days.

When using that as a teaching story, I tell my magick students, if she could do this, and she had no interest in magick, and was actually kind of afraid of magick, think of what you can do if you really set your mind to it and study and practice. She had great success with no knowledge, understanding, or real training. Those who are truly empowered with magick can do all this and more. It is in that spirit I share this material with you. I want basic magickal skills to be treated as life skills.

While magick is a huge part of my spiritual worldview, life, and profession, in times past, in ancient magickal cultures, magick was available to everyone. Even up to the generations of my Italian Catholic family, using Catholic magickal prayers, and special folkloric rites to break the evil eye and cure unexplained illnesses, had access to it. The modern world, though wonderful with many amazing innovations, has had the unwanted side effect of cutting us off from part of our birth right, as spiritual beings. The ancient Egyptians believed that magick, known as "heka," was a gift from the gods, and used to 'ward off the harsh blows of fate.' Temple priests, librarians, healers, and the pharaohs were the expert magicians, using it for the good of the community and nation, but everyone had access to household folk magick, and would consult a temple expert when the problem was more serious.

For those less familiar with the concepts of magick and want a deeper understanding of the philosophies of magick, I highly recommend the first book of this series, *The Casting of Spells*. It focuses upon the power of word and intention, and delves into the philosophy of the magician's will and purpose. *The Lighting of Candles* applies intention directly to the more primal, visceral act of flame and will, and builds upon many of the philosophical concepts in the first book, while keeping the information simple and able to stand alone for those only interested in candle magick. Like candles themselves, I intended this book to be simple and primal. While it builds upon the first book, subsequent books in the series will build upon this one. I want to offer tools that can be immediately used, and not overwhelm the reader with too much esoteric detail, theory, or philosophy—though I can't help adding some of the deeper mysteries sometimes.

While I know not everyone who reads this series of books will wish to be ritual magicians, shamans or Witches, just as everyone in the ancient world was not a temple priestess or priest, I do hope everyone who reads this book will try a candle spell, and thereby invite magick into their life.

CHAPTER ONE:
WHAT IS CANDLE MAGICK?

Fire is a primal element to our spiritual experience. We use the image of fire and light as one of the best descriptions of divinity. Ancient and modern people equate divinity with light. The Zoroastrians of Persia were considered fire worshipers by some, though the key to their beliefs was the purifying and uplifting nature of fire, leading to divinity. The Hindu pantheon has Agni, the god of fire, to whom many sacrifices are made by throwing the offering into the fire. Agni was sometimes thought as an intermediary god, transmitting these offerings from the worshipers to other gods, as fire ceremonies are important in many Hindu traditions. The Greeks and Romans honored hearth and home fire goddesses, such as Hestia and Vesta. The Celts honor fire in their agrarian fire festivals, such as Beltane, sacred to the mysterious god Bel, and then there is their fire goddess turned saint, Bridget. Most well-known god in the modern world is the manifestation of the Old Testament Yahweh manifesting through a burning bush or pillar of fire.

Even our description of spiritual mastery, en-*light*-enment, is an embodiment of light. Saints and holy people are often depicted in art with flame and bright halos. Light illuminates the darkness, the unknown, and the bright heavenly bodies of the stars, Moon and Sun have been the strongest symbols of divinity. When humanity first harnessed the power of fire to create light and heat, we also harnessed the power of magick.

With the use of fire to cook food, to protect us from predators, and to create a central gathering for story, song, drum, and ceremony, we advanced our culture. Many of the ancient traditions speak about those rebellious gods who steal fire from the heavens, from the gods of order, and in sharing the fire with humanity, create civilization. The light and fire are both literally fire, but also the fire of knowledge and enlightenment.

Ever since then, fire has played a major role in ceremony, religion and magick. You find it from the tribal cultures who are not far off technologically from those who first "discovered" fire. You find it in the orthodox churches with candles lit to illuminate churches and temples. You find it in the esoteric arts of magick, including the traditions of modern European Witchcraft, American Hoodoo, and Ceremonial Qabalistic magick. All of these traditions, seemingly so different in belief and practice, all light their fires in a sacred manner, with intention and, while not always a religious attitude, a spiritual awareness.

The Path of Magick

Those who light candles for magick, beyond veneration and illumination of the temple, or giving a focus for a ceremony, are intending on an outcome with the fire. They intend a specific result, making their light a form of magick. Magick is classically defined as the "the Science and Art of causing Change to occur in conformity with Will." This definition comes from a lovable and horrible magician, controversial and with many followers and detractors, named Aleister Crowley. Magick is the process of transforming our reality, performing ritual actions with intention that clearly communicates our desire to the powers of the universe, which then respond in kind, manifesting the result. Some see it as very personal, often involving religious views, while others see the process as mostly technique and impersonal.

A spell is a specific form of magick, a ritual act with a tangible result as the focus. While magick can be considered a lifestyle, an energy, or a process of life, spells are the specific steps that make up a magickal life. You can have a magickal philosophy about life, but if you are not exactly performing magick, you are not really living that philosophy. Magick is about the doing, as much as the thinking and believing. It's important to note that as you progress on the path, the separation between doing and being becomes less and less.

The Magick of Candles

Lighting a candle with intention is a very powerful, but very simple spell. It's a specific act of magick performed with fire and wax. Any successful spell requires three things: a clear intention, strong will, and a method to direct energy. Lighting a candle intuitively aligns all three of these things without the user always being consciously aware of these three parts.

When you cast a candle spell, you must set the intention just before you light the candle. Often you hold the candle to "charge" it with your intention. But even those lighting candles in a Catholic Church, who do not "charge" the candles as a modern Wiccan or Witch might, still has a clear intention in mind before lighting the wick. Some might even say a prayer to a saint, just as a magician might call upon an angel, spirit, or Pagan deity with the intention vocalized, even in a whisper. When hearing the term "charge" in modern magick, most people's minds go to the metaphor of a battery. One is filling the object with spiritual energy, just as a battery is filled with electrical energy. The older concept of "charge," tied with our magickal use of the term, means instructions. One is given a charge, a mandate, or an order on what to do. When we are charging a candle, we are giving it energy, but we are also giving the candle its "orders" based upon our intention.

Fire is a symbol of will. Fire is one of the four classic elements of magick, along with air, water, and earth. As each element is associated with a principle, and all are embodied in candle magick, fire is the most obvious element in a lit candle. Candles become synonymous with fire, as a tool to embody fire on a ritual altar. The element of fire is indicative of passion, drive, desire, creativity, and most importantly, your will. By lighting a candle, you are activating the power of will within you. Lighting the candle is the trigger, like lighting the fuse, to make the magick happen. Without this act of will, nothing will happen. When I work candle magick with clients, I can prepare everything for them, but I almost always require they light the candle, aligning their will and action with the candle spell I've prepared.

The candle ritual itself is a method of directing energy. The function of ritual is a spiritual technology to harness the intention and will, and direct this energy towards the desired effect. The candle and fire of the candle direct energy as they burn. The intention sets the direction of where the energy goes to manifest. The flame kindles your own will to connect with the intention set in the candle, and the literal burning of fire and melting of the wax helps release a tangible energy, as well as the stored psychic energy of your intention and will that you have added to the energy of the candle. The candle has energy from its wax, its color, and any additional "dressings" in terms of symbols and potions you've put to it. More on candle dressing will be found in **Chapter Four**.

What I think is the most effective aspect of candle magick is how every candle inherently embodies the qualities of all four elements within its physical makeup. The four elements are known as the fundamental powers of magickal creation. Their patterns repeat over and over again in metaphysics, philosophy, psychology, and science. We use tangible symbols for these primal energies, aspects of nature that best embody them, but the energy of the elements goes beyond their symbol. We use the terms fire, water, earth and air, but the elemental energies are more than combustion, H2O, minerals, and gases. The elements are often followed with "of the Wise" to distinguish them from their terrestrial symbols and embodiments. Fire is the process of combustion. Fire of the Wise is the energy of will, desire and passion. Combustion is the best embodiment of Fire of Wise that we can perceive and use in ritual, but Fire of the Wise is more than combustion, and has correspondences on many different levels. Combustion is its physical correspondent.

Here is an overview of the four elements:

- ✦ **Fire** – Light, Energy, Passion, Desire, Identity, Will
- ✦ **Air** – Life, Language, Structure, Thought, Communication, Travel, Truth
- ✦ **Water** – Love, Astral, Emotion, Healing, Flow, Form, Image, Compassion
- ✦ **Earth** – Law, Physical Form, Density, Manifestation, Tangibility, Sovereignty

They are even loosely compared to the four fundamental forces in physics (electromagnetism, strong nuclear force, weak nuclear force, and gravity), the four states of matter in chemistry (plasma, gas, liquid, and solid), and the four DNA nucleotide bases in biology (A-adenine, C-cytosine, G-guanine and T-thymine). Magical philosophers often consider our universe to be four fold in nature.

A fivefold division uses the human senses – sight (fire), smell (air), taste (water), touch (earth) and hearing (spirit). The famous sixth sense is the psychic sense behind the elements, associated with the third eye and the circle around the five-pointed star in the pentacle figure.

SPIRIT

AIR

WATER

EARTH

FIRE

Figure: Pentacle with Elements

When the four elements are present together, they "conjure" the fifth element, known as spirit, akasha, ether, or my favorite name for this mysterious force, quintessence. The fifth element is a mystery, for it is the sum of the four but greater than its parts. Some use the mathematical equation 1+1+1+1=5 to demonstrate this. Spirit is the element from which the four are created. They issue forth from what is called active spirit by ceremonial magicians. They also return to spirit upon completion of their work, returning to passive, or receptive, spirit. Spirit is that mysterious spark that brings something to life.

Rituals all over the world honor and call upon the four elements. The four directions are the most common way to embody and manifest the elements in harmony and balance. Envisioning working in a circle with the four directions, be it the Witch's Magick Circle, the Magician's Circle, or the Medicine Wheel, is a mandala, a pattern, of creation and intention. The elements themselves are symbolized by various combinations of the seasons associated with the directions, the winds, colors, a variety of spiritual guardians, including archangels, totem animals, or deities, and most often, their tools. Tools can include the wand (fire), blade (air), chalice (water), and stone or pentacle (earth), much like the suits of the Tarot deck. Other symbol sets can include a red candle (fire), incense (air), bowl or shell (water), and stone, salt, crystal, or bowl of dirt (earth).

While doing magick in a circle ritual is highly effective and more desirable in the long-term, it is not always practical or even traditional. Most candle spells do not occur, until fairly recently, in the context of a greater circle ritual. For those who want simple instructions on circle magick, *The Casting of Spells* has details on the magick circle ritual of modern Witchcraft, which can be adapted to other traditions and belief systems. When working with a simple candle spell, you really have all you need with just the candle. Many of my most effective candles spells did not involve complex or fancy rituals, as the simple candle spell embodies many of those aspects already.

The candle embodies the four elements in the following ways:

✦ **Wax – Earth** – The dense, physical body of the candle. You can feel the weight in your hand when you hold it. It has mass and gravity. It is the solid "fuel," the potential for energy, in the candle. Wax comes from mineral, plant, and even animal sources, but all come from the earth.

- ✦ **Flame – Fire** – The most obvious of the elements is the fire of the flame. It illuminates and warms. You feel the physical and spiritual presence of the flame. Out of all the elements, it is the closest to the element of spirit, the fifth element. As spirit is the least tangible element and can behave as a thing alive with personality and information to share.
- ✦ **Oxygen – Air** – The burning candle needs oxygen to burn and releases carbon dioxide and water vapor. Though invisible, like the element of air, actual air is needed to make a candle burn.
- ✦ **Melting Wax – Water** – Water of the Wise is really the principle of flow and liquid is the best symbol of it. As the wax liquefies, it takes on the traits of elemental water. It can drip and flow before hardening again. Likewise, the combustion will release water vapor, and depending on the candle type and holder, the vapor can condense on or near the candle as liquid water, though the heat often makes it evaporate quickly and unseen, if it condenses at all.

With all four present, the mysterious element of Spirit is also present in a balanced and tangible way, even without a ritual circle. A ritual circle can enhance the experience of a simple candle spell, or a candle spell can be part of a larger ritual working. The essential elements for a successful operation are all "hidden" within the ritual of a simple candle spell.

Maintaining Elemental Balance

Due to the specific balance of the elemental energies when a candle spell is cast, you must take care to maintain the correct balance, else your spell will go awry. Changing the balance of energies changes the spell, and can alter, even unintentionally, the outcome. Tradition tells us, whenever possible, let the candle burn down and extinguish itself. This process maintains the balance.

If the candle burns part way and does not finish, it might indicate that the spell is not necessary, or if part of your intention in the spell (**Chapter Six**) was "For the highest good, harming none" or something similar, then perhaps this is the candle's way of telling you the intention was actually harmful and not for your highest good. The way a candle burns can be a form of divination (**Chapter Eight**) to the candle's result and manifestation.

Generally, when the candle is done burning, the spell is done and set into motion. Some will try to relight an aborted candle, but a 'rule of three' usually applies, different from what some call the Wiccan Law of Three. I was taught if you try to light a candle three times, and three times it still extinguishes, it was not a just mechanical failure on the candle's part, but a clear omen not to continue. To do so is to do magick at your own peril. One could argue even if it is a mechanical failure on the candle's part, if you chose that candle for this specific spell, it was like drawing lots or a tarot card, it was the one you were meant to use, and the message it is giving you is still true, do not proceed, even if it's a message you don't want to hear.

For those who want to safely burn them all the way and never snuff, you have several possible methods, depending on your own living situation. Generally, common sense and safety precautions will say never leave a burning candle unattended, though I know many magickal practitioners who technically do. They often use one of the following:

Fireplace – If you have a fireplace, place the candle in the fireplace behind a fireproof screen. If it falls over, it will be upon a nonflammable surface and cause no damage.

Sink or Bathtub – Assuming your sink or bathtub is not made of a flammable plastic, does not contain a flammable substance, or is not near flammable substances, you can put the candle in it. Make sure your sink or tub is empty and shower curtains are far away. Often a little water at the base, in case the candle should fall, is a good safety precaution. I use a stainless steel sink that is ideal for this practice.

Cauldron – A flameproof iron cauldron large enough to catch a falling candle is ideal for those wanting to leave the candle upon an altar or other sacred space. A deep metal bowl can also be used.

Lantern – There are many metal and glass lanterns available in craft and home décor stores. The candle is placed safely within the lantern, in a steady base, and the door of the lantern is closed. They are designed with air holes to allow the candle to burn, but now allow any stray sparks out beyond the lantern. In our temple, we keep a seven-day jar candle burning in a lantern whenever possible.

Metal Cabinet – Some professional folk magicians, whose clients pay them for candle burning services, have some sort of "chapel" where candles can be safely and continuously burned. Some of the simplest ones are steel cabinets with metal shelves. Others include iron works similar to those in churches, to hold glass jar and votive candles. Despite the precautions, I've known more accidents with this method.

Please use common sense and what is right for you. If you have small children or pets that can knock over a flaming candle, then leaving it unattended is not the brightest of ideas and shouldn't be done. I've known a few pets to almost set the house on fire to the surprise of the Witch or Magician who assumed animals would know better and keep away from the flame.

Letting the candle burn all the way maintains the original balance of elements from the moment you lit the wick, setting the spell into motion. By not doing anything else, the balance is maintained. If you can't let a candle burn in one sitting due to safety issues, snuff the candle with a candlesnuffer, spoon, or the bottom of a chalice if you must, and relight it later. Continue that process of snuffing and relighting until the candle completely burns. Snuffing it allows the proper balance of energies to maintain within the candle. Snuffing contains the energies, ideally without changing their balance. They stay simply dormant until the candle is relit. The candle spell is usually not complete and fully set into motion until the candle has burned fully.

To blow out, clap out, or wet the candle, even with moist fingertips, can upset the balance of the elements and the energies. There is a belief you "blew away" the spell and it won't come back to manifest for you. In traditional magickal training, they would say that you "offended" the elemental spirits of fire or air, known in their Medieval forms as salamanders or drakes for fire (lizard-like creatures) or sylphs (small, winged faery-like creatures) for air. The offended spirit would stop your spell, or twist it, giving you something you didn't want, but close to your chosen intention.

Today, most believe offense is not given if offense is not intended and the spirits are not quite so vindictive, but doing these unbalanced techniques does tend to twist or negate your candle magick. This explains the perception that the elemental spirits are twisting your spell. I believe the mechanism causing this is the imbalance of the elements. The perfect balance is set with the spell to manifest your intention. Add a little more air energy or take a little fire energy away, and suddenly the balance shifts, but you continue to light it and set it into motion, unbalanced, so your result will be unbalanced or not manifest at all. My teacher, Laurie

Cabot, taught students of the Cabot Tradition that our breath contains prana, life energy, and blowing on the candles adds more life energy to the spell but upsets the balance of the candle. It wasn't a case of vindictive spirits but simply a disproportion of energy distorting the original intent.

Investing in a nice, decorative candlesnuffer as a ritual tool will help remind you to always snuff your candles if you have to put them out. I like the ones that the snuffing "cup" is on a hinge and can swivel, allowing you access into taller glass jar candles. Snuffers that are locked at a ninety degree angle don't allow such access, and instead you have to cover the top of the jar.

While admonishment against blowing out candles was the default teaching of occultism when I learned candle magick, today, with the sharing and exploration of other forms and traditions of magick, candle snuffing is not the hard and fast rule. There are forms of magick, to trigger the magick, that the candle is extinguished in dirt, water, or blown out. Many practitioners of folk magick feel it's silly to be "afraid" of blowing out candles and do it all the time, and simply relight them. I would never tell someone not to do what works for them, or to abandon the effective techniques learned from their own teachers and traditions. I can only share what has consistently worked for me and what I've observed in my experience.

Some believe we create our own magickal paradigms and filters. If we were taught something was "wrong" then we unconsciously manifest the result we were expecting. If we were not taught that particular filter of belief and expectation, then the unwanted result would not manifest. I think magickal systems do develop inherent filters and parameters that allow you to function in that system and often inhibit you from learning other systems and paradigms.

The benefit of such filters in a magickal system is to create the structure and contain the system, particularly when a novice is learning. Otherwise, if there are no guidelines and rules, there is no structure, and anything and everything can be a spell. Yet people do anything and everything all the time and don't seem to have success in magick when compared to the trained practitioner. The structure helps the process.

After all these years, I still do not blow out my magickal candles. Mundane candles for lighting at a dinner party, or ambience and general use, I'll blow out, distinguishing them from my intentioned candles. One of the personal reasons why I continue to do so is the observation of my clients. More than once, I've had the experience of an untrained client completing a candle spell at home from our session having the spell go awry when they ignored my instructions to snuff. I gave them no dire warning about blowing out candles but simply instructed them on what to do. Once, I simply snuffed out the candle, wrapped it up, and told them to relight it at home. I was remiss in my usual instructions to snuff if needed and relight. There should have been no real unconscious manifestation of failure or distortion. It was a small candle, and I didn't think they would need to snuff and relight. Each of these clients came back to tell me that the spell either didn't work or distorted in some way, manifesting something close to the intention but unwanted. In each of these cases, the client revealed with some prodding they blew out the candle.

One client did a candle spell to return and reconcile with a cheating husband. Her intention was to truly work through things, not simply command and compel him to return. For a short time, he appeared to return, and all was proceeding in the right direction, yet a few days later, he left again, with a letter explaining he only came back to retrieve their dog, and she was soon left with no husband and no dog.

Another did a money candle for a specific amount of money to pay off a looming debt. He received the money on time, but immediately was hit with another unexpected expense, slightly exceeding the original sum of money granted, all within three days of blowing out the candle. He was very upset and wondered if his additional debt was some sort of karmic payback for dabbling in magick.

A third client felt she was under psychic attack by a magickal practitioner. It was unclear if she truly was, or was manifesting her own bad luck. She was experiencing violent nightmares, an abnormally high amount of accidents, and her energy level diminished. As a magickal consultant, the remedy is the same. If someone believes they are under psychic attack, you treat it as such because either they are, or they are unconsciously attacking themselves. Protection magick will help in either case. We did a complex clearing followed by a protection candle spell with special protection incense. She read on a website, from another tradition of magick, to blow out the candle, and you would be "blowing away" the person harming you. This was not my instruction. I told her to snuff it and relight as necessary. For the first few days when the candle burned, before she read that internet article, her symptoms subsided. Nightmares eased up. No major or minor accidents occurred, and her energy was beginning to increase with more rest. She read this article, burned the incense and blew the incense over the flame, blowing the flame out, and believing she was "blowing away" her attacker. She felt confident and threw out the rest of the candle. That night, the nightmares returned with a vengeance and her health took a turn for the work. When we discussed it, I felt she "blew away" all the protection we had built up for her, undoing our magick.

Of course not all magick works for everyone, and these could be natural percentages of failure or unclear intentions, but after doing professional consultations for many years with a strong track record of success with my clients, I found it interesting that those without any real expectation of failure due to blowing out a candle, and even those with an expectation of success, still experienced failure. Perhaps they were unconsciously "infected" by my belief system through some unknown mechanism of telepathy. Perhaps there is something to the old adage of not imbalancing your candles. I think back to the Catholic church, letting the candles burn continuously until out, and despite my many criticisms of the dogma and politics of the church, wonder if they remembered a key teaching in their own candle magick, and that is why it continues to be so popular.

In my own magick, I'm always looking for cross-cultural connections, as I feel that if you find several different traditions with the same idea, you might find some truth. I was introduced to the Mayan folk medicine magick of Miss Beatrice Torres Waight through her biographical book *Fire Heart: The Life and Teachings of Maya Medicine Woman Miss Beatrice Torres Waight* in her own words as told to Katherine Silva. In it, she describes her sacred ceremonies, or *primicias*, and their view on blowing out candles.

"When the primicia is over, the candles are not blown out with our breath. We spit on our thumb and fingers to put the flame out or use a candle snuffer. We never blow out a candle that has been used for a sacred ceremony because then we disrespect the spirit of the fire, and blow away the good luck!"[1]

---

[1] Silva, Katherine. *Fire Heart: The Life and Teachings of Maya Medicine Woman Miss Beatrice Torres Waight.* 2011. p. 53

While I'm certainly open to the possibility of a cross-cultural infusion from the Catholic Church prominent in Belize could influence her view on candles, I doubt any traditional priest taught her anything about offending the spirit of fire. So this little cross-cultural connection, while not evidence, is a supportive piece to why many Witches and magicians today do not blow out candles. Yet, obviously, one difference is her willingness to use the spit and pinch method of snuffing.

Exercise: The Psychic Candle

This is one of the most basic meditation practices in occult traditions. Find a comfortable place where you can sit, either cross-legged on the floor or in a chair, back straight. In either position, have a surface before you, at least three feet away, that you can place upon a candle. Any candle will do right now, but perhaps a simple white taper is best. Light the candle and get comfortable before it. Set a timer if you like. Ideally, you can build up to fifteen minutes of this exercise, but if meditation and candle gazing is new to you, start with just five minutes. You might think that is an easy goal, but it's much harder than you think.

Gaze at the candle and breathe normally, but go a bit deeper in your breath. Relax your body. Start at the top of your head and scan your body, giving each part of your body permission to relax more deeply. Give your head, neck, and shoulders permission to relax. With each breath, feel your chest and back relax. Waves of relaxation move through you, down your body, sweeping away any tension as your belly and lower back, as your hips relax. The waves of relaxation flow down your shoulders and through your arms, all the way to your fingertips. Feel the waves flow through your legs and relax you down to the tips of your toes and the soles of your feet. Even in this relaxed state your spine is straight and you are breathing deep, gazing at the candle.

The Lighting of Candles

Focus on the light of the candle. It may flicker or stay steady. It doesn't matter. Focus all your attention upon the flame. If your eyes tire, you can blink, but keep your attention single-pointed upon the flame. If your mind wanders, bring all your thoughts back to the flame. Don't beat yourself up for letting your mind wander, but simply dismiss the thought and bring attention back to the flame.

If your timer has not yet gone off, close your eyes, and visualize the scene before you in your mind's eye. Be aware of the flame, the candle it is burning, and the surface the candle is resting on. Is there any candleholder to be aware of? Just recreate the scene in your imagination, and then put all attention onto the candle flame. Soon the candle flame will fill your mind's eye, and all else will fade away. Focus your attention upon the flame for as long as you can.

If you lose the vision, gently open your eyes, and gaze at the physical candle again, eventually repeating the process. Let the timer bring you back. It's easy with this exercise to distort time and think that you have been there for hours when it has only been minutes, or to think it's been minutes, and to have spent a significant amount of time. That is why I suggest starting with five minutes and building up to practice this technique.

This simple exercise is a core starting practicing of many different magickal and meditative traditions. It gives you focus, discipline and increases your visualization skills. Some say it even opens up your psychic abilities gently. For those who develop a proficiency with it, a non-traditional addition to the technique, appropriate for the work here of candle magicians, is to reflect upon the elements of the candle. As you gaze at the candle in your mind's eye, reflect on the earth that is the wax, granting it a physical, tangible presence. The wax is like your body. The wax is like this world. Reflect upon the melting of the wax, the liquid flow that drips from it or burns away, like water evaporating with the heat. To create change, all things must flow and take a new shape. Reflect upon the invisible air that feeds the flame. Your words, your intentions, and prayers have been carried upon this air. The sacred sounds you've heard have been carried to you on this air. Reflect upon the fire, the process of transformation via combustion that crowns the candle, shining its energy and passion. And if you look closely at the flame, near the wick is a small dark archway, like the door to an ancient temple. This is a gateway to the mysteries of magick.

The Lighting of Candles

CHAPTER TWO:
TYPES OF CANDLES

The first step in candle magick, after setting the intention of the spell, is to choose the appropriate candle that suits your intention. Candle choices can be divided into candle color (**Chapter Three**) and candle type. By first educating yourself on the types of candles available in magick and investing in a little bit of a stock for various intentions, you will be prepared for whatever your needs might be.

Beyond color, candle categories can generally be divided into the materials used to make the candle, primarily the wax, and the style in which the wax is shaped and poured. Some materials are not available in some styles for reasons of popularity, economics, and tradition. Finding a source of candles you like, or eventually learning to craft your own, is essential for an active candle magician.

Candle Materials

Candles are usually made from a solid to semi-soft fuel source that will maintain a flame over a period of time. Traditional candles were made from tallow, a byproduct of animal fat rendering. Most common in Medieval Europe was beef fat, but the first candles made in China were made from whale fat. Sperm whale oil was also used in Europe. While we see candles as a cheap tool to work with today, they were quite a pricy commodity at one time, and used only by the upper classes. Oil lamps, and the potential magick with the lamp, was a more common household item, and therefore a more common magickal tool in folk traditions. Tallow was replaced by the spermaceti, or sperm whale oil, as well as plant oils from rapeseed until the rise of paraffin. Now modern candles are usually made from one of the following sources:

Paraffin – Paraffin is the most common wax, as it is an inexpensive byproduct of petroleum refining. Most commercial candles are made from paraffin today. The easy accessibility of paraffin candles and cheap cost are an excellent reason to use them. The association with petroleum production often upsets more ecologically sensitive magickal workers, feeling the wax is too chemically potent and synthetic, and more natural substances are "purer" and carry a stronger inherent charge magickally.

Beeswax – The wax from the beehive, a byproduct of honey collection can be used in candle-making. Beeswax candles are a high-quality candle, and some religions require certain special candles, like the Catholic Easter candle, to be made from beeswax. They are considered pure and magickally potent, as many traditions hold bees sacred as a totemic animal of the heavens.

Soy – This plant-based wax is made from the soybean. The hydrogenated form of soybean oil has a lower melting temperature than most commercial waxes and works best in a glass container. Certain additives can be introduced to create pillars or tapers that will burn well without a glass container.

Palm Oil – A plant oil-based wax is made from the palm tree. It produces a high-quality, all-natural wax that is becoming more popular among magickal practitioners. Palm oil has been involved in great social and economic controversies since growing in popularity. Places where it is produced are often besieged by deforestation, animal abuse, environmental abuses, smuggling, and human rights violations involving the workers. If using palm oil candles, make sure it's from an ethically-sourced supplier.

Gel – Gel candles are a mixture of a resin with mineral oil to form the wax fuel. Some also mix other forms of wax, particularly paraffin. Gel candles have not gained much popularity in magickal practitioners.

Each has their benefits, drawbacks, and availability. Though many of us prefer to use all natural products, fairly traded, you'll find many of the most esoteric candles used by occultists are still in petroleum based wax, as they are too large and expensive to do otherwise. The only option for many environmentally-friendly candle magicians is to get molds and make your own using these other options, but soon after doing so, you'll begin to understand why petroleum is used unless you have a rather large candle budget. I think you should personally use what is best for you and available considering your economic means. At times it's a soy or palm oil candle for me, but other times it's a quick, cheap, and "unnatural" candle picked up at my local department store or flea market. Despite its reputation, paraffin is considered biodegradable and non-toxic.

The second concern is the wick used in the candle. "Wicking" is the process of capillary actions, where the wick draws up the melted wax as fuel to the flame. Wicks are made from fiber, paper, or cloth. Most common are cotton, and commercial candles are often treated with chemicals to make them flame resistant. They can be coated with a small amount of wax to provide the initial fuel before the candle begins burning. They are also braided to be flat and will curl slightly as they burn and be self-trimming, as a small portion burns away. Prior to this innovation, candle wicks needed to be constantly trimmed away as the candle burned, combining the original use of snuffers, which were candle scissors with what we think of as a snuffer today. Wicks often have a stiffening component, such as wire or plastic inside the wick, though that is becoming less common these days. There is some concern in using wire in wicks, particularly due to the fact that lead was once used as the wire. As it burns, toxic lead vapors would be released. Today, zinc is the most likely metal, and zinc is considered non-toxic, though the idea of zinc vapors is not comforting to most involved in holistic health practices. If you try to write with the wire of a candle wick, lead will leave a mark, zinc will not, if you have any concerns or need to test it. I'm unaware of any modern candle manufacturer that still uses lead, but if you get your hands on some old candles, it could still be possible.

Types of Candles

Candles come in a wide range of shapes and sizes. Each practitioner has their own favorite type they feel is most effective. For many of us, size, weight, and burn time are the contributing factors. While I have my favorite, I've found that most candles will work in candle magick if you're attracted to it for the spell.

Often the first type of candle you learn to do candle magick with is the type you like the most for future spells. In many magickal circumstances, you get pre-programmed, in that special magickal paradigm filter, with what you first learn and have a successful experience. There's nothing wrong with that programming as it's effective, but it can be helpful to learn to break such patterning and have success with any type of candle if you seek to be a more masterful magician over the long-term.

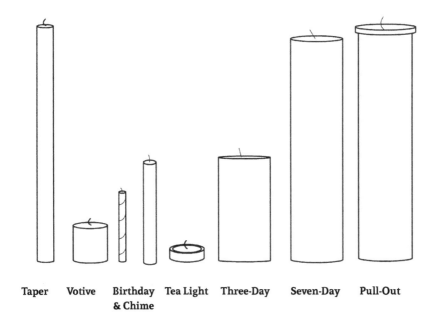

| Taper | Votive | Birthday & Chime | Tea Light | Three-Day | Seven-Day | Pull-Out |

Figure: Candle Types

Taper – A taper is a simple thin pillar candle that is wider at the base and thinner at the top, hence the name. They come in a wide range of sizes, with the most popular being six, ten, twelve, or fifteen inches. Tapers are an all-purpose candle for simple, basic spells. I find basic tapers have enough mass to them to hold a strong magickal charge but will burn relatively quickly.

Votive – Votive candles refer to smaller candles, usually two inches or so high with a one to a one and half-inch diameter. They take their name from the term votive offering, which refers to any offering that is not intended to be returned or retrieved, left at a sacred site. Votive offerings include all manner of stones, carvings, weapons, fetishes, and the like, often placed in bogs, wells, or buried in the Earth. Likewise, a votive candle is given as an offering, or used in spellcraft and will not be returned to the one making the offering. Votive candles are great in shrines and fit well into small, votive glass containers for safety and beauty. Like the ones in the Catholic Church, they are often colored, so the light shines through the glass in beautiful jewel tones. Due to their compact nature, most votives take slightly longer to burn than tapers, particularly when in a glass container to hold the wax. They are great when you want to prolong the burn of a candle for a time, such as sending healing or as an offering to a spirit or deity.

Miniature Taper or Birthday Candle – Very small candles, such as miniature tapers of three to five inches tall or simple small birthday candles used on children's cakes, can be used in magick. They are for short, quick spells that require less time and energy in their casting. Miniature candles are called Chime Candles, and before being adopted into metaphysical shops, were part of old-fashioned candleholders where their heat would make a small mechanical turbine with bells and often angels attached, turn, ringing the chime-like bells. These "Angel Chimes" were popular Christmas decorations in Europe and America, though now many popular manufacturers of such devices come from China.

Tea Light – Tea lights are a quarter of the size of votive candles, coming in a small metal foil container to hold them as they melt. Their burn time is shorter than a votive but longer than a birthday candle. They can be used as offering candles or for other simple spells. Usually they come in white, but other colors, sometimes with synthetic scents, are now available.

Pillar – A pillar candle is a large candle usually ranging from five to ten inches tall and two to six inches in diameter. They come in an array of colors and sometimes with added synthetic scents. They are excellent long-term candles or for large workings. Pillar candles have become a popular aesthetic in modern decorations.

Seven-Day Glass Jar Candles – Seven-Day Candles are like pillars poured into a tall glass jar to contain them, usually designed to burn for seven days straight though most burn for much shorter, being thinner than the old-fashioned seven-day candles. They come in an assortment of colors and are traditionally used for religious and magickal purposes. They are good for long-term spells, healing, and devotional work. In many folk magick traditions, a candle was left burning for seven-days because you were to repeat the intention or prayer for seven days in a row. Paint or marker, or Paper with symbols and images can be applied to the outside of the glass to decorate it. Often commercial seven-day candles will carry images of saints or deities upon them through a paper or plastic decal. They are also known as Novena or Vigil Candles in religious supply stores.

Three-Day Jar – Miniature version of the Seven-Day Candle, sometimes called Three-Day Candles even though the smaller three inches ones burn less than three full days continuously. Sometimes referred to as four-hour candles, depending on the size. They are used much the same way as Seven-Day Jar Candles, but for smaller or shorter workings.

Pull-Out Jar – Pull-out candles are seven-day candles made separate from their glass encasing. You are able to pull-out and remove the candle from the glass jar. You can anoint, carve or otherwise decorate the candle directly and then place it back into the jar. Popular among many magickal workers, particularly of the Hoodoo traditions, but now more popular in Neopaganism due to the crossover between such traditions in occult shops in major metropolitan centers. The author and teacher, Lady Rhea, "Witch Queen of New York," is famous for her intricate pull-out candles, and popularizing the technique in Wicca. Her book, *The Enchanted Candle*, outlines her techniques in detail.

Specialty Candles

Specialty candles, also known as shaped candles, are found more in occult shops than fancy candle stores. They are popular in the American occult movement, as the candles were primarily used in the practices of American folk magick such as Hoodoo. As occult shops, prior to the modern metaphysical and New Age movement, catered to a wide range of occult communities: Hoodoo rootworkers, Voodoo and Santeria practitioners, British Traditional Wiccans, ceremonial magicians, eclectic Witches and even Satanists, these specialty candles migrated into other magickal traditions and disciplines. They have been adopted by a wide range of modern Witches, and now are found in popular "traditional" spell books for Witches and Pagans.

Most shaped candles use cheaper paraffin and often come in the basic colors of white, black, red, and green, though some are catering to specialty colors such as blue, yellow, pink, and purple.

Baphomet/Devil – This horned god figure, the occultist's Baphomet, a creature associated with the Knights Templar and Éliphas Lévi; the pagan's Horned God; or the Christian's devil, is used in candle form for occult power, cursing, sex magick, revealing secrets or communion with the spirits of the Witch's Sabbat.

Cat – Feline shaped candles primarily burned in luck, gambling, wishing, and prosperity spells. Modern Witches also use them to attune to animal magick, specifically cat energy, as well as to honor the Egyptian cat goddess Bast.

Cross – A cross-shaped candle can be used for "uncrossing," a traditional name for curse removal, as you burn the cross, dissolving it. The curse is seen as harm crossing your path. It can also be used in religious devotion, ancestral magick, and in court success and justice spells.

Death/Grim Reaper – A candle of the Grim Reaper, most often in black, is used for luck, cursing, and working with ancestral spirits, or any form of operative necromancy.

Devil – A simple depiction of the "devil," when compared to the Baphomet-shaped candle is a taller, thinner image of a horned figure. This figure is generally used in cursing, sex, and gambling magick. Sometimes the devil figure is more like a Pagan satyr.

Double Action – Double action candles are not shaped differently than a normal pillar candle, but are poured differently, with the bottom half usually black wax and the top usually white, red, or green. Some are the opposite with the black wax on top and the other color on the bottom, for the special magick, as they are used to reverse curses and often use the motion of reversing the candle and burning it upside-down, though some are designed to cover the black bottom half with the new color above. Normally, they are burned by cutting off the top wick and then digging the wick out of the bottom end. The candle is turned upside down, with the old "top" now at the bottom, and burning the bottom half first. Often the black half is burned first to absorb and neutralize the harm, and then the color is burned to bring blessing. They are to stop harmful magick being used against you, with the white as all purpose, the red for reversing a love curse and the green for reversing a money curse. In a pinch, a traditional taper burned upside down can be used in such curse-breaking spells. I have found the action of turning the candle upside down is the most important.

Genitalia Candle – Candles shaped like a vagina or penis, primarily used in spells of sex, virility, fertility, and lust.

Human Candle – A human shaped figure candle, in male and female images. Used as a poppet, as well as in love and sex magick. There are many variations, including a united "couple" candles for marriage and separate couple, when burned will divide the couple back to back, for divorce, break-up, and separation spells.

Mummy – Shaped like an Egyptian mummy, complete with sarcophagus, they are used for gaining occult power, healing, and cursing. Naturally, such a shape can also help with spells to attune to the power of ancient Egypt and the Pharaonic mysteries.

Pharaoh – Like the mummy shaped candles, the pharaoh shaped candles are also burned for occult power, but also wisdom, material power of a king, success in business, and for contact with the Egyptian gods and spirits.

Pyramid – Pyramid shaped candles can be used for many purposes, but traditionally they add power and amplify a spell. They can be used in curse breaking, healing, and like the Pharaoh, contact with the Egyptian gods and spirits.

Reversible – Reversible candles are often confused with Double Action candles, as both "uncross" or "reverse" harmful magick. The reversible candles usually have an inner layer of red wax and an outer layer of black wax.

Seven Knob – A "taper" candle that will have seven equal knobs or balls on it. For spells that must be performed over a period of seven days, one knob a day is burned.

Skull Candle – Skull shaped candles are used for ancestral work and cursing, and sometimes healing, particularly healing brain or skull injury. Usually, they come in black and white.

Witch – A candle shaped in the medieval stereotype of the Witch, with the hag dressed in the pointed hat and cloak are burned for occult power, good luck, working magick on a Witch, and connection with the Mighty Dead, the Witchcraft ancestors.

Figure: Cat Candle

Figure: Male and Female Candles

Figure: Skull and Owl Candles

Figure: Pharaoh and Pyramid Candles

The Lighting of Candles

Figure: Satyr and Devil Candles

Figure: Witch and Cross Candles

You might have noticed with the specialty-shaped candles, many of the intentions behind the candles could involve ethically dubious purposes. It's important to realize that magick is like a fundamental force of nature, neither good nor evil, and carrying no moral judgement or safeguards. Teachers of magick describe this force like electricity. Electricity can be used to light up a room, and in that illumination people can read, talk, or otherwise engage in civilized and affirming behaviors. Electricity can also be used to electrocute someone. The electricity is neutral. Ethics and morality come into play through human use. Magick is the same way.

Many of the folk magick practices here that include cursing and control were traditionally developed among people who had less access to the justice systems of their society, such as the rural poor and in many cases slaves and the descendants of slaves. When you look across Europe, magick was a resource for both the privileged and underprivileged. The upper classes often had access to more learned advisors and magicians who could perform magick and create charms, while the poor would do things at home, and when needed, go to a specialist such as a Witch or cunning man.

Magick has no inherent morality or code to it, though systems of magick, and magickal religions certainly develop such things. *The Lighting of Candles* and related books in the series are not books on religion, but technique, so you must apply your own sense of ethics and morals to your magickal practices. Christian magickal practitioners will apply Christian morality, or at least their interpretation of it, to their magickal practices. Wiccan practitioners will also place their own ethics to the use of magick, believing in doing no harm, or as little harm as possible. The best rule of thumb I can give someone outside the context of a specific magickal tradition is that if you wouldn't do something through ordinary channels, then you probably shouldn't be doing it through magick. The use of magick doesn't make you exempt from the consequences of your actions, at least spiritually. Some traditions of Witchcraft say you must be willing to "pay the coin" of your magick. That doesn't mean some movie or comic book image of magick where every spell forces a karmic retribution for bending the laws of nature. Magick is nature. In fact, some of the oldest traditions refer to it as a natural science or natural philosophy. The "coin" refers to accepting the consequences of your actions on all levels. So be sure you really want to accomplish whatever your intention is before you light that candle.

Candleholders and Other Supplies

Some magicians are sensitive about every aspect of their craft, and fuss over the details, including candleholders. Others focus upon the main tools, and see such details as trivial. While I think I started my practice focused upon the details and as I've grown older, I've become less concerned, it's good to be knowledgeable about all the factors contributing, or deterring, your magick. At heart, I approach the occult arts like a scientist, taking good notes and seeking to understand the reasons behind my failures and successes, so those secrets can be passed on to new practitioners.

Candleholders are necessary for any candle that is not already in a glass container. Even standalone large pillars should ideally have something beneath them to catch dripping wax and allow them to burn to the end. Candleholders can come in many different materials, including glass, fine crystal, ceramic, and metal. Glass is most common, but if you are packing candles with herbs, or otherwise letting the candles burn till they self-extinguish, glass might not be best. Even though they are designed to withstand heat, glass can shatter or crack with fancy glass candleholders. Shattering doesn't seem to be a frequent problem for seven-day glass jar candles or smaller glass votive holders. But glass holders designed to hold tapers can shatter. Add some psychic energy to that candle through a spell, and I've found it more likely to shatter. The same can go for fine crystal. I've had glass holders shatter and send shards of glass across the room. Luckily no one was in the path.

Ceramic holders tend to deal with heat a bit better than glass, but they are not as common. Likewise, wooden candleholders are also available, but not as common and not advised for magick. Though I love the energy of wood, rarely do we know what kind of wood they are made from, and there is always a danger when a candle burns too far down, even if the inside of the socket for the candle is coated in something. Now there are also acrylic candleholders available, but they are designed for electric candles, and should not be used with flame.

The most common candleholder is made from metal. There are various metals, and the more modern candleholders are nondescript, simply named as metal. Others are clearly brass, bronze, chrome, nickel, iron, steel, and silver plated.

Brass and bronze can be difficult to tell apart, both being golden colored metals. Brass is an alloy of zinc and copper. Bronze is an alloy of tin and copper, sometimes with another metal. My teacher Laure Cabot insisted brass conducted magickal energy the best for candleholders, at least out of the affordable options to most Witches. Brass has astrological associations with Sun, Venus, and Uranus, while Bronze is ruled by Venus and Jupiter.

Modern magicians usually don't like to work with aluminum due to the belief it mixes poorly with potions and medicines and creates harm in the human body, but magickally, aluminum is a substitute for liquid quicksilver. It brings the qualities of the planet Mercury, and it is excellent for all forms of magick, but particularly communication. Modern magicians link it with Neptune or Uranus in planetary magick.

Copper is the metal of Venus, and aligns well with love, lust, and money magick. Iron candleholders bring the influence of Mars, and are used for protection. Many feel iron grounds out other magickal intentions, and should only be used in war and protection magick, and would be detrimental to other, more gentle intentions. Likewise, steel, made from iron, has similar properties. Sometimes highly polished steel is mistaken for aluminum or chrome.

You are less likely to find candleholders of pure tin or lead, but each is ruled by Jupiter and Saturn, respectively. More likely would be antique pewter candleholders, which might contain true lead in the mix, but today, most modern pewter is a mix of tin, copper, and antimony. Sometimes silver or bismuth is in the blend to make it "lead free." Old-fashioned pewter balanced the energy of Jupiter and Saturn, expansion and contraction. Some say it would neutralize both opposing forces, and was not the best for general magick.

Nickel is a metal for information and psychic exploration, so it doesn't make the best metal for manifestation of common goals, but is useful in more esoteric pursuits. Chrome is ruled by Pluto, and acts as psychic catalyst. It can bring power and force to any magickal intention.

Silver candlesticks, usually silver plated, are best for lunar magick involving psychic abilities, creativity, and emotions. While it's rare to get gold plated candlesticks, if you have it, it would evoke the power of the Sun, including success, prosperity, health, and optimism. Silver and gold are considered the best conductors of energy, and can be used for any type of magick.

Beyond candleholders are a few helpful stands for a candle. Lanterns that can hold candles have come back into home décor, when once they were a necessity of life. Formed from a variety of materials, they can safely hold a lit candle when you are not around. While you still shouldn't leave an unattended candle burning, it does provide a measure of safety. Temples with 'eternal' lights will often store the candle in a lantern for safer burning.

Most candleholders are single holders, though some decorative holders involve multiple candles, like a candelabra. Sometimes the pattern of candles can be conducive to the magick, while others, more chaotic, might detract from the overall spell.

Another safety measure is the use of trivets or trays. A trivet is usually considered an iron bracket or decorative "plate" that will lift up a kettle, cooking pot, or serving dish, preventing the hot bottom of the container from burning the surface of the table. Some use a trivet to lift a candle up off a surface to prevent scorching. Antique stores often have a variety of decorative ironwork designs.

Various trays, decorative or otherwise, and usually metal, are used to catch dripping wax, burning and falling herbs from a dressed candle rolled in herbs, or to create a barrier between the candle base and a flammable source to prevent scorching. Think of them functioning like a large plate or bowl. Circular trays make a nice focus for candle mandalas, and trays with a lip will usually contain wax that drips. A tray, rather than a simple plate, can usually contain more than one candle and maintain the patterns of stones, herbs, talismans, and other items around the candle in complex spells.

The last "accessory" of a candle magician is known as candle adhesive, sometimes known as tack or sticky wax. It's a putty adhesive that will burn like candle wax, but can be used at the bottom of a taper to ensure the taper will stay up right. Best for when a taper is not an exact fit for a candleholder. The adhesive makes sure a lit candle will not fall over. But when in doubt, put a tray beneath such a candle, in case the adhesive fails you.

Exercise: Candle Curiosity

Take a moment to reflect upon all the candle choices, from the material to the shape and size. When you think about the magick of candles, does that conjure any ideas or images for you? What candles are you most attracted to? What do you think is the most magickal? If money was no object, what would you use in your candle magick? Can you imagine yourself using such candles? How do they make you feel?

It's good to explore the ideas around magickal tools that we have. Often our intellectual understanding and goal is different than when we really try to imagine how we'd feel using something. Magick has its principles, but like art and music, there is a visceral quality that is not quantifiable, and those things that bring out the strongest visceral response are the most effective in spell casting.

With an understanding of candle materials and shapes, you can begin to think about how to stock up on candles for your own magick. Before you do, read the next chapter to understand the power of color, and how it influences your choices in magick, but at the very least, this chapter has opened your mind to all the different sorts of candles that are available to you.

Think about where you will store your candles too, as you build up a stock. Ideally, they should be in a cool, dry place. Higher temperatures can warp the candles, even with a simple hot summer afternoon, depending on your locale. If the candles are not individually wrapped, they can melt into each other and cause a real mess. Some place items of cleansing to keep unwanted influences from the "fresh" candles, such as bowls of salt, since they will readily absorb an intention. Others will just make sure to cleanse the candle before use, regardless.

Most magickal practitioners who are serious about their craft create some sort of supply closet or storage cabinet, separate from other mundane items. Candles, oils, and incense can be kept away from the household, as spell ingredients are of an exotic sort, and one wouldn't want to get them mixed up with the herbs of the spice rack when making dinner. Others don't have such a division between the magickal and mundane, keeping their candle assortment for the fancy dinner setting of the table in the same place as their magickal candles. There is a wisdom in that too, recognizing all things are sacred, and all things are part of everyday life.

CHAPTER THREE: COLOR MAGICK

Visible color is the reflection of specific frequencies of light. An object is a particular color because it absorbs other color frequencies and reflects the one we identify with it, sending that frequency out to our eye, to be interpreted by our retina and brain. In many ways, one can see the essence of candle magick, and perhaps all magick, being based upon the concept of light. Candle spells are activated by lighting the candle, sending forth frequencies of light from the flame itself. Without the flame, there is no candle magick.

The Magick of Universal Light

Light works on several different levels in the magickal paradigm. First, light can be divided into what we consider visible light and what is also known as psychic or universal light, which is invisible. Unlike other invisible energies of the electromagnetic spectrum, such as ultraviolet, infrared, gamma waves, or x-rays, psychic light has not be measured or catalogued by modern science. Many scientifically minded Witches and magicians believe it is only a matter of time before science does discover how to catalogue this magickal spectrum, believing this psychic light is in a higher level of the spectrum that cannot yet be detected, while more mystically minded practitioners think it is as elusive as the soul and science will not be able to find it.

This psychic light is the unseen light we create in our inner visions. If someone says "picture this," you hold in your mind's eye, an image of what they are describing, an image in "light" and color. But it's not physical light as it is within your mind.

In magick, we learn to direct these images and send them out as a part of our spellcraft. We believe this is a tangible energy, fueled by life force and will, that can be directed towards our intention. When receiving and "reading" this psychic light from other sources, we interpret it as a flash of vision and gut instincts. Light, including psychic light, is information, encoded by its vibration, and our inner psychic mechanisms, our chakras and etheric senses, decode the signal just as our retina receives frequencies and send them along the optic nerve to be interpreted as images by the brain. They are both forms of perception.

In fact, one scientific theory now conjectures that the universe behaves much like a hologram, a construct of light. Most succinctly detailed for the layman in the book *The Holographic Universe* by Michael Talbot. Essentially, the understanding of the universe with the principles of quantum physics, is that the universe is not as solid as we might like to think. The sub-atomic particles we like to think of as distinct particles, making up the other "solid" particles of our universe – atoms, molecules, and even living cells – can sometimes behave like a particle, and sometimes behave as a wave of energy, a wave of light. They can transfer information from particle to particle, non-linearly, beyond the speed of light. Observations of linked particles show that one is communicating with another in relationship to their course of direction and the other one is responding, but there is no known mechanism under the normal laws of physics to justify that effect. They are operating faster than the speed of light. How the observed substance manifests, particle or wave, all depends on who is looking at them and how. Much of the universe is about our perception, and our visual perception of light is one of the main ways we receive information about the universe. There is even the theory among physicists that the observer of a phenomenon changes the outcome on the quantum level. Magicians have always known the observer, and the observer's intentions, influences the outcome of magick.

One of the best models to understand how the universe operates under these principles is the hologram. The hologram is a three-dimensional construct of light created from the interference pattern of two overlapping systems or patterns of light waves. So if the universe can move information faster than visible light and behaves much like a three-dimensional solid construct of light, the concept of visible light, and this invisible psychic light that mystics believe transfers information in a non-linear manner faster than the speed of visible light should become a more important concept in our understanding of the universe.

The Psychic Eye

The inner organ, or gland, that corresponds to our inner eye, the *ajna* chakra, also known as the brow, the psychic eye, or the third eye is the pineal gland. Like the eyeball itself, the pineal gland, found in the brain with no access to direct light, has rods and cones, the same mechanism our physical eyes use to detect light and color. If it has no direct access to light, what are these sensory mechanisms detecting? Many mystics believe the pineal senses the psychic light moving along with the physically visible light. While the physical light is blocked by the body, the skull and brain, the psychic light passes through such obstacles with no problem. We do find the pineal gland is sensitive to physical light as well, and works differently in those people with seasonal affective disorder, who react poorly to the lack of light in the winter time. Magicians and Witches believe this is the organ that receives and can send psychic light information. This is one of the places where the "inner light" described by spiritual traditions across the world resides within us.

Through candle magick, we unite our inner light with the light of the candle flame, and use the additional visible light of the candle, both the color reflected off the wax and the flame itself, to fuel our spell. For many who are not confident with magick, and even more so for those who are, the candle provides an additional focus. We imprint our inner vision and intention upon the wax and release it with the fire, sending forth both visible and invisible light to manifest our goal. You don't have to have supreme concentration or visualization skills to make candle magick work.

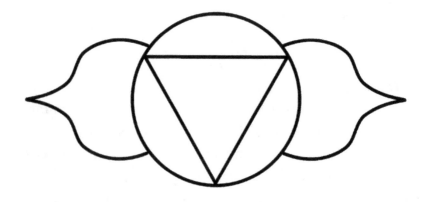

Figure: A Traditional Symbol of the Ajna Chakra

The Levels of Light

Light, both visible and universal, operates on several different levels simultaneously. The first operation of light is considered physiological. Certain colors, when viewed by humans, create particular responses in the body and in the mental and emotional levels. Studies have been done to show that certain colors naturally quiet and calm while others are more likely to agitate. Some are conducive to study, and others are not. This physiological association of color accounts for why the wall color of certain rooms changes our mood. While our personal psychology and experience might influence specific choices, we can generally categorize rooms as peaceful, empowering, healing, or agitating, and color plays a large role in those characterizations.

The second level light operates on is more psychological. Some colors have specific learned associations with them. Some learning is primal programming. If we have a favorite room growing up as a child where we felt the happiest, we will associate that shade of color in the room with such happiness. If we were attacked by a man in a yellow rain jacket, any number of studies can say bright yellow is a color of happiness and joy, but we will still personally associate it with pain or fear. So there is an added layer beyond the foundational color responses.

Magickal systems associate different colors with different intentions, energies, and psychological states. Many would assume the mystic masters of these systems attuned to the natural power of the energy and determined its correspondence. Yet different, working systems can have radically different correspondences. The biggest divide is between systems in the East and West. For example, Eastern Feng Shui suggested painting your door the color red for prosperity and success, while in western Qabalistic magick, royal blue is the color of prosperity. Both have slightly different reasoning behind them. The red door is for the vital life force necessary for success, while in the Qabalah, red is more military and combative. The blue of Qabalah is for the planet Jupiter, the planet of expansion and good fortune and in some forms of Feng Shui blue is feminine, and for healing and calming the family and home, not success. One might argue these systems of magick are a form of psychological programming, particularly some in the traditions of Chaos Magick, who believe all symbolism is arbitrary.

If you learn and believe a particular color does something, then it will fulfill that function for you as long as you truly believe it. Belief becomes a magickal tool.

Color and light works also, and possibly most importantly, on the power of vibration. Each frequency of reflected visible light, and its corresponding internally visualized psychic light, resonates at a particular vibratory rate, just as sounds do. Light waves are measured, with red being the lowest on the visible spectrum, just above infrared, and violet being the highest on the visible light spectrum, just before reaching ultraviolet. Every vibration works on us beyond our visual perception but through the entirety of our body. As sound influences our body so does light, and in particular, so does psychic light. It allows us to read the "vibes" of a room or gain other non-linear psychic information, from hunches to full-fledged visions.

The Colors of Magick

In the traditions of western candle magick, influenced by Hoodoo, Qabala, and Witchcraft, a range of generally accepted traditional color meanings and spell correspondences have arisen. Many are based upon the Qabalistic associations of the colors with the elements and planets and their various magickal correspondences. Others are based on modern interpretations of the Hindu chakra system as a rainbow. Additional color meanings and correspondences are based on folk wisdom and stereotypical associations, such as green with money because in the United States, money is green or black is for cursing because black is traditionally seen as "bad" due to its association with decay and absorbing all light. Red is for love and lust, as we depict the heart as blood red. While the list is not absolute, it does give us a starting point when deciding what color candle would be most appropriate for our spell intention.

Elemental Colors

Element	Color	Associations
Fire	Red, Orange, Yellow	Passion, Will, Creativity, Sex, Soul
Air	Yellow, Light Blue	Thought, Communication, Travel
Water	Dark Blue, Sea-Green	Love, Healing, Relationships
Earth	Black, Brown, Green	Prosperity, Home, Stability, Money

Planetary Colors

Element	Color	Associations
Sun	Gold, Orange, Yellow	True Self, Identity, Power, Essence, Health, Romance, Success, Father
Moon	Silver, Yellow, Violet	Emotions, Karma, Emotional Memory, Mother
Mercury	Orange, Gray	Mind, Thought, Perception, Magic, Androgyny, Travel, Technology, Writing
Venus	Green, Pink	Love, Attraction, Completion, Feminine, Sensuality, Sexuality, Friendship
Mars	Red	Action, Aggression, Initiation, Will, Masculine, Competition, Success

Element	Color	Associations
Jupiter	Purple, Blue	Expansion, Experience, Spirituality, Good Fortune, Prosperity
Saturn	Black, Wine	Limitations, Binding, Tests, Death, Earth, Crystallization
Uranus	Electric Blue, White	Individuality, Outer Expression, New Thoughts, Unorthodox
Neptune	Sea-Green	Inner Expression, Dreams, Romance, Unconditional Love
Pluto	Black, Red, Magenta	Death, Transformation, Rebirth, Obsessions, Sex

General Color Correspondences

Color	Associations
Red	Energy, Passion, Aggression, Sexuality, Lust, Destruction, Power
Red-Orange	Critical Intense Healing, Life Force
Orange	Strong Healing, Energy, Strength, Willpower
Gold	Unconditional Love, God Energy, Divine Will, Power, Wealth, Health
Yellow	Spirituality, Communication, Thoughts, Logic, Health, Clarity, Optimism, Cheer
Green	Healing, Love, Growth, Life, Mother Earth, Money, Prosperity, Success, Gambling
Turquoise	Higher Love, Higher Heart, Unconditional Acceptance, Divinity, Balance
Blue	Peace, Prosperity, Spirituality, Dreams, Spirit Healing, Luck, Good Fortune
Pink	Love, Happiness, Self-Esteem, Romance, Family

Color	Associations
Indigo	Psychic Energy, Visualization, Opening the Senses, Deep Peace
Purple	Spirituality, Tranquility, Balance, Prosperity, Psychic Ability
Violet	Cleansing, Neutralizing, Balance, Divinity, Psychic Powers
White	Healing, Love, Connection to All, Spirit Contact, Ancestors, Angels, Blessings
Silver	Goddess Energy, Moon, Maiden, Emotional Healing, Psychic Powers, Cycles
Black	Grounding, Magic, Meditation, Mystery, Crossroads, Crone Goddesses, Cursing
Brown	Healing, Grounding, Animal Powers
Rust	Removing Unwanted Energies, Release

One of the critiques of modern candle magick is the idea that the color of the wax is irrelevant, and it's the color of the light itself that matters. Regardless of the color of the wax, the flame is the same and radiating out the same color no matter the intention. Some would say that the color of the wax is to align the practitioner, and to contain the appropriate intention to be released in the melting process as the flame burns, but critics say it's the flame color that is the most important.

They look to another tradition encoded in the church's form of candle magick, colored glass containers. Most are in red and blue, and clear votive glasses tend to reflect the white candle. In fact, all the candle wax colors are the same because the wax doesn't matter as much as the light passing through the colored glass to fulfill the intention. Modern ceremonial magicians often have altar lamps, and place either colored glass, color tissue paper, or plastic "gel" filters used in stage lighting, around the lamp or candle to cast the temple in a particularly appropriate elemental, planetary, or zodiac energy. If you want to commune with a spirit associated with the planet Mars, literally fill your room with red light to make the physical environment more conducive to the communication. Likewise, if you hold a Mars or fire intention, putting the candle in a red glass container will help send that intention out into the universe with the red light frequency more than a red wax candle. Though, one could argue the candlelight is also being reflected off the colored wax.

Though I have a great appreciation for the argument and aesthetically appreciate the colored glass for various rituals, I've not found it to be detrimental to my spell casting. Again, it could involve belief systems and the way we are first taught magick, but I've done just fine with colored wax candles. I have used colored gels upon glass seven-day candles to change the quality of light for ritual and enjoyed that, and I have bought colored glass votives, but I also enjoy candles in different colors and shapes, and won't stop using these candles as they have proven effective for me in the past.

I also remember learning from Laurie Cabot, about how when she was young and in training as a Witch, they did not manufacture colored candles. That came later. At that time, candles were all white. You set your intention by placing things around the candles, and since white is the all-purpose color today, it worked for her then, before Witches even thought about having colored candles.

Use colored glass and colored lanterns as you feel called. Explore the idea of passing the spell's light through such frequencies, and see what works best for you as we progress on this path.

An excellent exercise in color magick is to meditate upon each color individually and see what associations you naturally come up with for that color. How does it make you feel? What do you think about? What are your magickal associations with the color? Many people will pick a color a day, focusing on that color and wearing it as an article of clothing, journaling the experience each day until they have a good set of personal color correspondences. If you need more structure to explore color meditation, try the exercise below.

Exercise: Color Reflection

Start this exercise by performing The Psychic Candle exercise from **Chapter One**. Once you have held the image of the candle in your mind's eye, try evoking the different colors. You can imagine the candle you are visualizing is changing color, or better yet, imagine the light itself is changing color, as if it's passing through a colored glass or colored screen. The colored light is bathing you in its glow. Notice how you feel, intuitively, with each color.

If you have difficulty imagining the colors casting from the candle, think of something easy to imagine that is that color, then imagine it so large the color fills the room, surrounding you. Red can be imagined with an apple or fire engine. Orange with the citrus fruit of the same name. Yellow is called forth with a lemon. Green is envisioned with grass or other vegetation. Blue is imagined with a clear blue sky. Indigo and related shades are the color of the night sky, and violet is found in the flowers.

When you first try this, do it with elemental colors. Start with the quality of Fire of the Wise, and imagine the light in red, then orange and finally yellow. Does one feel more like "fire" to you? Then evoke the quality of the Air of the Wise. Envision the candle casting a paler yellow, and then a light blue. Does one feel more like "air" to you? Then summon forth the quality of Water of the

Wise. The candle casts colors of dark blue followed by sea-green. Does one feel more like "water" to you? Lastly call the quality of Earth of the Wise. As paradoxical as it sounds, let the candle cast a "dark" light of black, then brown and dark green. Does one feel more like "earth" to you? Reflect on the colors of the elements. Take notice of the feelings of each color and how it can influence your magick on an elemental level.

The next time you do this exercise, try it with the planets. You can do the first "seven" planets of the ancients, or all ten used by modern astrologers and magicians today. Start with the Sun, and envision the candle casting gold and orange light upon you, conjuring the qualities of the Sun. Next is the Moon, casting a pale yellow, silver, and light violet or lilac color. Mercury's traditional color is usually orange, but grey is also appropriate. The light of the Venus candle will be green, and then pink. Mars' light is always red. Jupiter casts the royal colors of blue and purple, rich and deep. Saturn's colors are dark, black, or a deep wine. The outer three planets are unusual in their colors. Uranus will always have an electric color, ranging from an electric blue, blue-white, white, or electric yellow. Neptune's candle casts a sea-green hue upon everything. Pluto, like Saturn, has dark shades. Black again, as well as a deep red and magenta. Again take notice of the qualities each color has upon you for future reference in your magick.

The third time you do this exercise, dispense with the elemental and planetary schemes, and simply choose the colors as you will, exploring them on their own as simple vibrations and energies. You can follow the list in the book or create your own, keeping it complex or simple as you see fit. Like the previous two times, note your feelings and thoughts with each color, and how these impressions can help you in your magick.

The Lighting of Candles

CHAPTER FOUR:
CANDLE DRESSING

I've always found the idea of "dressing" a candle to be funny. When my teacher first spoke of it, I imagined us putting little doll clothes onto a candle, and making a doll, or poppet, out of it. I learned much later that my juvenile idea could actually be used in traditions of sympathetic magick, using a carved candle as a substitute for the stereotypical "voodoo doll." That is why the human-shaped candles are so popular in magick. They combine the idea of a candle spell with a poppet. But what my teacher referred to as "dressing" a candle might be considered adornment or decoration of a candle, to add to its power.

The simplest form of dressing is to anoint a candle with an oil, potion, ointment, or other spreadable substance. Sometimes dried herbs, rather than oils, are mixed with the candle wax when making it, or coat the outside of the candle. The magickal charge of a well-crafted potion, or the natural properties of herbal oils add their inherent power to the candle. Just as each color has its own vibration, each plant has a more complex combination of vibrations, rooted in the chemicals that constitute its make-up and medicine, and correspond with properties in herbal healing and magick. Choosing an appropriate potion or oil can add to the energy of the candle and increase your chances of success with a spell. As the wax with the dressing on it burns, it also releases the magick of the plant substances. If using an essential oil, or essential oil blend, the scent releases as the candle heats and burns and is also a method to engage and project the energy of the plant substances, what is known as their vibration in the modern era, or "virtue" in more traditional circles. The act of anointing the candle itself helps empower the magician. When you are crafting the spell, you will be influenced by the scent of the dressing, helping conjure a magickal atmosphere. Its magick will work first upon you, helping create the necessary internal changes to then manifest the spell's results externally.

Along with substances applied to the candle, the next most common form of dressing is to carve the candle, or mark its container, with magickal symbols and glyphs relating to the candle's intention. Extending the idea of sacred geometry and pattern to candle magick, a design can be made from a number of candles. Each is an individual spell, but together, they contribute to the entire working. Candles can be arranged in certain formations, and utilizing the formation of the candles on the work space lends itself to the purpose of the spell. Creative magicians link candle magick with other forms of spell casting, and might extend the idea with stones and crystals, incense, animal bones, photos, and other talismans. The candle or candles can be the engine of the spell. The dressings of herbs, oils, and magickal carving contribute to it. The overall pattern sets the energy for the larger working.

Dressing Techniques

Candle dressing customs differ from tradition to tradition, and from practitioner to practitioner. In days past, with limited resources and communication, there were techniques common to most occultists that were considered tried and true. Practitioners then based their own personal techniques on these foundations. With the access to more information, more materials and seeing the work of other candle magicians through the use of photos and even social media, a new wave of candle customs have been created. Traditionalists often wonder how effective they truly are, but we each have to judge for ourselves how effective a spell is in our life.

Here I share with you some of the standard ideas as I learned them, and encourage you to adapt them as you choose. Always write down your magickal experiments and spells in a journal, so you can go back and evaluate what really worked, and what just looked good. My advice is to favor effectiveness over artistic expression. While I think art is a huge component of magick, if something is wonderfully expressive, but the operation fails to meet its objective, then the art was not an effective spell.

Anointing

While dressing a candle with a liquid is not a requirement for some of the other techniques, it is the most basic form of preparing a candle for magick, beyond simply holding and lighting an unadorned candle. The art of formulating complex potions and herbal preparations is the aim of the third volume of this series, but a candle magician can use herbal recipes before learning the greater mysteries of formulation. Many shops and professional practitioners have blends already prepared that can be used on their own as a personal perfume, or in conjunction with spellcraft, including candle magick.

The oil is first placed upon your hands, adding to the magician's natural power when holding and consecrating the candle when casting the spell. The wafting scent of the oil is a magickal trigger for the magician, appropriately altering their own state of mind and energy to match the virtue of the oil. Magicians who have an animist perspective, believing that all things are alive and have an indwelling or animating spirit, believe that each plant has a plant spirit, and that plant spirit can be contacted through the plant substances. When your intention is in alignment with the plant spirit, it lends its power to the spell. Dressing a candle is a way of adding not just the energy of the plant, but aligning with the consciousness of the plant.

Ideally, all natural substances are used to add the natural plant spirit power to the spell, though some gain benefit also from using synthetic fragrance oils. The scent becomes a memory trigger to empower the magician, even if no plant spirit is actually present in the materials, though most herbal magicians prefer the natural oils over synthetics. There are simply certain scents that are not easily or cheaply obtained from essential oils and natural plant extracts. Such scents can evoke something magickal in their scent memory, despite the lack of natural power. Many find the scent of strawberry, blueberry, or various florals enchanting for magick, though they're not easily available in natural forms. One must make sure that any synthetic oils used on candles are designed to be burned. Those that are not will smell like burning plastic when used upon candles, a factor you don't have to worry about with natural substances, though not all natural substances smell pleasant when burned!

Rather than start with a complex personal or store-bought formula, many of us use a single oil for a spell, choosing the most appropriate oil for the spell, factoring in what we have access to and what is financially affordable. A huge amount of aromatic plant matter is needed to make a small quantity of natural essential oil, so making many oils is quite expensive, particularly popular and elusive scents such as true rose and jasmine. Other more plentiful flowers with easier to extract oils, such as lavender, are more available and affordable.

Magickal Essential Oils

Oil	Element	Planets	Uses
Amber	Fire	Sun	Health, Success, Well Being, Happiness, Protection
Black Pepper	Fire	Mars	Protection, Power
Catnip	Water, Air	Venus	Attraction, Mystery, Relaxation
Cinnamon	Fire	Jupiter	Success, Money, Prosperity, Love, Friendship
Elder	Earth	Saturn	Faeries, Protection, Health
Frankincense	Fire	Sun, Jupiter	Protection, Optimism, Success, Health, Cleansing, Blessing
Heliotrope	Fire	Sun	Health, Regeneration, Success, Happiness
Jasmine	Water	Moon	Psychic Power, Love, Lust, Attraction
Lavender	Air	Mercury, Jupiter	Relaxation, Healing, Peace, Faeries
Lemon	Water	Moon	Purification, Love, Optimism
Lemongrass	Water, Earth	Moon, Venus	Protection, Purification, Love, Healing
Mimosa	Fire, Water	Sun, Moon	Enchantment, Glamour, Illusions, Shapeshifting
Mugwort	Water	Moon	Psychic Power, Spirit Contact, Purification, Protection

Oil	Element	Planets	Uses
Myrrh	Earth, Water	Moon, Saturn	Protection, Preservation, Ancestors, Dark Goddesses, Blessing
Orange	Fire, Water	Sun	Health, Success, Happiness
Patchouli	Earth	Saturn	Protection, Love, Manifestation, Binding
Peppermint	Air	Mercury	Communication, Memory, Peace
Pine	Air, Fire	Jupiter	Leadership, Strength, Purification, Health
Rose	Water, Air, Earth	Venus	Magick, Mystery, Love, Healing, Beauty
Rosemary	Fire	Sun	Memory, Health, Purification
Sage	Fire, Air	Jupiter	Protection, Purification, Health, Money
Vetiver	Air, Earth	Mercury, Uranus, Earth	Psychic Travel, Grounding, Protection, Horned God
Ylang Ylang	Water	Moon, Neptune	Psychic Power, Love, Illusions, Dreams

While an essential oil can be applied directly to a candle, since you'll usually be touching it, it's recommended to dilute the oils. Just because they are all-natural does not mean they are all safe. Many oils are quite caustic to the skin. They are medicines as well as being magickal tools, and can have a biochemical reaction in our body through both scent and skin absorption. For a simple single taper candle, I would suggest mixing 3 to 5 drops of the essential oil with 10 to 20 drops of a "carrier" or base oil. While we

The Lighting of Candles

label these essential extracts as "oils" they are not true fats, but some pretty powerful chemicals. Base oils are true fats, usually plant-based fats.

Base Oils

Base Oil	Planet	Associations
Olive	Earth	All Purpose, Healing, Strengthening
Sunflower	Sun	Success, Health, Prosperity, Beauty
Hazel	Mercury	All Purpose, Communication
Apricot Kernel	Venus	Love, Friendship
Grapeseed	Jupiter, Neptune	All Purpose, Dreams, Psychic Ability
Jojoba	Earth	All Purpose, Preserving, Protection
Hemp Seed	Moon, Sun	Healing, Dreams
Almond	Sun, Moon, Mercury	All Purpose, Mystery
Sweet Almond	Venus, Mercury	Attraction, Good Luck, Friendship
Macadamia Nut	Venus, Earth	Beauty, Health, Home Blessings
Sesame	Mercury, Earth	All Purpose, Prosperity, Travel
Castor	Mars	Protection, Strength
Coconut	Moon, Saturn, Earth	All Purpose, Dreams, Psychic Power, Binding
Palm	Mars	Protection, Uncrossing, Power

For those who don't wish to delve into making simple blends from a recipe, or risk using the wrong essential oil, you can use a simple scentless oil considered holy in many traditions, olive oil. Along with being an excellent base for oils being used more immediately, it has a rich history of magick. Olives were the sacred gift of Athena to the people of Athens and the oil is considered both a staple and a medicine in the Mediterranean. It has a history of a holy oil in Jewish and Christian traditions, and many Witches have used it as a base for their own oils and ointments. Unfortunately it can turn rancid more quickly than other oils, so commercial oil producers and even handcraft artisans will usually use a more stable oil as a base oil to mix their blends, such as a liquid wax known as jojoba oil, or grapeseed or apricot kernel oil. Almond oil is another holy oil used in magick and it has a wide range of healing and holy properties. Sunflower is also used, with its obvious associations to solar magick. You can use any of these as a base oil for a solitary oil blend to be used on a candle, or for a mix of oils. One of the most long-lasting oils used in some forms of earth magick but usually shunned by aromatherapists and holistic practitioners is mineral oil. Some magickal companies will use mineral oil as its base, since unlike plant products, it won't turn rancid. I personally think the plant oils hold plant magick and medicine better, but under certain circumstances I'm not averse to using mineral oil.

Any of these oils can be used as a base in magickal blends for candle magick. Here are some basic formulas that can be used for dressing a candle. Their ingredients are not incredibly exotic, nor should they be too expensive, and can be found at health food stores, herbal shops, occult supply shops, and online.

Magick Power Anointing Oil

8 oz. of Base Oil
1 Teaspoon of Dragons Blood Resin, powdered
½ Teaspoon of Vervain

¼ Teaspoon of Frankincense Resin, powdered
¼ Teaspoon of Myrrh Resin, powdered
10 Drops of Vitamin E Oil

Place base oil in a double boiler, or simply make one by putting a Pyrex glass container in a bowl of warm water upon the stove. Gently heat the oil in the double boiler and add the herbal ingredients to the oil. Turn off the heat and let cool. Strain through cheese cloth, separating the oil from the herbs and resins. When in a clean bottle, add the Vitamin E oil to help preserve it. This oil can enhance any magickal purpose, and packs a serious energetic punch to most spells. Not to be used in spell intentions calling for a gentle manifestation of the results.

Holy Oil

8 Oz of Base Oil
4 Drops of Frankincense Essential Oil
2 Drops of Myrrh Essential Oil
1 Drop of Cinnamon Essential Oil
1 Drop of Rose Essential Oil (substitute a pinch of Rose Petals)
10 Drops of Vitamin E Oil

Place the oil in a mixing container and add the essential oils, drop by drop, swirling them in with a clockwise motion, to blend them with the base oil. When all the essential oils are in, repeat the swirling motion with the Vitamin E oil to preserve it. A great all-purpose oil to be used in almost any spell with balanced energy and results. Use rose petals if rose oil is unavailable.

Blessing Oil

8 Oz of Base Oil
3 Drops of Pine Essential Oil

3 Drops of Lavender Essential Oil

2 Drops Rosemary Essential Oil

10 Drops of Vitamin E Oil

Like the Holy Oil, mix the essential oils into the base oil drop by drop, swirling in with a clockwise motion to blend them fully, followed by the Vitamin E. This is a great gentle oil, for when you want slower and more gentle results in your magick.

Dark Power Oil

8 Oz of Base Oil

3 Drops of Myrrh Essential Oil

2 Drops of Patchouli Essential Oil

1 Drop of Vetiver Essential Oil

1 Pinch of Black Pepper

10 Drops of Vitamin E Oil

Mix each of the essential oils into the base oil, but in this instance, with a counterclockwise motion. Use this oil for rituals that are for diminishing or removing, for aggressive protection, and for intentions that some might consider to have a high "coin" to pay, having personal spiritual consequences.

The motion of the dressing is very important to many candle magicians, though the systems used in determining the motion differs from one practitioner to the next. The most common system suggests you anoint the candle in the center with both hands, and move outward to the tip with one hand and the base with the other, making the energy of the candle balanced as you dress the candle and focus upon your intention.

The second method is determined by your intention. If you are seeking to manifest something, you anoint the tip of the candle and draw the substance down to the base. You are symbolically drawing it from beyond down into manifestation to you. This is most often done for those performing waxing Moon magick if following customary lunar cycle teachings. In such teachings, if you are seeking to manifest something or create, you do your spell when the Moon's light is waxing, or growing towards the full Moon. If you are seeking to banish and diminish something, you would anoint the base of the candle and move away to the tip, symbolizing moving it away from you. This is done for waning Moon magick in lunar teachings, when the Moon's light is diminishing, from the Full Moon to the Dark Moon.

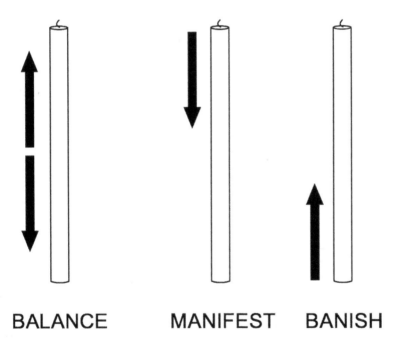

BALANCE   MANIFEST   BANISH

Figure: Candle Dressing Oil Motions

Others feel it doesn't matter how you dress a candle as long as you get the candle covered in the liquid. Likewise, many candle magick practitioners don't care about the tides of the Moon, and simply do whatever magick they need, whenever they need it. While there can be a power in such a confident strength of will, drawn from need and desire, I personally have had a lot of good fortune with following the astrological tides of the Moon, Sun, and planets. How you can use such timing with candles and other forms of magick, will be covered in **Chapter Five**.

There are several other adornment and embellishment techniques you can use in conjunction with anointing to add even more power to your candle spell. You don't have to use every technique in every spell, but each one can add a little extra energy. Practitioners should follow their intuition to determine which of these techniques is necessary for each spell.

Rolling

Rolling refers to literally rolling an anointed candle in a magickal powder, letting the powder stick to the candle. Some, rather than literally rolling the candle, will simply sprinkle the powder on the oiled candle. While it can work with various anointing methods, it usually works best with a blended oil, a mix of a thicker true base oil blended with volatile essential oils for scent and power. In a pinch, our old friend and ally olive oil can be used with great success to adhere powders to the candle. The rolling powders can be a finely ground herb or a mixture of herbs, although some use glitter and finely powdered minerals like pyrite. Though safety should be taken with any candle magick, even more so with rolled candles. Burn them on a tile or dish, in a cauldron, or on other flame-proof surface, for bits of burning powdered herb will often fall from the candle, and create a greater risk for fire.

Some rolling herbs for this technique include:

Magickal Herbs

Herb	Element	Planets	Use
Allspice	Fire	Jupiter	Good Fortune, Blessings
Angelica	Fire, Air	Sun	Angelic Magick, Healing, Protection
Basil	Fire	Mars	Passion, Sex, Fast Cash
Bay	Earth, Fire	Sun, Jupiter	Success, Legal Power, Prophecy, Dreams
Calendula	Fire	Sun	Health, Fidelity, Psychic Power
Catnip	Water	Venus	Dream, Rest, Psychic Power, Cat Magick
Chamomile	Fire, Water	Sun	Healing, Dreams, Meditation, Success
Chickweed	Water	Moon	Friendship, Lightening, Ease
Cinnamon	Fire, Earth	Jupiter	Influence, Prosperity, Riches, Love
Cinquefoil	Earth, Air	Sun, Mercury, Moon	Curse Breaking, Protection, Understanding
Comfrey	Earth	Saturn	Regeneration, Protection, Past Life Memory
Cloves	Fire	Jupiter	Success, Fame, Stop Gossip, Stop Pain
Copal	Fire	Sun, Jupiter	Protection, Blessing, Banishing Harm
Coriander	Fire	Mars	Lust, Passion, Love, Energy
Damiana	Fire, Earth	Venus, Mars	Lust, Sexuality, Vitality
Dill	Air	Mercury	Prosperity, Multiplication, Safe Travel
Dragon's Blood	Fire	Mars, Pluto	Power, Strength, Energy
Elder Flower	Water, Earth	Moon, Venus, Saturn	Protection, Faery Magick, Health
Fennel	Air, Earth	Mercury, Neptune	Calm, Peace, Soothing, Prosperity
Feverfew	Earth	Venus, Sun	Protection, Healing, Motherhood, Love

Herb	Element	Planets	Use
Frankincense	Fire	Sun, Jupiter	Protection, Blessing, Success
Garlic	Fire, Earth	Mars	Protection, Prevents Psychic Vampirism
Galangal	Fire	Mars, Pluto	Protection, Sex, Spirituality
Jasmine Flowers	Water	Moon	Psychic Powers, Dreams, Healing
Juniper	Earth	Jupiter	Blessing, Cleansing, Psychic Sight
Lavender	Air	Mercury, Jupiter	Peace, Clarity, Rest, Prosperity
Licorice	Air, Water	Mercury, Venus	Controlling Addictions, Clear Speech
Lobelia	Fire	Mars	Clearing, Opening, Catalyzing
Lovage	Water, Earth	Venus, Neptune	Love, Beauty, Glamour
Myrrh	Earth, Water	Moon, Saturn	Protection, Binding, Preserving
Mugwort	Earth, Water	Moon	Psychic Power, Protection
Mullein	Earth, Fire	Sun, Saturn	Protection, Psychic Contact, Ancestors
Nutmeg	Earth, Fire	Venus, Mars, Jupiter	Psychic Power, Aura Cleanse, Happiness, Success
Oak Bark	Earth	Jupiter	Leadership, Strength, Protection, Endurance
Orris Root	Water, Air	Venus, Moon	Love, Protection, Psychic, Spirit Contact
Mistletoe	Fire	Sun, Moon	Spirit, Catalyst, Blessing, Power
Parsley	Earth, Fire	Mars	Cunning, Secret Knowledge, Protection
Patchouli	Earth	Saturn	Protection, Love, Grounding
Black Pepper	Fire	Mars	Power, Aggression, Protection, Lust
Peppermint	Air	Mercury	Clarity, Healing, Communication
Pine	Air, Earth	Jupiter	Purification, Health, Leadership

Herb	Element	Planets	Use
Rose	Earth, Water, Air	Venus	Love, Spirituality, Balance, Healing
Rue	Earth, Fire	Mars	Protection, Grace, Blessing
Sage	Earth, Air	Jupiter	Healing, Clearing, Prosperity
Skullcap	Air	Mercury	Success in Education, Intelligence, Memory
St. John's Wort	Fire	Sun	Light, Protection, Clear Nightmares
Tansy	Earth, Fire	Sun, Venus, Pluto	Protection, Ancestral Reverence
Tarragon	Fire	Mars, Saturn, Pluto	Dragon Magick, Independence, Strength
Thyme	Air	Mercury	Speeds Magick, Wishes, Love
Vervain	Air	Mercury, Venus	Blessing, Protection, Love, Success
Yarrow	Water, Fire	Venus, Mars	Boundaries, Flow, Love, Health
Willow Bark	Water	Moon	Psychic Power, Faery Magick
Wormwood	Fire, Earth	Mars, Pluto	Spirit Contact, Protection, Banishment

Along with herbs, some will include some minerals, particularly for protection rituals, and include things like salt, sulfur, or iron filings. Powdered eggshell is a potential ingredient for such magick. As with the basic oil blends, you can use the following blends for various forms of magick. A "part" can be any measurement. Just keep the proportions by volume for the formulas, and realize this is not an exact science, but like cooking, an art as well. Many of the measurements, when done by volume rather than weight, will differ on the consistency of the grinding of each substance before mixing them. Ideally, make sure all substances are as ground up as possible prior to rolling or sprinkling the candle with the powder.

Power Powder

2 Parts Dragon's Blood
1 Part Wormwood
1 Part Tarragon

Money Powder No. 1

1 Part Pine Needles
1 Part Oak Bark
1 Part Calendula

Money Powder No. 2

1 Part Basil Leaves
1 Part Patchouli

Love Powder

3 Parts Rose Petals
2 Parts Patchouli
1 Part Orris Root
1 Part Cinnamon

Lust Powder

2 Parts Damiana
2 Parts Basil
1 Part Coriander
1 Part Dragon's Blood

Good Luck Powder

2 Parts Frankincense
2 Parts Cinnamon
1 Part Clove

The Lighting of Candles

Healing Powder
1 Part Chamomile
1 Part Catnip
1 Part Lavender
1 Part Vervain

Protection Powder No. 1
2 Parts Frankincense
2 Parts Myrrh
1 Part St. John's Wort

Protection Powder No. 2
1 Part Garlic Powder
1 Part Oak Bark
1 Part Vervain
1 Part Rue

Psychic Powder
2 Parts Jasmine Flowers
1 Part Mugwort
1 Part Sandalwood
1 Part Orris Root

Safe Travel Powder
1 Part Dill Seeds
1 Part Sage
1 Part Peppermint

Legal Success Powder
2 Parts Calendula
2 Parts Galangal
1 Part Cinnamon

1 Part Blueberry Leaves or Berries

Creativity Powder
1 Part Catnip
1 Part Lavender
1 Part Chamomile
1 Part Nutmeg

The more finely ground these mixes are, the more easily they will stick to the candle. You can grind them by hand with a mortar and pestle, or some modern practitioners use a coffee grinder designated only for magickal work, as sometimes the most powerful magickal substances are also the most poisonous and should not mix with items used for consumable foodstuff or herbal medicine. I even keep separate mortar and pestle sets: one is for magickal work; specifically, one is for medicines and food, and one is for poisons.

Carving

To carve a candle is to etch letters, symbols, and images into the wax using a sharp instrument. Carving combines symbol and sigil magick with candle magick, and the etching provides a space for anointing fluids and powders to cling. Some carvings are fairly simple, with just a letter or two. Others are geometric designs and images involving great complexity.

The symbols carved can be from a variety of systems and traditions, and popularly include simple letters and initials from the Latin alphabet, foreign languages such as Greek or Hebrew, astrological glyphs, Nordic runes, Celtic ogham, sigils, simple shapes, and images. The meaning of the symbols adds to the power of the candle magick. Some symbols are considered to be archetypal powers in and of themselves, such as the runes. Their power is inherent in the symbol itself. Nothing further is really needed.

More traditional candle magicians feel that symbol systems shouldn't be mixed in one candle spell, while others feel free to mix symbols from several different systems in one spell. Traditionalists wouldn't mix astrological glyphs with Norse runes, while a less traditional practitioner would have no problem mixing Greek letters with Celtic tree symbols. I must admit, I had no such early admonishments from traditionalists, and tend to fall under a more modern view, using the tools that intuitively call to me, or systems I've had a relationship with already. I've had no adverse effects mixing systems. I think such traditions started in the ancient world of Alexandria and the well-respected Greek Magical Papyri, where a variety of cultures and systems were mixed, to great effect.

A simple use of candle carving is to carve the name or initials of the person who you want the spell to affect. You can also carve the astrological glyph of their birth, or Sun, sign. If the spell can be summed up by a particular word or short phrase, it can be carved along the side of the candle in English or your native language. Some carve simple pictures into the candle, such as hearts, $'s, X's, Moons, Suns, and stars. Emojis in social media are not so far off from what candle magicians have been carving for some time. They have a hieroglyphic quality. Sometimes when evoking the favor of a particular saint or deity, the candle is carved in the image of the figure, with eyes, ears, face, hands, and mouth.

The carving tool can be any sharp instrument conducive to carving. The traditional tool, a pointed wooden or metal instrument, is known as a burin, but most modern practitioners use a sharp nail, the edge of a small knife, a penknife, a thorn, or even their fingernail.

Consider the following candle carving examples:

+ Runes for Healing
+ Money Spell for Jane
+ Protection Candle for Harry
+ Apple, Hawthorn, and Willow Ogham for Faery Communication

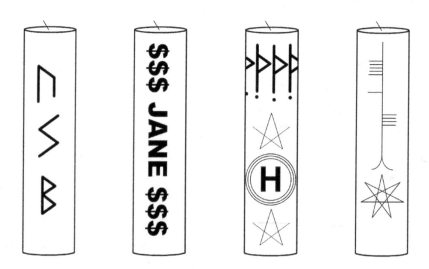

Figure: Symbols on Candles

Packing

Packing is probably the least used of these candle techniques as it can be the most work-intensive, difficult, and potentially dangerous. Packing a candle refers to carving out a small portion of the candle base. A pinch of powdered herb or herb mixture is placed into the hollowed-out section, and then sealed with wax from another candle. The sealing wax does not necessarily have to match the first candle color. Usually, a simple white candle is used to seal. When the candle burns down, the herb burns. Depending on how the candle melts, the herb can be infused in a pool of wax without setting on fire, or catch flame and burn in a small and fast blaze. Sometimes the herbs can smolder like incense. In any case, it releases an additional bit of energy right at the end to give the spell an extra blast of magick.

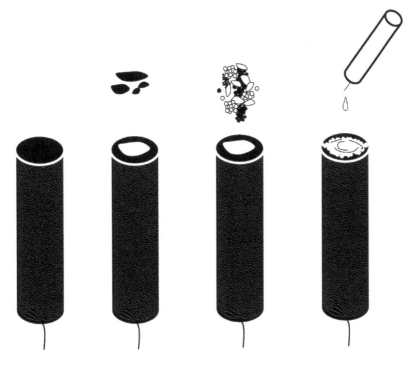

Figure: Candle Packing

If you are using this technique, it is important to make sure that you have an appropriate holder for the candle. If using this technique on a standard taper, make sure the candleholder is metal. Glass, crystal, and stone can shatter under the excess heat generated by the burning herbs, and the various fragments can travel across and room at a speed and temperature to damage other objects and people. While many consider that a sign of a really powerful spell, it is often simply a sign of poor planning and foresight.

Some consider it safer to make their own candles and add the herbs during creation, rather than preparing and packing a commercial candle. Candlemakers spread herbs into the cooling wax, or even drop small crystals or stone chips at the bottom. When done effectively, the candle releases the stone when burned, and it can be used as a talisman to further the spell, or the final act of magick to seal the intention can be to bury the stone on your property, to keep the effect close to you, or release it somewhere else if seeking to banish an unwanted force.

Designing Candle Art

Complex designs carved upon candles and decorated with powders or glitter, are more common on larger pull-out and pillar candles. These symbols are combinations of designs infused with complex meaning to manifest your goal. They are most prevalent in Hoodoo and African Diaspora traditions in the botanicas, but have been brought into Neopagan traditions popularly through the work of Lady Rhea, former owner of Enchantments in New York City, though many Witches and Wiccan have been using such techniques.

Such carvings go beyond the simple symbols inscribed upon the side of a taper candle. Some are geometric in form, create balanced and complex patterns of lines. Often at the heart of the patterns is a star or some other geometric shape. Esoteric lore tells us numbers encode magick just as much as color and scent, so the number of points on the star references the type of magickal intention for the spell. While there are several different systems of numerology, often disagreeing with each other, the systems of Qabalistic numerology and geometry influence most western magicians on some levels, even those American Hoodoo practitioners who absorbed grimoire traditions, planetary hours, and Hebrew letters into their practices.

Basic Shapes, Stars and Correspondences

Triangle (Trigon)	Square (Tetragon)	Pentagon	Hexagon	Septagon (Heptagon)
Three Points	Tetracle	Pentacle	Hexagram	Septagram (Heptagram)
Saturn Dark Goddess	Jupiter Sky Father	Mars (Venus) War God	Sun Sun God	Venus Love Goddess
Stillness, Shadow	Good Fortune, Guidance, Law	Victory, Destruction	Wealth, Awareness	Romance, Lust
Black, Wine	Purple, Blue	Red	Gold, Yellow, Orange	Green, Pink

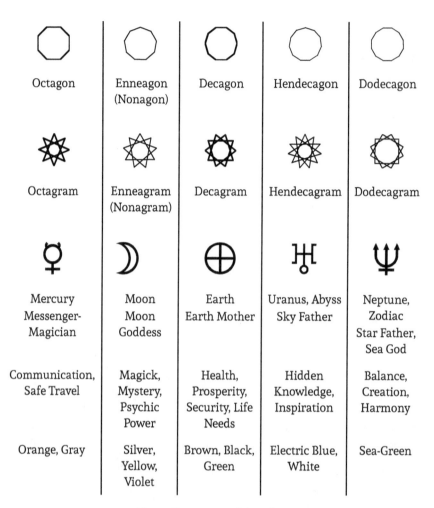

Octagon	Enneagon (Nonagon)	Decagon	Hendecagon	Dodecagon
Octagram	Enneagram (Nonagram)	Decagram	Hendecagram	Dodecagram
Mercury Messenger-Magician	Moon Moon Goddess	Earth Earth Mother	Uranus, Abyss Sky Father	Neptune, Zodiac Star Father, Sea God
Communication, Safe Travel	Magick, Mystery, Psychic Power	Health, Prosperity, Security, Life Needs	Hidden Knowledge, Inspiration	Balance, Creation, Harmony
Orange, Gray	Silver, Yellow, Violet	Brown, Black, Green	Electric Blue, White	Sea-Green

Figure: Geometry and Astrology

While most of the associations in this chart are from Hermetic Qabalah teachings, Venus, and the Five-pointed Star, or Pentacle, are often associated together as an overall symbol of magickal power and Witchcraft. Venus' orbit with the Sun and Earth makes a pattern noticeable from the Earth that is akin to a five-petalled flower. In modern Qabalistic lore, Pluto is most often associated with the top of the Qabalistic Tree and the number one.

With or without such stars and shapes as a basis for the carving, other symbols can be used, including astrological glyphs, religious signs such as crosses or Om signs, mystical symbols like the caduceus, chakra mandalas, and simple shapes like dragons, snakes, birds, rabbits, claws, trees, mountains, wheels, coins, knives, purses, and flowers.

Cross	Snake	Flower	Mountain	Wheel
Balance	Change	Nature	Travel	Movement
Christianity	Healing	Love	Spirituality	Vacation
Ancestors	Power	Healing	Adventure	Escape

Figure: Simple Shapes

Heart Chakra	Eye	Caduceus	Purse	Rose
Love	Vision	Healing	Winning	Romance
Healing	Protection	Travel	Prosperity	Mystery
Balance	Inspiration	Magick	Good Luck	Royalty

Figure: Complex Shapes

Different symbols can be added to a central "base" image upon the candle, or a free-standing image or collection of images and symbols, based upon the intention of the spell, can be carved.

Figure: Angel of Protection with Pentacles and Hexagrams

Figure: Cupid Heart Love Spell

Once a pull-out has been carved, many will oil it, but first oil specific sections and then decorate them in a powder, most often colored glitter. Imagine your carving is like stained glass, with the lines like the connecting metal between the panes of glass. Oil one "pane" of the drawing. Sprinkle the appropriate colored glitter upon it. Gently blow off any excess glitter and any glitter that struck a non-oiled surface. The lack of oil makes it less likely to stick, but glitter is quite tricky and no candle will be "perfect." Let it dry a little and then repeat again, until all the different "panes" of the drawing are appropriately glittered.

For those who don't have easy access to the larger pull-out candles, similar art, created or collaged from magazines and computer printouts, can be adhered to the outside of glass. They can be black and white, and colored in yourself, or printed in full color. The art can simply be affixed upon the glass with tape, or in a more traditional and artistic style decoupaged upon the glass. Others draw or print on adhesive "sticker" paper and stick it directly upon the candle as a label.

Spellcasters have used, quite successfully, traditional grimoire images and amulets, even without a deep understanding of how they were crafted. Popular in both Hoodoo and Wicca is the use of the "pentacles" which are really geometric designs, from *The Greater Key of Solomon* grimoire. Some would simply place the image under the candle, but today, they are mounted right upon the glass holder. Likewise, images of tarot cards, woodcuts, etchings, famous pieces of art, and even photos of famous practitioners and movie stars, can be used for candles to honor the dead.

Figure: Seal of Archangel Michael

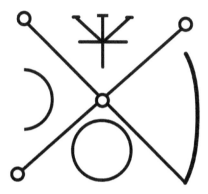

Figure: Seal of the Planetary Intelligence of Venus

Figure: Candle Art

For the more artistically inclined, but lacking the fortitude for glitter and candle carving, you can find a variety of paints that work on glass, ranging from traditional acrylics, to the pen-bottle style fabric and "puffy" paint available at craft stores. Using brushes, paint pens, permanent "Sharpie" pens, or bottle markers, you can draw directly on the glass. The thicker puffy paints often peel off, allowing you to more easily reuse the glass candleholder again.

Arranging Candle Grids and Mandalas

Though technically not a "dressing" for the candle, the last type of candle preparation is creating the artistic symbol not upon the candle itself but with the candle upon the altar or workspace. Such patterns are akin to what crystal practitioners call "grids" but instead of using just crystals, the candles become the primary focus for the grid. The patterns formed by the grid are reminiscent of the spiritual art form known as mandalas, as expressed in Hindu yantra designs, alchemical etchings, and the sand paintings of the Navajo and Tibetans. Modern psychologists use the art of making, or at least coloring, mandalas as a method to balance and calm the mind and give awareness to deeper perceptions.

Similar to the geometric art carved upon pull-out candles, the candle mandalas arrange the candles in a star or polygon shape. They can be done on a simple bare workspace or altar surface, an altar cloth of the appropriate colors, or placed upon a drawn (or printed) geometric design. The center of the design can have a "main" candle for the working, sometimes larger than the rest. The center of the design can also have an object, picture, or symbol of who or what will be influenced by the spell.

The mandala can be as simple as placing the candles in their proper arrangement or as complex as connecting the various candles with lines of a mineral, such as salt, to connect and conduct energy. Additionally, lines of fresh or dry herbs, herbal powders, various polished or pointed crystals, or bowls of water, herbal tea, or oil-and-water mixes can add to the energy.

Here is a list of stones commonly used in magick today that are fairly accessible to practitioners. They can be used as a part of your candle mandalas.

Stones and Crystals

Stone	Element	Planets	Use
Agate	Air, Earth	Mercury	Communication, Travel, Clarity, Change
Agate, Blue Lace	Air	Mercury, Jupiter	Peace, Clarity, Spirit Contact
Amethyst	Water	Moon, Neptune	Sobriety, Good Fortune, Psychic Ability
Aventurine	Earth	Venus	Good Fortune, Money, Healing
Calcite, Yellow	Fire	Sun	Health, Clarity, Optimism, Self Esteem
Calcite, Blue	Air	Mercury, Jupiter	Clear Mind and Speech, Prosperity, Influence
Calcite, Green	Earth	Venus	Attractiveness, Glamour, Wealth
Carnelian	Air, Fire	Mercury	Healing, Strength, Communication
Citrine	Fire	Sun	Health, Happiness, Success
Clear Quartz	All	Sun, Moon	Magnifies Any Intention
Emerald	Earth	Venus	Success, Health, Love, Attraction, Beauty

Stone	Element	Planets	Use
Fluorite	Air, Water	Mercury, Venus, Jupiter	Cleansing, Clearing, Protection, Health, Happiness
Jasper	Earth, Fire	Mars	Protection, Grounding
Garnet	Fire	Mars, Saturn	Success, Lust, Vitality, Grounded Strength
Hematite	Fire, Earth	Mars, Saturn	Protection, Grounding, Centering, Strength
Lapis Lazuli	Air, Water	Jupiter, Venus	Prosperity, Health, Good Fortune, Influence
Moonstone	Water	Moon	Psychic Power, Emotional Health, Past Life
Obsidian	Fire, Earth	Pluto, Saturn, Mars	Reflection, Protection, Mystery, Wishes
Onyx	Earth	Saturn	Protection, Grounding, Karma, Heal Grief
Peridot	Earth	Venus	Love, Beauty, Art, Success
Pyrite	Fire, Earth	Sun, Venus	Money, Fortune, Health, Love
Rose Quartz	Earth, Water	Venus	Love, Self Esteem, Happiness, Relationship
Selenite	Water, Earth	Moon, Neptune	Protection, Clearing, Psychic Power, Spirit
Tourmaline, Black	Earth	Saturn	Protection, Neutralization, Grounding
Tourmaline, Green	Earth	Venus	Heart Healing, Prosperity, Beauty
Tourmaline, Pink	Water	Venus	Heart Healing, Love, Romance

Stone	Element	Planets	Use
Turquoise	Air, Earth	Jupiter, Venus	All Purpose, Protection, Health, Success

Love Candle Mandala

Seven Red Candles in Septagram Star, Rose Quartz in Center, Copper Wire Connecting Candles

Place seven red candles in a seven-pointed star formation with a piece of rose quartz in the center of it. Cleanse and charge each candle for love, as well as cleansing and charging the stone for love. Take a spool of copper wire and connect the candles not in a circle but by tracing a seven-pointed start clockwise, starting at the top candle and moving downward until you complete it. Seven-pointed stars can be tricky. While you can embellish this with other techniques such as carving the candles with hearts and anointing with an oil for love, this shows you the basic setup for a love candle mandala.

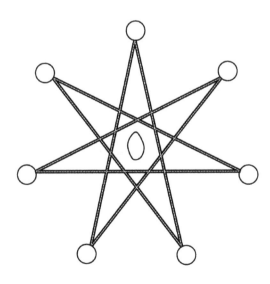

Figure: Love Candle Mandala

Healing Candle Mandala

Six Yellow Candles in Hexagram connected by lines of Vervain, Central Bowl filled with Water and six drops of Frankincense Oil, Central White Pillar Candle

Grind vervain up fine, and make a six-pointed star on your work tray or space. Cleanse and charge six yellow candles for the Sun, and place them in their holders upon the six points evenly. In the center of the hexagram place a glass or bronze bowl half-filled with water. Add the six drops of frankincense oil to the water, and place a cleansed and charge white pillar candle in the bowl of water as the central focus.

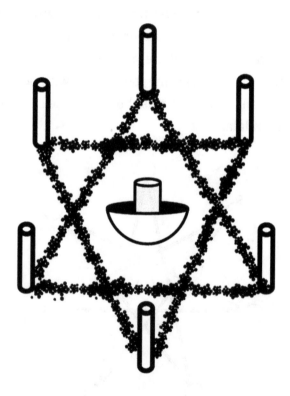

Figure: Healing Candle Mandala

Protection Candle Mandala

Five Black Candles in Pentagram. Photo of Protected Person with Smokey Quartz Point in Center of Pentagon. All connected by salt.

Draw a pentagram in sea salt or kosher salt upon your altar space or work tray. Place five cleansed, anointed and charged black candles at the points. Some are averse to using black candles, and while a very protective color, they are predisposed to think of protection as white and doing harm with black, so if that is a strong internal program, you can certainly use white, but I find the black candles more powerful for this spell. The anointing oil can be either Magick Power Anointing Oil, Dark Power Oil, or another Protection Oil, and they can be dusted in Protection Powder No. 1 or No. 2 herbs. Place the photo of the person who needs protection in the pentagon in the center of the star, and place a smokey quartz point that has been cleansed and charged for protection upon the photo. This will create a powerful protection for the recipient.

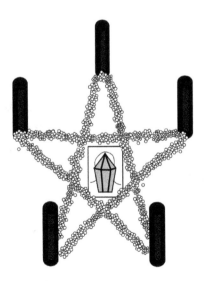

Figure: Protection Candle Mandala

Increase Psychic Power Mandala

Nine Purple/Silver Candles, Silver Coin, Parchment with Enneagram Printed, Nine Pinches of Mugwort.

Upon parchment paper, draw or print a nine-pointed star. In the center place a true silver coin, cleansed and charged. Place the nine candles upon the points, and between the candles place a pinch of mugwort herb or Psychic Powder. The candles can be anointed with Magick Power Anointing Oil or a Lunar Oil and carved with crescents prior to anointing. When the spell is done, carry the silver coin in the left pocket or left shoe.

Anointing, carving, rolling, packing, designing, and arranging are the main methods of preparing and dressing a candle for deeper magick. These simple techniques turn a simple candle spell into a more profound ritual. While I love to make my spells complex and add aspects of other forms of magick, we shouldn't discount the primal power of simply picking the right colored candle and lighting it. We don't need all of these additional techniques to have a successful spell. I've had many a simple, dry, and unadorned candle serve my needs well, but we can enjoy these techniques. Magick isn't simply utilitarian. It's emotive and expressive. Magick should help connect us to nature, and through nature, to ourselves. Our goal is not always just to have success with the single spell, but to expand our understanding of ourselves, our relationship to nature, and the forces of the universe. Working with plants, stones, planets, and geometry, through the medium of artistic expression, coupled with operative magick, can do just that for us.

Exercise: Dressing Supplies

Obtain some basic items for dressing your candles. Determine what you will use for a carving device, a burin. You can find specialty carving tools at some magick shops, or decide to use a more common item for the work. Likewise, get a small assortment of oils and herbs, as well as a grinding tool, either a traditional mortar and pestle, or an electric grinder. Craft one of the basic anointing oils to have on hand for future candle work, or wait until you complete the next chapter, on Astral Tides, before you make your oil, so you can time the creation of it with the most fortunate moment.

CHAPTER FIVE:
THE ASTRAL TIDES

Tradition tells us that the timing of a spell is critical, though different traditions have different techniques in determining what the most appropriate time to cast a spell is. Some work in the traditions of Witchcraft and focus upon the Moon. Others work within the cycle of the day and its own time. Some disregard magickal timing totally, but learn to follow an "internal clock" of knowing when the need and desire arises and feels right.

For most of us, though, learning about the tides helps us feel them in the future and learn to go with the flow. Astrology can play an important aspect in candle magick. The simple method of invoking astrological energies, requiring no special knowledge, is based on the days of the week. Who is right? Who knows? There is really no right or wrong, only effectiveness and failure. When you work with a technique that is measurably effective for you, then you've found a right way, not simply a way that appeals to your aesthetics and biases.

If a particular timing technique seems intuitively important to you, then it probably is, and you should use it. If a technique seems unimportant or even silly to you, disregard it for now. Did your spell work? Then whatever you disregarded probably wasn't important. If your spell failed, try to use that technique you might have disregarded before. If effective, work with that timing technique more. Sadly, sometimes the techniques we aesthetically like the least turn out to be the most effective for us. It's almost like diet and nutrition. The things we like the least turn out to be the best for us in terms of health and nutrition, while the things that taste the best and we consider treats are usually not great for our health. Experiment to find what works best for you. Talk to other practitioners. What works for them? Learn from their wisdom as well.

All the timing involving the Moon, Sun, and planets are considered "astral tides" as the old translations of astral referred to "stars," and a tide describes the flow in and out of particular powers. When fortunate energies are with us, it's like the tide has come in and brought what we need. When the time is ill for our magick, the tide has gone out, sending away the power required for success. As the Moon governs the ocean tides, the planets are all said to govern the flow of esoteric energies as they rise and fall upon and within the Earth. In older astrological teachings, rather than modern astronomical, the seven ancient "planets" included the Sun and Moon and referred to them as wandering stars, rather than fixed stars set in the constellations. So in that sense, they are "astral." Learning to feel the flow, and go with it, is an important step in your work as a magickal practitioner.

This chapter is a simple guideline of some of the most effective techniques commonly used in candle magick.

Lunar Tides

The simplest magickal understanding of the Moon occurs through the observation of its waxing and waning periods. The Moon's general motion can be divided into two broad categories, waxing and waning. When the Moon is waxing, it is growing in light. When the Moon is waning, it is diminishing in light, or growing in darkness. In the northern hemisphere, the light grows from right to left, as does the darkness. In the southern hemisphere, it is reversed.

Conventional modern magick states that when the Moon is waxing, the time is right to gain things in your life. Waxing magick is to manifest specific goals, material goods, or conditions. The flow is directed to bring things towards you. Even if they manifest later, the magick you set in motion at this time, through your candles and other craft, is to materialize your desires.

When the Moon is waning, it is the time to remove things from your life. The flow is conducive to diminishing effects, banishing people and forces, and removing harm. Protection magick is particularly powerful at this time.

The Moon's cycle can be divided into four quarters, two waxing and two waning. The first and second quarters are the waxing phase with the Full Moon occurring at the end of the second phase. The third and fourth quarters are the waning phase, with the Dark Moon occurring at the end of the fourth quarter, the time just before the Moon becomes the New Moon, and enters the first quarter. The Moon is still without visible light once it starts waxing in the first quarter, taking a few days to show the first tiny crescent, and some magicians will wait until that crescent is visible before doing any waxing moon magick, even though geometrically the Moon is technically waxing. Some magicians believe that no magick should be done when the Moon is dark, considering it either a rest period, a time of potential misfortune and misuse of power, or a time better utilized for introspection, not magick.

The most powerful time for waxing Moon magick is just before the Moon goes full. The most powerful time for waning magick is just before the Moon goes dark. To plant seeds for long-term projects that do not require immediate manifestation, the new Moon works well. And when you want to gently diminish something, not banish it all at once, just after the full Moon, as the Moon is in the third quarter, is a good time for gentle release.

Depending on the vision and phrasing of the spell intention, you can work around these cycles. You can have a traditional waning intention on the waxing Moon by wording the spell to manifest the situation in a "positive" statement that would be the result of something being diminished or banished. Likewise, you can do waxing moon magick on the waning Moon by phrasing the spell as removing the obstacles to manifestation of your goal. For instance, instead of doing a spell to banish illness because the Moon is waxing, you can do a spell to manifest the conditions of health. You could do a spell for prosperity on the waning Moon by banishing blocks to wealth and good fortune.

Solar Tides

Just as the Moon waxes and wanes, the Sun does as well, though in a somewhat less obvious manner. In the yearly cycle of the Sun, the day grows or diminishes in light, even though the orb of the Sun always appears to be one hundred percent illuminated. Due to the seasonal shifts caused by the amount of light visible during the day due to the axis of the Earth, our summers are warmer with longer days full of light and the winters are colder with shorter days of less light. The solstices mark the transition points, like the full and dark Moon. The summer solstice is the peak of light and the longest day, after which the Sun's power diminishes. The winter solstice is when the day is shortest with the longest night after which the Sun's power begins to grow again. The equinoxes are the midpoints of balance between the two, being times of equal darkness and light. So with this conventional wisdom, Sun magick to increase power, light, and life force is best between the winter and summer solstice, while magick to diminish light and power is best between summer and winter solstice. But when doing personal magick, it can be hard to wait many months for such a shift. That is why Moon magick, with a single month cycle schedule, is more popular.

One can also use the cycle of the day as a solar waxing and waning pattern. From when the Sun rises until noon, the Sun's power is growing. From noon to sunset, the Sun's power is diminishing. Just as timing magick by the Moon, if you want to manifest, regardless of what the Moon's quarter is, do your spell sometime between dawn and Noon. If you want to banish, do your spell between Noon and sunset.

The Magick of the Week

A simple and effective way of working planetary magick is through the days of the week. It requires no math skills or special equipment beyond an ordinary calendar to tell you what day it is.

According to occult traditions involving the seven major planets, our cycle of the seven-day week is attuned to the planets. The names we use for the planets are derived from the classical gods associated with them. In English, we associate them with Teutonic deities, except the Sun, Moon, and Saturn, though they are associated with cognates with the Roman equivalents. The pattern of the week is the Sun, Moon, Mars, Mercury, Jupiter, Venus, and Saturn. When we do magick on a particular day, we can better evoke the power of the planet and align it to our intention.

Days of the Week

Day	Planet	Deity	Correspondence
☉ Sunday	Sun	Sol	Success, Health, Power, Energy, Purpose, Drive, Optimism
☽ Monday	Moon	Luna	Psychic Power, Healing, Emotions, Karma, Family, Cycles

Day	Planet	Deity	Correspondence
♂ Tuesday	Mars	Tyr	Protection, Aggression, Will, Power, Action, Destruction
☿ Wednesday	Mercury	Wotan	Thought, Memory, Writing, Speaking
♃ Thursday	Jupiter	Thor	Success, Good Fortune, Luck, Legal Victory, Prosperity
♀ Friday	Venus	Freya	Love, Romance, Attraction, Beauty
♄ Saturday	Saturn	Saturn	Protection, Binding, Grounding, Manifestation

Using this simple timing method, you can simply do the spell when the day of the week corresponds to your intention. Love spells are more effective on Freya's Day, or Friday. Use a green or pink candle, as they are the colors of Venus. A black candle lit for protection is most effective on a Saturday, as both correspond to Saturn, a planet of binding, protection, and manifestation.

Planetary Hours

Beyond the pattern of the days of the week, are the planetary hours. The magickal tradition comes from the concept that not only each day of the week is ruled by one of the seven planets, but also each hour of the day is ruled by a planet. The tradition is said to go back to Chaldea, a Semitic-speaking country that was absorbed into Babylon, famed for their astrological knowledge. The use of planetary hours allows you to combine the blessings of two planets at one time period. The day will be the dominant energy, and the hour will be the modifying energy.

For example, if you want to do a love spell, then you would naturally choose the power of Venus for your spell, and if following the planetary days, you would pick Friday to do your spell. If it is to attract a lover, the waxing Moon would also be ideal. If the most important trait in the new lover is clear communication, you might perform the spell on the Day of Venus, Friday, in the hour of Mercury, for clear communication. The Mercury hour occurs several times in the day of Venus, so you must choose the time that is most conducive to your personal preferences.

The pattern of hours follows a Qabalistic sequence based upon the perception of how far away the planets are from the Earth. The sequence is Saturn, Jupiter, Mars, Sun, Venus, Mercury, and Moon, and starts with the first hour of the day as the same planet associated with that day. So the first hour of Sunday is the Sun. The second hour would be Venus. The third hour of Sunday is Mercury, and so forth. Following through with twenty-four hours, the twenty-fifth hour, or first hour of the next day, would automatically follow the pattern and flow into the appropriate first hour of the day. The last hour of Sunday corresponds with Mercury, and the first hour of Monday belongs to the Moon, following the established pattern. This "Chaldean Order" or Qabalistic order gives us the pattern of our days of the week.

Technically the system divides the hours of the day into twelve day hours and twelve night hours. The method of what constitutes an "hour" is up for some debate among magicians. Three basic methods of planetary hour definitions, and thereby systems of calculation exist.

Modern Clock – The modern clock method follows our modern timekeeping. The first hour of the day is from midnight to 1 a.m. The second hour is 1 a.m. to 2 a.m. the pattern continues until Noon, which then starts the "night" hours. Each hour is a normal sixty-minute hour. This is the least traditional, but for a time before computers, it became a favorite technique among modern magicians.

Basic Sunrise Method – While we look to the modern clock, most in the ancient world using something akin to this style of planetary magick and timekeeping started the day with sunrise. Many modern Witches look to the Celtic traditions, whose people started the day with sunset, but planetary magick of this sort traces its spiritual roots to the Middle Eastern magickal tradition, not the Celtic. With this method, the first hour starts at sunrise, and goes for sixty minutes. As the waxing and waning of the yearly solar cycle occurs a few negligible minutes are shaved off here and there.

Traditional Sunrise-Sunset Method – By far the most orthodox method is the one involving the most math. It involves the time of sunrise, sunset, and the sunrise of the next day. Hours are not set standard sixty-minute hours, unless it is the equinox, but fluctuating "hours" depending on the time of year. The minutes between sunrise and sunset are added up if doing a spell during the day, or the minutes between sunset and the following sunrise for magick timed at night. The total number of minutes added is then divided by twelve, and that number is considered to be the length of a planetary "hour" for that day. When the year is waxing, the day "hours" will be longer than the "night" and when the year is waning, the reverse will be true. One then plots out along the modern clock the time period of each planetary hour for the day, and the appropriate time for the magick is chosen. Thankfully, modern computer applications and spreadsheets, along with almanacs, newspapers and online resources make this work much easier than it has been in the past.

Daytime Planetary Hours

Hour	Sun	Mon	Tue	Wed	Thu	Fri	Sat
1	☉	☽	♂	☿	♃	♀	♄
2	♀	♄	☉	☽	♂	☿	♃
3	☿	♃	♀	♄	☉	☽	♂
4	☽	♂	☿	♃	♀	♄	☉
5	♄	☉	☽	♂	☿	♃	♀
6	♃	♀	♄	☉	☽	♂	☿
7	♂	☿	♃	♀	♄	☉	☽
8	☉	☽	♂	☿	♃	♀	♄
9	♀	♄	☉	☽	♂	☿	♃
10	☿	♃	♀	♄	☉	☽	♂
11	☽	♂	☿	♃	♀	♄	☉
12	♄	☉	☽	♂	☿	♃	♀

Nighttime Planetary Hours

Hour	Sun	Mon	Tue	Wed	Thu	Fri	Sat
1	♃	♀	♄	☉	☽	♂	☿
2	♂	☿	♃	♀	♄	☉	☽
3	☉	☽	♂	☿	♃	♀	♄
4	♀	♄	☉	☽	♂	☿	♃
5	☿	♃	♀	♄	☉	☽	♂
6	☽	♂	☿	♃	♀	♄	☉
7	♄	☉	☽	♂	☿	♃	♀
8	♃	♀	♄	☉	☽	♂	☿
9	♂	☿	♃	♀	♄	☉	☽
10	☉	☽	♂	☿	♃	♀	♄
11	♀	♄	☉	☽	♂	☿	♃
12	☿	♃	♀	♄	☉	☽	♂

While I, too, love the ways modern technology makes our lives easier, I think every student of magick should try calculating the planetary hours by hand at least once in their life, if not a few times. Here are the steps to do it by hand.

+ **Determine Day or Night Hours** – Are you looking to do your spell during the day or night?
+ **Obtain the Times** – Find out the times of sunrise to sunset for a day hour spell or sunset to the next sunrise for a night hour spell. They will vary based upon your location and the date.
+ **Total Time** – Add up the total number of minutes between the two sunrise/sunset times for your particular time period.
+ **Divide** – Divide that total number of minutes by twelve, for there are twelve hours in the day, and twelve hours of the night. Whatever number of minutes you get is a planetary "hour" of that time period.
+ **Clock Adjustment** – Using the previously calculated "hour" period, adjust the planetary hours to the traditional time to determine "when" a planetary hour starts and stops. There may be a short period of time that is unaccounted for at the end, since we are rounding when doing it by hand.

For example, I wish to do an evening spell on the night of Samhain, also known as Halloween or simply October 31st. Let's pick the year 2012. On October 31, 2012, in my area, sunset was at 5:38 PM and sunrise the following day, November 1, was at 7:19 AM. Between 5:38 PM and 7:19 AM, 13 traditional hours and 41 minutes elapsed.

5:38 PM – 6:38 AM = 13 Hours
6:38 AM– 7:19 AM = 41 Minutes

The Lighting of Candles

13 Hours = 13 x 60 minutes = 780 Minutes

780 + 41 = 821 minutes of the Night

821 divided by 12 = 68.4155

Each magickal hour of the night is approximately 68 traditional minutes, slightly higher than our traditional hour.

Hour	Starts	Ends
Night Hour 1	5:38 PM	6:46 PM
Night Hour 2	6:46 PM	7:54 PM
Night Hour 3	7:54 PM	9:02 PM
Night Hour 4	9:02 PM	10:10 PM
Night Hour 5	10:10 PM	11:18 PM
Night Hour 6	11:18 PM	12:26 AM
Night Hour 7	12:36 AM	1:34 AM
Night Hour 8	1:34 AM	2:42 AM
Night Hour 9	2:42 AM	3:50 AM
Night Hour 10	3:50 AM	4:58 AM
Night Hour 11	4:58 AM	6:06 AM
Night Hour 12	6:06 AM	7:14 AM

Due to rounding, we are off by about five minutes, so to compensate, don't start your magickal workings in the exact minute when a planetary hour begins, but a few moments after, to make sure you are in the correct moment. Planetary hour calculators will take into consideration the time fractions and provide a more precise calculation.

The candle(s) will have the astrological energy of the moment when it was lit, so subsequent relighting does not have to be astrologically timed if you have to snuff out a candle and relight it at a later time to complete the spell. Magick, or truly anything, always contains the energy of when it is initiated, but the following work can be done under any conditions.

Exploring the astrological, or zodiac, sign the Sun, Moon, or other planets occupy, the aspects or angels those planets make to each other, and the effects of these phenomenon upon spell casting, will be a topic for the subsequent volumes of this series. For now, focus upon the basics of the Sun, Moon, and Planetary powers as they manifest in the year, week and day.

Exercise: Watching the Tides

If you don't keep a journal, magickal or otherwise, commit to keeping a basic record of your day for a short period of time, anywhere from one week to one month, depending on your desire for data. This exercise will help you understand how the astral tides flow in your own life, and hopefully train you to intuitively perceive them in more meaningful ways. In your record, keep track of the details of your life in terms of fortunate or difficult experiences. Did you have a bad day? Was it personal or business? Did you have any conflicts? Any good exchanges with people? Who? Any day with really great food? Sex? Creativity? Injury? Note all things in this manner, even if they seem insignificant. Make sure you note the time when these things occur during the day.

Once the (first) week is over, go back, and notate on each day the energy of the Moon. Is it waxing or waning? Is it in the first, second, third or fourth quarter? The Sun's yearly tide will most likely be the same during the week, unless your week has a solstice. If your week does have a solstice or even equinox, notate it on that day. Then look at the character of each day in association with the daily planet. Choose a few significant moments from specific days, and calculate the planetary hours for that day. In what hour did those events occur? Can you see a correspondence?

With time, you might grow to feel the pulse of the astral tides in a daily flow, though some of us pick out particular aspects of the astrological tides to be sensitive, and it's not always the flow of planetary hours.

Another note on planetary hours is taking into consideration the considerably non-magickal Gregorian Calendar. We determine the days of our week based upon the Gregorian Calendar, a refinement of the older Julian Calendar. While an effective civil calendar, magickal practitioners note that it does not flow with any pattern of magickal time and since our days of the week are based up on it, it can be quite arbitrary from a magickal perspective. Yet modern magicians still use it effectively, believing the overall cultural thought-form of everyone recognizing the same day of the week wins out over every system. Likewise modern numerologists use the birthdates and years to effectively create numerological charts and readings.

While I understand the sentiment, and often feel the same way, with such dates as the New Year, January 1st, having no astronomical or magickal association, the Julian Calendar was influenced by the late Egyptian Calendar. While imprecise on many levels, it sought to fix imprecisions on the previous Roman Calendar, and fused Greek, Egyptian, and Roman elements. The Gregorian Calendar was an attempt to fix imprecision in the Julien.

The roots of our calendar come from some very magickal traditions, even if we are unaware of them. In some ways, it's our discomfort with the imprecision of time and our need for mythologies to account for intercalendary days and fractions that don't fit into clockwork processions that causes our need for new, rectified calendars.

Author Jean-Louis De Biasi, initiate of the Ordo Aurum Solis tradition, proposes a new understanding of planetary hours for the serious ritual magician in his book *Rediscover the Magick of the Gods and Goddesses*. He essentially tackles the question of how we know on a magickal level that "Tuesday" is really "Tuesday" as the calendar we use has been adjusted so many times. Is there a sequence of the days of the week and a way of generating them that is more in harmony with the natural flow of time as known by the ancients. Drawing upon the work of Roman historian Cassius Dio, the start of the weekly cycle is indeed Saturn and Saturday, rather than Sunday or Monday, as well as the pattern of eight gods found on a Romany bracelet in Syria, starting with Tyche for fate and then continuing Kronos, Helios, Selene, Ares, Hermes, Zeus and Aphrodite, and fusing it with the ancient's idea of the month, and its four weeks being tied to the Moon, with the cycle starting on the new Moon, Jean-Louis proposes days of the week based upon the lunar cycle. This alternative system aligns planetary days with the natural cycles and aligns them in harmony with the Moon. It requires a bit more work, but can provide some fascinating results.

Essentially Week 1 starts on the day of the New Moon when the Moon enters the first quarter and begins waxing. Day 1 of any week starts as a Saturday. Count out seven days for Week 1 and start Week 2. Continue the pattern until you have four weeks of seven days.

Day	Week	Planet	Day	Lunar Phase
1	1	Saturn	Saturday	Fourth Quarter New Moon
2	1	Sun	Sunday	
3	1	Moon	Monday	
4	1	Mars	Tuesday	
5	1	Mercury	Wednesday	
6	1	Jupiter	Thursday	
7	1	Venus	Friday	
1	2	Saturn	Saturday	First Quarter (Variable)
2	2	Sun	Sunday	
3	2	Moon	Monday	
4	2	Mars	Tuesday	
5	2	Mercury	Wednesday	
6	2	Jupiter	Thursday	
7	2	Venus	Friday	
1 (Variable)	3	Saturn	Saturday	Second Quarter Full Moon
2	3	Sun	Sunday	
3	3	Moon	Monday	
4	3	Mars	Tuesday	
5	3	Mercury	Wednesday	
6	3	Jupiter	Thursday	
7	3	Venus	Friday	
1	4	Saturn	Saturday	Third Quarter (Variable)
2	4	Sun	Sunday	
3	4	Moon	Monday	
4	4	Mars	Tuesday	
5	4	Mercury	Wednesday	
6	4	Jupiter	Thursday	
7	4	Venus	Friday	
1	Intermediate			
2	Intermediate			

As the lunar month is not a simple, even twenty-eight days, with a sidereal/tropical lunar month as 27.32 days (time it takes to go through the twelve zodiac signs) with the synodic, or lunation, month (time it takes from new Moon to new Moon) being 29.53 days, there will be some discrepancies generated between the weekly cycle of seven days and the next new Moon. Any days between Day 7 of Week 4 and the new Moon Day 1 of Week 1 are considered to be intermediate days ruled by no planet specifically, or under the domain of the eighth sphere, Aethyr, and the fixed stars. Presumably, the deity would be the goddess Tyche, or Fate.

In the Temple of Witchcraft community, we use a similar system with a modern variation, starting the first day of the new Moon cycle with Sunday, not Saturday, and then following the pattern. We have a divination and magick system called the Witch's Runic Stones, based upon the traditional eight Witch's Runes, and expanded into a system of twenty-nine symbols, one for each day of the lunar cycle. You can explore this pattern to see if it works better or worse for you than the Roman one proposed by Jean-Louis.

Personally, I've done quite well with the traditional calendar days of the mainstream modern calendar, and calculating the necessary hours. I've also explored this new method and find it quite interesting, and workable too. I've tended to use the modern calendar for more mainstream manifestations and explored this new method with larger, more mystical spells of personal evolution and healing. As always, experiment, explore and see what will work for your own magickal path.

CHAPTER SIX:
SIMPLE CANDLE SPELLS

The technique of candle magick is powerfully intuitive and creative. You can adapt it to your own style. At its most basic level, a simple candle spell needs a clear intention and strong feelings to kindle the energy and catalyze the spell. Candle spells can ideally take a few minutes to set in motion, but those who are more ritually inclined can take as much time as they like, and have as much ceremony around the process as desired. Candle magick adjusts to the personality and desires of the magician. Use the techniques that make you feel the most empowered and magickal.

Preparing the Intention

What do you want the spell to do? Get clear in your intention. While it can help to write out a simple statement, like a petition spell, you can also simply verbalize it. Sum it up as simply as possible. If the intention is clear in your mind, that is all you really need for candle magick. Many who have done spells and have had them go awry, because the intention was not clear, will choose to write out the spell with any caveats or conditions in the written document, and either place the written petition beneath the candleholder, or burn the petition from the flame of the candle.

One of the most common questions is how many spells, or how many different intentions, can I have in one candle? I've found that just one is effective. There can be many aspects to that one intention, conditions that appear to be separate intentions, but in essence, the final results will be one specific goal. Do a separate candle spell for other goals, or look to the next chapter on more complex spells involving more than one candle. For now, keep it simple, and keep one specific intention per candle spell.

Preparing the Candle

With your intention in mind, determine what kind of candle you will need. What do you have on hand or have easy access to get? What is your budget for this? What powers will be best to call upon in terms of elements and planets? What shape and materials will work? Is it a quick and fast spell with a smaller candle, or a long-term spell requiring more wax? With that in mind, determine the day and time most conducive to your candle magick.

Once the candle is chosen, will you be using any other techniques beyond just the candle itself? Determine if you will be anointing it with any fluid, carving it with any symbols, rolling it in any powder, or packing it with any herbs or minerals. Do you want to do this work as a part of the ritual itself or prepare it in advance? I suggest doing packing and carving in advance, outside of the formal ritual, while anointing and rolling techniques can be done in ritual, but that is simply my own preference. In either case, make sure you have everything you need on hand for when you need it, including any supplies to clean up the mess you make.

Candle Magick Ritual

When you are prepared to do the ritual, you can be as formal or informal as you like. Some like to do it in the context of their own religious traditions. Catholics performing candle magick, or candle "prayer," might perform the rosary before and after to set the right space. Hindus could use a mantra chant. Many will simply meditate, clearing the mind and focusing the energy. Magicians like to set a sacred space, doing what is called "Casting a Circle" in modern magick, by creating a circular boundary to keep harmful forces out and energy for the spell within the space. Formal circle casting can be found in the previous book in this series, *The Casting of Spells,* but a simple method of making sacred space, either out loud or silent, is to acknowledge the directions around you.

I, (state your name), call upon the sacred powers of the directions all
*   around me.*
I call upon the powers and blessings of the North.
I call upon the powers and blessings of the East.
I call upon the powers and blessings of the South.
I call upon the powers and blessings of the West.
I call upon the powers and blessings of the sky Above.
I call upon the powers and blessings of the world Below
And I call upon the powers and blessings of the Center.
Hail and welcome.

You can call upon specific deities, ancestors, spirit guides, or angels if you'd like to do so. Many successfully use their candle magick without anything so formal. They simply move directly to the body of the candle spell.

Hold the candle in both your hands after any preparatory dressing work has been complete. While holding it, feel your energy from your hands mingle with the energy of the candle, its wax, color and any dressing. While holding it, visualize your intention as a final result. What would you see? If you can't see clearly with internal imagination, and even if you can, more importantly, ask yourself how it would feel when the spell is successful. Feel it. Play pretend for a moment. Think about your intention in clear, concrete statements. Speak them. If you have a written intention, read it out loud. Then feeling as if it's real, and engaging whatever senses you can to make that feel true, even for just a few moments.

Feel as if your hands are flowing with energy, like water. The candle is like an empty glass, filling with water. Fill the candle to the rim of the metaphoric glass until it can take no more of your intentional energy. Then light the wick. Let it burn. Your candle spell is set in motion. If you called to the powers from the directions, make sure to thank and release them as well.

Where to Burn the Candles?

When I began my training, where to burn your magick candles was not even a question. My teachers taught to create your own special place to do magick, a working altar, ideally behind a closed door. Some were hidden in secret closet hiding holes to prevent any guests or visitors from knowing you were a Witch. As magick has become more accepted, at least in general, we have more choices. I still favor keeping magickal candles, specific spells, burning in the temple room where all my magick is done. There is also benefit for moving the candle to where you wish it to have the most influence. Depending on your place of work, if doing a job prosperity spell, you could have a simple candle burning at your desk. Candle burning is frowned on by many workplaces, though I was lucky at my last office job as it was fine to use a small votive on my desk. Although we were an eccentric artistic company. Romance and sex spells can have the candle burning in the bedroom. Happy home spells will naturally have the candle where the family gathers, the living room, kitchen, or upon the hearth if you have a mantle. Healing spells can be near the one in need. Protection candles can go near thresholds, but be careful the opening and closing of doors does not accidentally extinguish them. So the short answer to this question is to burn them wherever you feel they will be most effective.

The Working Candle

Many in magickal traditions, particularly Wicca, Witchcraft, and ceremonial magick, will have a "working candle" as a part of any more elaborate ritual. Whatever the general intent of the ritual is, a specifically chosen candle for the working will be lit, along with any religiously significant candles, such as those associated with the goddesses and gods. They are often coordinated with the planetary day, hour, or Moon associations, or if a seasonal celebration, with the colors associated with that celebration. Items burned, from incense charcoal to spell petition papers, are burned from the working candle to infuse them with this "working" energy.

Like other spells, the timeframe for manifestation is not set. Various traditions suggest that a week or month is traditional, and if the spell does not manifest by then, it failed, but I've had spells manifest many months, and sometimes even years later, so it can be important to put clear intentions of a time frame into your spell. **Chapter Eight** will deal with issues of omens and divination about the timeframe of the spell, based upon the remaining wax or how the candle burned as well as disposal of the candle remains.

It's important not to throw out a candle that is still burning just because it appears the spell has manifested successfully already. Some "miracle" spells can happen in an hour or day, before the candle has fully burned itself out. Magick works beyond the bounds of space and time. By throwing it out, you might be short-circuiting the spell, thinking it is done, but it truly isn't. The few I've known to do that often believe the spell has manifested, and they snuff and get rid of the candle without it fully burning. They soon find the solid "result" is not so solid, and the manifested sure thing collapses before they can collect whatever manifestation they intended. Be safe, rather than sorry, and once you put something in motion, commit to it until the candle burns out on its own like any other candle spell.

Disposal of Candle and Spell Remains

What do you do with whatever is left over with your spell remains? Like many things, it depends on who you ask. Pragmatic spellcasters will say that the magickal energy is spent, so just throw it out. Many keep leftover wax and remelt it into new candles, not for other spells, but for devotional and functional purposes, not wanting to waste the wax. Others store ashes of paper, matches, herbs, woods, and wax in an ash pot, and use them as ingredients or a base in other spells that require a powder or a dark ash, such as the creation of black salt, or rituals to darken the brow to increase psychic ability.

In the Hoodoo traditions along with other forms of folk magick, where you dispose of something depends on the intention. To get rid of something in the spell, it was always disposed of off your property, or at a crossroads or graveyard. Crossroads are particularly powerful to invoke some deities' aid, like Hecate or Legba, and graveyards are especially helpful if your spell involves aid from the ancestors. To keep something close to you when it manifests, you bury it in your yard, near the front door, or under a tree. Burial by a tree or bush also helps the magick grow over time, for long-term spells. Running water helps spells manifest, while stagnant or ocean water helps remove forces from you. Swamp water is to destroy something completely. The various directions, North, South, East, and West, have associations with them, varying in different traditions. Bringing the remains to those directions from your area of magickal working will invoke those powers. Generally, east is for beginnings and west is for spells of ending.

Urban Witches in the traditions started in New York City, popular among the clientele of shops like The Magickal Childe and Enchantments would put the remains between two halves of an orange and wrap it in a brown paper bag before disposing of it in a river to keep the results "sweet."

Ask yourself two questions at the end of each candle spell if you don't have a standard disposal method: Are there any remains? What feels most appropriate to do with them? Then follow your intuition.

Before disposing of the remains, you might want to contemplate divination techniques involving the remaining wax, and if using a glass case candle, the soot in the glass. Look to **Chapter Eight** before you get rid of anything.

Simple Candle Spells

While I suggest exploring basic candle spells before advancing to more complex ones in the next chapter, I would also advise reading the entire book all the way through, particularly the sections on Candle Divination, before attempting any of these spells. While the most basic spell can be successful with little knowledge, the more you know, the better the experience will be for all involved.

Prosperity

Candle Color: Blue, Green, Gold
Moon or Sun Tide: Waxing
Day: Thursday, Sunday, Friday
Hour: Jupiter, Sun, Venus
Dressing: Powdered Cinnamon, Sunflower Seed Oil

For overall prosperity, to help your success flourish, I recommend taking a simple jar or pillar candle to hold a larger amount of energy, for a long-term successful result. Simply anoint the exposed surface with oil and sprinkle powdered cinnamon upon it. Charge the candle for a general sense of prosperity and success. Light it and let it burn, drawing to you the bright and expansive powers of success.

Quick Cash

Candle Color: Green
Moon or Sun Tide: Waxing
Day: Friday, Sunday, Thursday
Hour: Mercury, Venus
Dressing: Money Powder No. 2 or just Basil, Sunflower Seed Oil

While general prosperity is a wonderful thing, sometimes we need quick cash to pay a bill. While generally, we focus on the end results of our magick, sometimes, unexpected money is the best solution to the situation at hand.

Take a green candle and carve your initials upon it to indicate the money will go to you personally, unless your spouse or another person legally linked to you, who is also in need of the money, could solve your need for quick cash. Then put the other person's initials upon it too. Carve the amount of money you need on the candle, and decorate the remaining space with dollar signs. Anoint the candle with simple olive oil and sprinkle Money Powder No. 2 on it, or if you lack the Patchouli, just use the Basil as a strong money herb. Before you light the candle, charge it with the words and intentions:

To immediately get $_____ for _____ in a manner that is correct and acceptable to me.
So mote it be.

The Lighting of Candles

Light the candle and let it burn on a trivet or tray, as many "fast acting" spells often make the most mess and create the most sparks.

New Job

Candle Color: Blue or Purple
Moon or Sun Tide: Waxing
Day: Thursday, Sunday
Hour: Jupiter, Sun, Mercury
Dressing: Magick Power Anointing Oil, Good Luck Powder

Dress your candle with the Magick Power Anointing Oil and dust it with Good Luck Powder. Charge it while envisioning the type of job that you desire. If you'd like to be more precise, start with a list of all the things that are absolute requirements – general field or industry, minimum payment, maximum distance from your home, required benefits. Don't get hung up on a specific title or company. Place this list under your candleholder and then charge your candle. If you have resumes you are printing and sending out, place them in a container, such as a large manila envelope or file folder, to protect them from accidental wax, oil, or herb spillage, and place a tray or trivet between the papers and the candleholder. If you electronically send your resume, then simply print out one token resume to empower in all forms of media. Once the candle has fully burned, send out your resumes and apply in earnest.

Luck and Fortune

Candle Color: Orange Candle and a Blue Candle
Moon or Sun Tide: Waxing
Day: Wednesday
Hour: Mercury, Jupiter

Dressing: Hazelnut Oil, Magick Power Anointing Oil, Good Luck Powder, Money Powder No. 1, Photo of Yourself

Use the orange candle for luck and the blue candle for fortune. Carve four simple shamrock images down each candle, so with the two candles; you'll have eight images of shamrocks. Anoint the orange candle with Hazelnut Oil and sprinkle Good Luck Powder on it. If you can't obtain Hazelnut Oil, then any base oil will do. Likewise, anoint the blue candle with Magick Power Anointing Oil or another base oil, and sprinkle Money Powder No. 1 on it. Place your photo between the candles, with the Orange candle to your left and the blue candle to your right. Light the orange first and then the blue with the words:

> I conjure good luck and good fortune. Many the fates bend my way and may I be wise enough to see and accept their blessings. So mote it be.

Let the candles burn, and when done, hide the photo somewhere it won't be found by another.

Love
Candle Color: Green, Pink, Red
Moon or Sun Tide: Waxing
Day: Friday
Hour: Venus
Dressing: Rose, Ylang-Ylang, Catnip, and Lemongrass in an Apricot or Sweet Almond Base, Love Powder

While I think the topic of love spells on their own is so complex, so much so that I wrote a whole book on love magick entitled *The Witch's Heart*, love candle spells can be quite simple. Start by writing out a list of the qualities you wish for in a lover or partner. Be specific in qualities, but not how they manifest. You can say you want someone attractive to you, but I wouldn't list hair color, eye color, height, or weight. You can ask they be successful, but don't list a minimum yearly income. When you have the list of qualities you truly desire written on a paper, place it under the candleholder, trivet, or plate for the candle. Choose a simple taper, or a human figure of the appropriate gender image, and anoint the candle with a mix of the oils above that are available to you. If using a traditional candle, you can carve two interlocked hearts on the candle. Sprinkle the herbal love powder on the candle, hold it and charge it with your desire.

Figure: Interlocked Hearts

I ask in the name of the Goddess and God
To find a lover who embodies the qualities I have listed
I ask this be for our highest good.
I thank you for this and all other blessings.
So mote it be!

If you work with any specific Venusian goddesses in your private practice, such as Aphrodite, you can tailor the incantation to suit your own preferences. Light the candle and let the magick work. Once it's burned, make yourself available by going to places where you could meet the right person and, be open to mutual friends introducing you to new people. You never know how the magick will manifest!

Fast Sex

Candle Color: Red
Moon or Sun Tide: Waxing
Day: Friday, Tuesday
Hour: Mars, Venus
Dressing: Coriander Oil in base or Dark Power Oil, Lust Powder

One of the most simple candle spells in the world is a Fast Sex or Lust candle. It's a spell for an immediate lover, rather than a spell for sex with a short duration. One simply charges a red candle, chime to taper in size, no larger, for an immediate sexual partner, and then looks out where there are potential mates. The other option is to use the stylized genitalia candle, for the genitalia you desire, not necessarily the genitalia you have. The trick of this spell is one cannot be too picky, so any stipulations, like "safe" or "acceptable to me" should be used, but you can't expect a supermodel on short notice. To spice it up, anoint the candle with either coriander essential oil in a sweet almond base, or use the Dark Power Oil formula. Then sprinkle it with Lust Powder. Once the candle burns out you will most likely find a playmate.

Gay Male Love

Candle Color: Green, Pink, Red
Moon or Sun Tide: Waxing
Day: Friday
Hour: Mars, Venus
Dressing: Hyacinth Oil, Lavender Oil, Basil Oil, Fennel Oil, or Coriander Oil in base, Love Powder

Lesbian Love

Candle Color: Green, Pink, Red
Moon or Sun Tide: Waxing

Day: Friday
Hour: Venus, Mars, Moon
Dressing: Patchouli Oil, Sandalwood Oil, and Myrrh Oil in base, Damiana and Rose Petals

While any love spell can be used in almost any situation, the history of magick has been decidedly heteronormative in the case of love and sex magick. Those seeking partners of the same gender, or those differently gendered, don't have a lot of classic resources, but the intersection of magick and queer community in modern times, often quite publicly, has created new traditions. Either of these spells can be used in the same way as the general love spell, but with the intention of a same sex partner. You can use the appropriate gender image in the form of the human-shaped candles, or genitalia-shaped candle, or any other form of traditional candle. Like above, you can carve interlocked hearts, or you can use dual interlocked male (Mars) or female (Venus) symbols. For those who are gender non-binary, any androgynous combination can be used.

Figure: Interlocked Male and Female Symbols

Beauty

Candle Color: Green
Moon or Sun Tide: Waxing
Day: Friday
Hour: Venus
Dressing: Rose Oil, Lady's Mantle

To increase beauty and, most importantly, self-love and self-confidence, take a green candle and anoint it with rose oil, or any scent that evokes a sense of beauty. Sprinkle the candle with lady's mantle herb, a plant renowned for renewing beauty and youth. Envision your most idealized and beautiful self when charging the candle, and light it to bring that self to reality.

Stop Gossip

Candle Color: Black
Moon or Sun Tide: Waning
Day: Saturday
Hour: Saturn, Mars
Dressing: Clove Essential Oil in Castor Oil Base, 1 Whole Clove, Slippery Elm

While we might think we know who is speaking or writing against us, I found this spell is best to be left open-ended, without naming a particular person, so the magick can seek out the right result guided by divine wisdom.

Take a black candle, if possible, a human-shaped candle. Using your carving tool, make an opening for the mouth. If using a simple taper, pillar or pull-out candle, carve eyes, nose, and a mouth, and make sure the mouth can fit a bit of herb in it. Stuff the mouth opening with the slippery elm herb, and then place the clove, narrow end in first, to "cork" it. Dress the candle with clove essential oil in a base of castor oil. Charge with the incantation:

In the name of the binding powers of Saturn,
I charge this candle to stop all gossip, all harm, all venom spoken or
  written against me
I ask this for the highest good.
So mote it be.

If possible, let the entire candle burn without snuffing it. Beware of the herbs catching fire. Have a plate beneath the candle to catch the potentially falling clove. You can cast it in a crossroads when the candle is done burning.

Gain New Friends

Candle Color: Pink
Moon or Sun Tide: Waxing
Day: Friday
Hour: Venus, Mercury
Dressing: Catnip, Lodestone, Magnetic Sand (Iron Filings)

Do this spell if you have trouble making or keeping new friends. It is particularly good for those suffering from social anxiety, and will just make you more approachable in general, and foster rapport. Anoint a pink taper, of if you can find it, a pink cat-shaped candle, with catnip essential oil. Old Occult shops often have an oil called Black Cat, which can be used instead. It has some magnetic properties within it. If neither is available to you, sweet almond or apricot kernel oil would work well too. Charge the candle to attract and keep good quality, new, emotionally available friends to you. Reflect on the type of friend you want, and the type of friend you want to be while holding the candle. Then light it.

While the candle can work well on its own, if you want to add extra power to it, put a natural lodestone or magnet at the base of the candleholder and sprinkle iron filings on it, to emphasize the attraction to you.

Basic Healing

Candle Color: Green, White
Moon or Sun Tide: Waxing to Bring Healing Energy
Day: Wednesday, Monday
Hour: Mercury, Sun, Moon
Dressing: Chamomile, Lemongrass, or Eucalyptus Essential Oil, 3 Green Crystals

Basic Healing spells are great for a simple illness that doesn't require serious medical attention, such as colds, the flu, or minor injuries and infection. They work by bolstering the immune response and increasing vital life force. Because of this reason, it's best to do these spells in a waxing tide, but you could use a waning tide to remove illness instead of bolstering vitality. Anoint your candle and place three small green stones (emerald, green aventurine, green fluorite, green calcite, etc.) in a triangle around the candleholder base. Name the person you are sending healing to, even if it's yourself, through this incantation or something similar:

*In the name of the Divine, I send green healing magick to
_____, for their highest healing good. So mote it be.*

In the ethics of healing magick, it is always important to make sure you ask permission to heal if the recipient is able to answer. Some ask the recipient if they can "Pray in their own way," meaning magick and spells, to get a "yes." Let the candle burn, and offer the stones to the recipient in a green bag to carry for continued health and well-being.

Serious Healing

Candle Color: Red or Orange, White
Moon or Sun Tide: Waxing to Bring Healing Energy, Waning to Remove Illness
Day: Sunday, Wednesday
Hour: Mercury, Sun, Moon
Dressing: Blessing Oil or an essential oil specific to the illness, Healing Powder or an herb specific to the illness, Photo of Recipient, Citrine

Serious healing involves long-term, chronic, or life-threatening illnesses. For serious healing, I prefer either a human-shaped candle that best conforms to the gender identity and image of the recipient of the healing, or a seven-day pull-out. If you cannot obtain either, any candle will work in a pinch. Anoint the candle with the oil and sprinkle healing powder on it. Sprinkle healing powder upon the photo, placed before the candle. Charge the candle with these words, while holding it:

In the name of the Divine, we ask for complete and total healing for _____, on all levels in a manner acceptable to them and for their highest good. So mote it be.

Then light the candle. Repeat the spell as often as needed for long-term illness. Even when the candle is done, you can leave the stone, herbs, and photo on the altar to continue the work.

Like minor healing, one should ask permission of the recipient whenever possible. When that is not possible, a magickal practitioner can consult a divination device, particularly a yes/no oracle such as a pendulum, to confirm this healing energy would be welcome and accepted on some unconscious or higher level.

Banish a Headache
Candle Color: Back
Moon or Sun Tide: Waning
Day: As needed, but ideally Saturday, Monday or Wednesday
Hour: As needed, but ideally Moon, Mercury or Saturn
Dressing: Any mix of Lavender, Peppermint, Eucalyptus, Chamomile (Roman) Essential Oil, Feverfew

Take a black candle and anoint it in a mix of these soothing oils. Sprinkle powdered feverfew upon the candle. Charge the candle to completely and immediately banish your headache. Light the candle and imagine lifting your headache out of your head, and placing it into the candle flame. As the flame burns, it burns away any pain you have.

Healing Grief
Candle Color: Dark Blue
Moon or Sun Tide: Waning
Day: Saturday or Sunday
Hour: Saturn, Sun, Moon
Dressing: Melissa, Frankincense, Neroli, Lavender, Ground Hawthorn Berries or Rose Hips, Seven Pins

Anoint your dark blue candle, ideally a taper, with any combination of the uplifting essential oils such as melissa (lemon balm), frankincense, neroli, and lavender. While not required to be effective, you can add the heart healers of hawthorn berries or rose hips sprinkled upon the candle. Add seven evenly spaced pins along the side of the taper candle. You will burn a section of the candle for seven days. You could get a Seven Knob candle, but they usually come in more primary colors. Use of a darker color is more appropriate for healing grief.

Along with the herbs on the candle, drinking a cup of hawthorn and rose hip tea would aid the magick immensely, though hawthorn should be removed if you are on any cardiovascular medications or have any heart or circulatory disease. Ideally, 1 tablespoon of dried herb added to 1 cup of boiling water. Let it steep for 5 minutes and strain. Drink the tea as you sit before the candle, and gaze at the flame. Pour your grief into the flame. Talk. Cry. Simply be. Do anything you feel is right. Let it burn until the pin falls out, and snuff the candle, repeating, with another cup of tea, the next day for seven days in a row. You will notice a significant shift in your grief, though time is the true healer in these situations.

Quit Smoking

Candle Color: White, Grey
Moon or Sun Tide: Waning
Day: Saturday, Sunday
Hour: Saturn, Sun, Mercury
Dressing: Base Oil, Lobelia, Mullein, Coltsfoot, One Cigarette

Work with a health care practitioner to provide additional support in quitting smoking, but for the magickal side, I've found this candle spell helpful for many clients. Unroll a cigarette and use some of the tobacco to pack the bottom of the candle. When you burn the candle, make sure you use a metal holder, and have an appropriate tray or trivet beneath it. It can also be helpful to have proper ventilation, as the end of the spell will smell like a cigarette burning. Mix equal parts of dried mullein leaf, coltsfoot, and lobelia, though choose the herbal medicine *lobelia inflata*, not an ornamental lobelia variety. It is known as Indian tobacco.

Anoint the candle with a base oil of your choosing and roll the candle in herbal mix. Charge it to completely remove any addiction to nicotine, tobacco, and cigarettes/cigars. Once the candle is lit, take any remaining herb mix and sprinkle it counter-clockwise around the base of the burning candle. Let it burn down until it reaches the packed tobacco. Sweep everything up and bring the remains of the herbs and wax to a crossroads you do not frequent. Leave it at the crossroads, and when you leave, do not turn back to look at it again.

Quit Drinking

Candle Color: Purple, Indigo, Lavender, Sea-Green, Turquoise. A Black Human Figure Candle can also be used
Moon or Sun Tide: Waning
Day: Monday
Hour: Moon
Dressing: Grapeseed Oil, Oakmoss, 3 Amethysts

Addictions, but particularly alcoholism, fall under the realm of Neptune in planetary magick. While proper medical and psychological support is the key, evoking the blessings of Neptune, and in other systems, the Moon, helps alleviate conditions and make successfully quitting a stronger chance.

Anoint the candle with grapeseed oil and dress with powdered oakmoss. Place three amethysts in a triangle formation around the base of the candle. Light the candle and envision the candle sucking up and burning away the addiction. When the candle is done, carry the three stones as a talisman in a purple bag and hold them when facing difficult situations around alcohol addiction.

Weight Loss

Candle Color: Pink

The Lighting of Candles

Moon or Sun Tide: Waning
Day: Friday, Sunday
Hour: Venus, Sun, Mercury
Dressing: Grapefruit Oil in base, Chickweed, Blue or Yellow Apatite, 7 Pins

Like smoking and drinking, weight loss is another topic that can be aided by magick but works best when partnered with medical, emotional, and psychological support as necessary. With excess weight there is either a medical reason or a personal reason contributing to obesity. More often than not, issues can stem from self-esteem and societal expectations. Magick should always focus upon what is best for the individual's health, as many might not fit their idealized image but can still be healthy, and many who do fit a societal ideal might be dangerously unhealthy. The key is for healthy weight loss or ideal body weight for health and well-being.

On the waning moon, anoint the pink candle, possibly a human figure candle of the appropriate gender identity, with grapefruit oil in a base. Sprinkle dried chickweed herb upon it. At the base of the candle, place the mineral known as apatite, which helps with metabolism and digestion. While it comes in many colors, the best two for this intention are blue or yellow, for the throat and solar plexus chakras respectively. This is a spell that works well by dividing the candle into seven segments marked with pins and burning only one segment per day for seven days. As the pin falls, so does weight "drop" from the recipient of the magick. You could use a seven knob candle, but the pin dropping as sympathetic magick is helpful. When the candle is done, use the mineral as a talisman and reminder for proper eating habits and appropriate exercise.

Animal Healing

Candle Color: Brown, Tan, Orange
Moon or Sun Tide: Waxing to Bring Healing, Waning to Banish Illness
Day: Sunday, Monday, Wednesday
Hour: Moon, Sun, Mercury
Dressing: Base Oil, Healing Powder

While the principles for healing are essentially the same for humans, animals and even plants, practitioners have found some different correspondences work better when working with animals. Healing farm animals was a tried and true part of Witchcraft that is mostly forgotten now, as the Witch is less close to the farm these days. Most of us now are working animal healing for our beloved animal companions.

Take a brown or other "earth tone" candle and carve the name or even a crude picture of the animal into the wax. Anoint it with a base oil and dress it with basic healing powder, unless there is a specific herb appropriate for the specific ailment. Charge the candle for complete healing of the animal in question and let it burn.

Regeneration

Candle Color: Red or White, Human, Mummy, or Pharaoh Candle
Moon or Sun Tide: Waxing
Day: Sunday
Hour: Sun, Moon
Dressing: Magick Power Oil, Power Powder, Six Garnets

A regeneration candle is done when you feel that you have expended a lot of vital life force, often on a project or conflict, and need to recoup and regenerate your health and well-being. You don't necessarily have to be ill, though it can also be used after a period of extended illness when you are on the road to recovery. It is not a healing spell, so it shouldn't be used in place of rectifying any illness or injury. It just can aid the recovery process – physically, emotionally, or magickally.

I like to do this with a shaped candle – either a human figure, a mummy (life after death) or a pharaoh, as the pharaoh's had their own regeneration mysteries. Do it when the tides are waxing and filling with life. If on a solar holiday such as Winter Solstice, Vernal Equinox or Summer Solstice, or on a full Moon, even better. Anoint the candle with Magick Power Oil, sprinkle the Power Powder on it, adding any personal power herbs if you'd like, and then surround the candle with six garnet stones, in a hexagram formation. Let it burn completely and be open to the tide of life force returning to you.

Protection
Candle Color: Black or White
Moon or Sun Tide: Waning, Ideally Dark Moon
Day: Saturday, Tuesday
Hour: Saturn, Mars, Sun
Dressing: Frankincense & Myrrh Oil, Protection Powder No. 1

Protection is one of the most sought after spells. It can be good to do protection magick for general protection, but it can also be done when we feel a need for protection or when circumstances are different and we feel vulnerable. This basic candle spell for protection can serve either case. While I traditionally use black candles to absorb and neutralize any harm, some people are so culturally conditioned to use white for protection and associate black candles with "evil," so go with the color candle you feel strongest. Carve your name, or the name of the person to receive the protection on the candle. Mix equal parts of frankincense and myrrh essential oil in a base, and use it on the candle. Sprinkle Protection Powder No. 1 and let it burn. It will generally boost the spiritual "immune" system and strengthen boundaries, and tend to absorb and neutralize any harm being directed to the recipient.

Uncrossing

Candle Color: White, White Cross-Shaped Candle
Moon or Sun Tide: Waning or New Moon
Day: Saturday, Sunday, Thursday,
Hour: Saturn, Sun, Jupiter, Mars
Dressing: Holy Oil, Protection Powder No. 2

When you are "crossed" it means that something is blocking, thereby "crossing" your path. Often it implies intentional harmful magick, or at the very least, intentional malice manifesting as blocks to your health and well-being. Nothing tends to go right. Sometimes we can even cross ourselves, manifesting our own blocks, and a good uncrossing ritual can be helpful in either situation, whether we have outer world enemies or inner world conflicts.

Before doing uncrossing work, it's great to take a cleansing ritual bath. Dissolve a cup of sea salt in your bathwater. A few drops of cleansing essential oils can be helpful as well, including lavender, frankincense, hyssop, lemon, lemongrass, or lemon eucalyptus. Soak for five or ten minutes and imagine breathing out any unwanted energies from your pores into the water. When done, sit in the tub as the water drains out, taking everything down the drain. Then rinse and dry off.

An effective symbol of being crossed is a cross or an "X." You can use a cross-shaped candle, or if working on a taper, votive, or pull-out candle, carve a cross or an X upon it. Anoint with Holy Oil

The Lighting of Candles

and dust with Protection Powder No. 2. Charge the candle to dissolve all blocks and remove any forces crossing your life path. As the cross dissolves with the melting wax, so too will these forces. Light the candle and let it burn. This is a particularly important candle to observe for divination signs, as outlined in **Chapter Eight.** If the crossing is strong, it might need be to done more than once.

General Reversal

Candle Color: White, Reversal or Double Action
Moon or Sun Tide: Waning
Day: Saturday, Sunday, Thursday
Hour: Saturn, Sun, Jupiter, Mars
Dressing: Holy Oil

My favorite form of minor curse breaking and general reversal of harmful influences is a reversal ritual. There are several kind that can be done. In most of these rituals, the black wax embodies the curse or ill fortune, or it absorbs the harm as part of the ritual. Some use true reversal candles that have an outer layer of black wax and an inner layer of a color, usually red or white, and in the burning process the inner layer covers the outer layer, signifying the new color "beats" the "evil" of the black colored wax. Others use double-action candles. Depending on how they are made, they are usually two-toned color candles. Some have the black on the bottom of the pillar candle, and the color above covers it, much like the true reversal candle. Others that burn more cleanly are sometimes made with the black on top, signifying you "burn through" the "bad" and all you are left with, in the end, is the "good" color of the blessing you are seeking. Some practitioners dig the wick out of the base and turn it upside down, in a ritual action of "reversing" any ill intent or specific spell.

In my own experiences in learning such reversal spells, we lacked fancy two-colored candles. I was taught to use a simple taper candle of the color pertaining to the situation that needed to be reversed. When in doubt, use white. Dig out the wick in the base. You are digging to get at the truth, and your own reality, not what someone has placed upon you. Digging gets anything that has been put on you "loose" and ready to be lifted. Set the top of the taper on fire as the situation "as it is" while holding the candle vertically. Then turn counterclockwise as you are looking at it, and hold the candle horizontal. From your altar candles, light the wick sticking out of the base. You now have a horizontal candle burning from both ends. Make sure to have a tray or cloth beneath to catch the dripping wax. Then turn the candle vertical, but with the first flame at the bottom and the base flame at the top. Stick the bottom flame into the candleholder, letting enough wax melt to secure it if that end tapers. By extinguishing the flame, you are extinguishing the unwanted situation and manifesting your own situation, signified by the base of the candle being on top. You have turned the tables on any ill-wisher and reversed the situation.

As with the Uncrossing Candle, it can be helpful to take a ritual salt bath before doing the reversal working. If you want specific correspondences for specific situations, use those listed below with the same basic ritual as the general reversal candle.

Reversal of Bad Finances

Candle Color: Green, Green/Black
Moon or Sun Tide: Waning or New
Day: Thursday, Friday
Hour: Venus, Jupiter, Sun, Moon, Mars
Dressing: Basil Oil

Reversal of Bad Romance
Candle Color: Red, Pink, Red/Black
Moon or Sun Tide: Waning or New
Day: Friday
Hour: Venus, Mercury, Mars
Dressing: Yarrow Oil

Reversal of Bad Health
Candle Color: White, Yellow, White/Black
Moon or Sun Tide: Waning or New
Day: Sunday, Wednesday
Hour: Sun, Mercury, Mars
Dressing: Angelica Oil

Open the Way
Candle Color: Yellow
Moon or Sun Tide: Waning
Day: Any
Hour: Sun, Mars, Jupiter, Moon
Dressing: Open the Way Oil No. 1 or No. 2

Open the Way is also known as a Road Opener spell, and sometimes described as a Road Block Remover. It's similar to an uncrossing or reversal candle, though is used when the blocks are not placed by supernatural or psychic means, but more mundane or karmic sources. It is a great spell when you are the biggest obstacle in your life.

Traditionally in folk magick, it is named after the herb Abre Camino (*Eupatorium villosum*), which literally translates as Road Opener. Many would say that any Road Opener spell that does not contain Eupatorium villosum is not truly a road opener and they would have a point, but I learned doing similar spells simply with cleansing and clearing substances. Sometimes such spells of a similar nature are called Cut and Clear, but indicate setting a boundary disconnecting you from a source of harm or the past, and then opening the way. Cut and Clear often uses lemon scents, though I had learned to add a small amount of nightshade, for its botanical name, Atropos, is named after the fate who cuts the threads of life and fate. Since Eupatorium villosum is a tropical plant, it's not one I've had a strong relationship with so my own experience with it has been cursory at best. Yet opening spells and candles with traditionally purifying herbs have been quite effective for me and my clients. Here are two formulas for opening the way. The first is more gentle, and the second a bit stronger.

Open the Way Oil No. 1

4 Drops of Lemon Balm Oil
3 Drops of Camphor Oil
1 Drop of Sage Oil
1/8 Oz of Base Oil
Pinch of Cinquefoil
Pinch of Pine Needles
Pinch of Sea Salt

Open the Way Oil No. 2

3 Drops of Lemongrass Oil
3 Drops of Cedar Oil
2 Drops of Palmarosa Oil
1 Drop of Citronella Oil
1 Drop of Camphor Oil
1/8 Oz of Base Oil
Pinch of Rue
Pinch of Cinquefoil
Pinch of Sulfur

The Lighting of Candles

Carve your name into the candle, along with the words OPEN THE WAY three times upon it. Anoint with oil. When you light the candle say, "I open the way to health, happiness, good fortune and success on all levels. So mote it be!" If there is something specific you are blocked from, make that a part of your declaration. Let the candle burn and when it is done, the way shall be open and blocks are removed!

Win in Court

Candle Color: Dark Blue or Purple
Moon or Sun Tide: Waxing, Ideally the change from First to Second Quarter Moon, or the Vernal Equinox – both time of balance and justice
Day: Thursday, Friday, Sunday
Hour: Jupiter, Venus, Sun, Mercury
Dressing: Olive Oil, Legal Success Powder

Winning legally can often depend on whether you know you are legally and morally "in the right" or if you know that you are not, as both require different strategies. When you feel you are justified, attributes of Jupiter for influencing people in high places, particularly to do the right thing, are best. Those who feel they are not entirely justified, would do better to use more Mercurial options for trickery, or Mars options for strength and intimidation. Venus can be used in either case for getting what you value, as Venus rules Libra, the sign of the scales of balance. Usually I won't take on a client to do this work if they and I don't feel they are justified, so my experience is more with Jupiter oriented spells.

Carve any details pertinent to the case on the candle. If the issue is to be awarded specific amount of money, write "WIN" with the currency number and your name. If working a larger seven-day pull-out jar, draw scales with one scale up and one scale down.

On the "up" side, put symbols associated with your victory: your initials, the amount, and anything else you can think of. On the lower "losing" scale, put the initials of the one(s) you are going against. Anoint the candle with basic olive oil, sprinkle with the Legal Success Powder and let it burn. If there is any remaining powder from the spell, sprinkle some in your pocket or shoe when going into court.

Courage
Candle Color: Red
Moon or Sun Tide: Waxing
Day: Tuesday
Hour: Mars, Sun, Jupiter
Dressing: Castor Oil, Power Powder

When you have to take a stand against something, or otherwise take an action that requires strength and courage and is not part of your everyday experience, a simple candle spell can boost your resolve and will to do so. Simply light a red candle charged for courage. It is that simple. You can dress it by carving your name, anointing it with castor oil and Power Powder, but if you don't have those things on hand, just light a red candle for courage and go take your stand.

Safe Travels
Candle Color: Orange
Moon or Sun Tide: Waning
Day: Wednesday
Hour: Mercury or Moon
Dressing: Safe Travel Powder, Agate

Charge an orange candle for safe travel, and if specifically looking for safety on a particular trip, name and envision yourself or your loved one needing protection on that trip. If you have a picture of the destination, place it under the candle. Be sure to include the intention of travel to and return from the trip. Place a cleansed agate stone next to the candle. You could also enhance the spell by putting eight agates around the candle, for eight is the number associated with Mercury. Sprinkle a ring of Safe Travel Powder around the candle and crystals counterclockwise (clockwise if in the southern hemisphere), to remove harm before your light it.

Home Blessings
Candle Color: Light Blue
Moon or Sun Tide: New Moon, Waxing
Day: Any
Hour: Any
Dressing: Blessing Oil

This candle spell is done best at a housewarming gathering filled with people who wish the occupants of the home well. If they are open to magick, it can be done at the gathering, or if the guests are not magickal practitioners, done just before they arrive. Simply anoint the blue candle with the general blessing oil and charge it for a happy, healthy, harmonious home. Let it burn and radiate the blessing out, and if done before or at the house warming, it will help magnify and radiate out the good wishes of the guests.

Stop Arguments
Candle Color: Black, White, Blue
Moon or Sun Tide: Waning
Day: Saturday
Hour: Saturn, Mercury, Jupiter
Dressing: Lavender Oil, Licorice Root Powder

This is a gentler version of magick that is used to stop people from talking negatively, such as a Stop Gossip, or what some refer to as "Shut the Fuck Up" spells. Rather than using herbs to inhibit and numb, we use things to bring peace. Take your candle and carve the names of the two (or more) people generally arguing. Between the names, carve what is now known as the "Peace Symbol" consisting of a circle with a downward trident-like symbol. Designed by Gerald Holtom as a symbol for the British Campaign of Nuclear Disarmament, it does bear a striking similarity to the "Crow's Foot" or "Witch's Foot" mark inverted, as well as the Elder Futhark rune Algiz. Sadly the similarity has made ultra-conservative Christian groups try to paint the Peace symbol as a symbol of evil, equating it with a broken cross, but the deep meaning in our general collective is one of peace and harmony after it was adopted by activists first in the United States.

Figure: Peace Symbol

Anoint the candle with lavender oil, and any other oil you think would bring the participants peace and harmony. Then dust the oiled candle with licorice root powder. As an herb with demulcent qualities, like slippery elm, it can be used to soothe and quiet the throat, but it has a sweetness to it that helps calm a situation. Let it burn, ideally in the area where the majority of

The Lighting of Candles

arguments are occurring, and let the magick bring some tranquility.

Bayberry New Year's Eve Candle

Candle Color: Bayberry (Olive Green)
Moon or Sun Tide: If not Yule or New Year's Eve, New Moon
Day: Yule Eve, New Year's Eve
Hour: Any
Dressing: None

Despite living in New England all my life, I learned this colonial "spell" tradition from my very good friend author and teacher Stephanie Taylor Grimassi, a transplant to New England from California. Candles would be made from the wax of the bayberry. When the berries were boiled, the residue on the surface could be used in making candles, and these candles were wonderfully clear and smelled great compared to the candles of the time. The finite yearly supply made them a treat, and they would only be burned on holidays, and particularly for this holiday "spell."

Burn a bayberry taper in a candleholder, for the candleholder's "socket" is part of the magick. Burn it with intention on New Year's Eve, speaking these words:

Bayberry candles burned to the socket, bring health to the home and wealth to the pocket!

Often they were given as gifts at the Yuletide season and then burned on our modern New Year's Eve. When given, it was a sign of wanting to renew and strengthen the bonds of friendship over the coming year. Or if obtained as a pair of candles, one could burn on Yule or Christmas Eve and the second on New Year's Eve. Some modern practitioners use bayberry seven-day jar candles, and burn them for the first forty days of the New Year to ensure prosperity for the rest of the year.

Awakening the House Spirit
Candle Color: White
Moon or Sun Tide: Full Moon
Day: Saturday or Sunday
Hour: Saturn, Sun, Moon
Dressing: Blessing Oil, Cup and Plate

Pagan people have long believed in the spirit of the house influencing the home and the people living in it. Called House Elves, Brownies of the British Isles, or the Lares of the Romans, they were once venerated by families, and embody the spirit of the land where the home is built, as well as the materials, particularly the wood, that go into building it. You can commune with the house spirit, but if you choose to awaken it, you should put out a cup and plate, along with the candle, and make offerings of food and drink to it to bring health and happiness to all who dwell in the home, and repeat this working monthly to "feed" the spirit. Simply consecrate the candle with the Blessings Oil and place it, along with a filled cup and a plate with some snack, usually a sugary treat, near the heart of the home, either the kitchen, or if you have a hearth, near the fireplace. Recite this or something similar:

I call to the Spirit of this Home.
I call to the Spirit of this Dwelling
I invite you to be present in our lives
May we honor you.
May you bless us.
May there only be peace between us.
Blessed be.

Let the candle burn, and when done, remove the offerings. If possible, dispose of them upon the land nearby outside. If not, take whatever methods of disposal seem appropriate for you. Repeat this ritual once a moon cycle to keep blessings flowing between you and the house spirit.

Meditation

Candle Color: White, Light Blue
Moon or Sun Tide: Full Moon or Dark Moon – Points of Balance
Day: Any day
Hour: Moon, Sun, Saturn
Dressing: Holy Oil

Dress your candle with Holy Oil and use it as a focus for meditation. Carve the triangular meditation symbol into the candle. Charge it for aid in achieving and maintaining a meditative state, and the discipline of keeping a meditation practice. This can be your central candle if you keep a meditation altar.

Figure: Meditation Symbol

Attract Spirit Allies

Candle Color: White, Black
Moon or Sun Tide: Waxing – Ideally on the Full Moon
Day: Any day
Hour: Moon
Dressing: Magick Power Oil, Psychic Powder or an equal mix of Wormwood and Mugwort

Ideally, if you can obtain a Grim Reaper candle, a Skull candle, or a Baphomet candle in an appropriate color, use it. Otherwise, a standard candle will work. If using a standard candle, carve upon it a glyph used in the Temple of Witchcraft tradition to attract your spirit allies and guides. Anoint it with Magick Power Oil and sprinkle Psychic Powder on it so you can perceive the spirits. Meditate before the candle, asking your spirits to commune with you on a level you can sense and comprehend.

Figure: Spirit Allies Symbol

Lucid Dreaming

Candle Color: Blue, White, Silver, Yellow
Moon or Sun Tide: Either
Day: Monday
Hour: Moon, Mercury
Dressing: Blessing Oil, Psychic Powder

This candle is for clear dreams you can remember and control. Dream control is a highly desired skill among occultists both east and west, and is a skill to develop over time. I prefer using a larger jar candle or pull-out, and only light this prepared candle as I'm going to do dream work. Anoint it with Blessing Oil and Psychic Powder. Charge it to achieve the lucid dream state. Before bed, meditate before it for a few minutes, setting your intention for what kind of dream, and what you seek to experience. You can lucid dream about anything. Then snuff the candle and go to bed. Keep a notebook by your side to write down all you remember. It can take perseverance to develop lucid dreaming skills, but this can help jumpstart it.

Magickal Power

Candle Color: Red, Black
Moon or Sun Tide: Waxing
Day: Tuesday, Saturday
Hour: Moon, Mars, Saturn
Dressing: Dark Power Oil, Dragon's Blood Resin, Parsley, Tarragon

If possible, obtain a Witch, Skull, Pharaoh, Mummy, or Baphomet candle in the appropriate color. If you cannot obtain a shaped candle, carve this power symbol into a traditional candle, or if you do obtain a shaped candle, it can be carved upon the bottom.

Figure: Magickal Power Symbol

Anoint the candle with the Dark Power Oil, which isn't so much about dark power, but dark herbs and oils to manifest things, unlike the less tangible inner blessing oils. Sprinkle a mix of powdered dragon's blood resin, parsley, and tarragon on the candle and set it in a tray or bowl, as most shaped candles will drip a lot. Charge the candle with this incantation:

I call upon my Ancestors
And the Ancestors of the Magickal Way
To prepare me for, and open me to, a deeper magickal power
May my spells always be cast true
May my insights grow and flower
As I follow the Golden Road for the rest of my days
So mote it be.

Let the candle burn fully, and be aware of the evolution of your magickal self and the power you gather. Use it wisely.

The Lighting of Candles

Wisdom

Candle Color: Yellow, Black, White
Moon or Sun Tide: Waxing – Ideally, the New Moon
Day: Sunday or Thursday
Hour: Jupiter, Sun
Dressing: Holy Oil or Base Oil of Sunflower or Almond, Sage and Oak Bark

Wisdom is an ephemeral thing. It's hard to define, but we know someone wise when we speak with them. While many on the magickal path focus on power or psychic ability, academics, or leadership, I think the true goal is wisdom. For me, wisdom is knowledge in balance with power and love. It is knowing when and how to use knowledge, and just as much, knowing when not to take action. This is a simple spell to invite the blessings of wisdom to grow more strongly with you as a practitioner.

A Skull or Pyramid candle would work well for this spell, but any candle can work. If you use a pull-out or pillar, you can carve the images of a pyramid and/or skull upon them. A pyramid with the all-seeing eye would also be appropriate. Anoint the candle and sprinkle a mix of powdered sage and oak bark upon the candle. Charge the candle for Wisdom:

By the Divine Mind, Divine Will and Divine Heart,
I consecrate this candle to Wisdom
Holy Sophia, grant me the Understanding that is yours to give
And may my thoughts, words and deeds be guided
By the most ancient wisdom of the stars.
Blessed be.

CHAPTER SEVEN: COMPLEX CANDLE SPELLS & FIRE MAGICK

While simple candle spells are quite effective, and in my mind, preferable, many feel that complex candle spells improve the chance of success. While some magicians hold to the adage "less is more" for certain situations, more is actually more. With more complexity, there can be more energy and more intent. With several candles, there are more vessels to carry intention, and with a variety of candle shapes or colors, more complex intentions can be woven into the spell working.

What makes a candle spell complex is either the number of candles used, the movement of the candles, or the deeper intentions of the candle work. Multiple candles are chosen based on astrological or numeric values associated with the intentions, as described when talking about candle grids and mandalas in **Chapter Four**. Most western magicians use the Qabalistic system of number and shape to align with the candle's color, scent and intention, whether they realize it or not, but there are other esoteric systems of numerology and astrology, and some that are simply based free-form and upon intuition.

You can create candle mandalas or grids using stones, herbs, candles, tarot cards, and any other items that seem appropriate, and mix them with the techniques previously outlined. Carve and dress the candles as desired, and link them with the appropriate astral tides and planetary timing. Usually, the candles will make the points of the shape, but some will use just one central candle, and stones or other items as the points.

Beyond the grids are candle altar rituals, as the movement of the candles also makes candle spells more complex. Rather than allowing the candle to be lit and simply burn, complex candle rituals will have you snuff the candles for a particular number of days, relighting them, often with offerings of incense or other items to set the proper vibration, and move the candles around to change the energies involved. Either a special altar is created for the work, or a space would be cleared on the magician's or Witch's regular working altar.

A traditional Hoodoo practitioner will make the distinction between candle rituals and "setting lights" or "setting the lights" for a client. Setting lights does not move the candles and is more deeply based in prayer. Candles are often arranged like they would be in a church, in simple rows, and perhaps even on metal holders or racks.

In more active rituals, candles are moved closer together to bring forces together during the ritual, or moved apart to separate them. Candles might be lit in a specific order and candle flame carried by a neutral taper or chime candle from one specific candle to the next. Various items are placed between the candles to evoke energies between the forces, or people, present in the ritual. The geometry of the candles can shift, taking it from a symbol grid or mandala into a deeper ritual working, using shape and number to change the situation, along with light, color, and scent. A chaotic pattern can be transformed to order by aligning candles and removing unnecessary ones. The candle altar, like any good altar, becomes the microcosm of the magician's or client's life. What is done to the altar is done to the life. For this reason, some will "sequester" such rituals upon large trays of circular, rectangular and square design to contain the changes. The magician working for a student or client wants to make sure the changes are for the individual's life, and not their own, though there is always the possibility of side effects when doing magick

The Lighting of Candles

for others. When you work magick for others, there is the risk it
will change your own life, too.

Candle Manifestation Grid

Candle Color: 1 White, 1 Red, 1 Yellow, 1 Blue, 1 Green
Moon or Sun Tide: Waxing
Day: Saturday, Friday
Hour: Saturn, Venus, Sun, Mercury, Moon
Dressing: Magick Power Anointing Oil, Power Powder
Tools: 5 Polished Obsidian Stones, Salt, Incense Burner

While this spell can be used for any intention, the setup
requires a lot of energy and focus, and can help manifest goals
more quickly and powerfully than a simple candle spell.

Create a pentagram, point up, in Power Powder upon a tray or
altar space. Moving clockwise from the top point, place a white
candle at the top point for spirit, a blue candle for water, a red
candle for fire, a green candle for earth, and a yellow candle for
air. When you trace the pentagram from the top, you get the
elements in the order of manifestation, spirit, fire, air, water, and
earth before returning to spirit again. Where the downward
pentagon is in the inside of the pentagram, place the obsidian
stones at the points of the pentagon, cleansed and charged for
manifestation of intentions. Place the incense burner at the top
point of the pentagram, using a burner that can contain a heated
charcoal. Cleanse each candle and anoint with Power Oil,
returning them to their proper places.

Write out the intention in either simple language or a more
formal spell as outlined in the writing techniques of *The Casting of
Spells* book. Then fold the paper. If the intention is to manifest
something in your life, you traditionally fold the paper towards
you. Light your charcoal in the incense burner. Sprinkle Power

Powder on the charcoal as incense. Waft the paper through the smoke. Place it in the center of the pentagram, in the center of the obsidian stone pentagon. Pour a bit of salt on it for crystallization of your intention. Then light the candles in the order of manifestation – white, red, yellow, blue, green.

By Spirit I light this white candle to align my intention with the Holy Spirit
By Fire I light this red candle to align my intention with True Will.
By Air I light this yellow candle to align my intention with Divine Mind.
By Water I light this blue candle to align my intention with Perfect Love.
By Earth I light this green candle to align my intention with Sacred Sovereignty
So mote it be!

Let the candles burn. When they are all gone, gather up the Power Powder, salt, and intention paper and bury them somewhere on your property or near your home if you do not have property that is specifically yours. You can keep the obsidians in a pouch until the spell manifests, and then once it does, cleanse them and use them again.

Warding with Candles

Candle Color: 4 White Candles
Moon or Sun Tide: Waning
Day: Saturday, Tuesday
Hour: Saturn, Mars, Sun
Dressing: Holy Oil, Protection Powder No. 1
Tools: Peyton, Frankincense Incense, Incense Burner

This spell will establish magickal wards, a form of protection shield, around a particular area. They can be cast for an entire building, a section of a building, or a room. Take four white candles, ideally jar candles or candles that can be placed in a lantern. If the candle is in glass and can be removed from the glass, carve a pentagram upon each of the candles, starting with the bottom left point and moving toward the upward point, continuing until you complete the five-pointed star. This motion is known as a banishing pentagram. If poured directly into a glass container, use a black permanent magic marker upon it, and draw a banishing pentagram.

Anoint each candle with Holy Oil and roll in Protection Powder, or sprinkle the powder on the top of the candle if using a poured glass candle.

Take a peyton, which is a ritual pentacle (five-pointed star in a circle) as the center of your work. A peyton may be a wooden disk or shallow dish with a carved or painted pentacle, or made from copper, brass, aluminum, or in some rare cases, gold or silver. It embodies earth and spirit in a Witch's Circle, and is a place where items are charged to be empowered. The pentagram is also a powerful symbol of protection, so the peyton is an ideal vessel of protection, being a shield against harm.

If you have a ritual method of creating space, such as casting a Magick Circle, do so. If not, take a few deep breaths and burn some cleansing incense such as frankincense incense and move from the center to the north, back to the center again, then out to the east and center, to the south and then center and finally to the west and center. Take your candles and pass them through the incense smoke. Charge them first for protection, and place upon the peyton for a few moments. Envision the energy of the peyton connecting to the deep earth and, like a fountain of white light, the energy rises up from the deep earth, through the peyton, and fills the candle. Say:

I charge this candle with the light of the Earth,
with the Soul of the World.
By your light, life, love and law,
may this place be completely protected from all harm on any level.
So mote it be!

Then place the candle to the north of the peyton and light it. Continue this process moving candles to the east, south and west. If you cast a circle, release it before moving the candles out of the circle space. Move the candles to the furthest edge of where you seek protection for your wards. Take the north candle, and move through the dwelling to the furthest point of the north of the dwelling. If you can put it outside, you can, but the inside most northern point is fine too. Simply envision the light of the candle radiating outside as well, protecting the outside of the dwelling.

Continue moving the east candle to the furthermost east point, the south candle to the furthermost south point and the west candle to the furthermost west point. Envision the field of protection anchored by the candles, centered by the peyton, and encompassing the whole area you wish to protect. Let the candles burn as much as you can, and snuff and relight until they have completely burned.

Your wards are set. You can repeat this spell annually, or as you feel it is needed.

Seven-Knob Attracting a Partner Candle Spell

Candle Color: 2 Red (or Pink or Green) Seven-Knob Candles
Moon or Sun Tide: Waxing
Day: Friday
Hour: Venus, Mars, Sun, Mercury
Dressing: Almond Oil, Dragon's Blood, Rose Petals
Tools: Tray

Anoint the candles with almond oil and sprinkle crushed Dragon's Blood resin upon them. Designate one candle as "you" and another candle as your future correct romantic partner. Charge each to attract the other, for the good of all involved. Place on opposite ends of the tray at least a foot apart. The tray is to "hold" the spell and contain the herbs used. Sprinkle rose petals in a clockwise circle on the tray around the two candles. Say:

In the name of the old gods of love and trust
I call for a lover, a partner kindling both romance and lust
I call for the one who is right for me now
I call to draw to me (describe the partner you desire)

Then light the candles and let one knob burn on each. The next day, move the candles slightly closer together and repeat the incantation. Burn another knob on each. Continue for seven days, bringing the candles closer and closer together until they are next to each other by the last of the seven knobs. When the candles are done burning, take the rose petals and scatter them to the wind, repeating the incantation. Be confident that you and your partner are moving now closer together to meet. Make yourself available to opportunities to meet new people, and if you have a feeling that someone might be a good match for you, take the risk of rejection and introduce yourself. You will be pleasantly surprised.

Healing Hexagram

Candle Color: 7 Taper Candles – 3 Green, 3 Red, 1 Gold
Moon or Sun Tide: Waxing
Day: Sunday, Wednesday or Friday
Hour: Sun, Mercury
Dressing: Chamomile Oil, Self-Heal Herb
Tools: Photo of Recipient of Healing or Full Name Written Out on Paper, Frankincense Incense, Incense Burner, 6 Citrine Stones

Place the photo or name paper of the recipient of your healing intention in the center of your workspace. Arrange a downward pointing equilateral triangle of the green taper candles. Arrange an upward pointing equilateral triangle of the red taper candles intersecting it evenly, creating the hexagram or Star of David formation, with the photo/paper in the center.

Light your frankincense incense. Pass each of the citrine stones through the smoke, and charge each one for complete healing. Moving clockwise around the hexagram, place them between the candles.

Starting with the upper point red candle furthest from you, pass it through the frankincense smoke and then anoint it with chamomile oil in a base and sprinkle the candle with self-heal herb. Specifically charge it with the intention of healing the recipient "fully and completely, in a manner that is correct and for the good of all involved." If you are allergic to chamomile, as many are, frankincense oil can be used instead. Light the candle. Move clockwise around the hexagram, repeating with the candles, alternating colors until all the candles of the hexagram are lit.

Repeat the same process with the gold candle, but place the gold candle in the center, right upon the photo/paper of the recipient. Let the incense burn out and the candles burn down. Place the citrine stones in a gold, green or red charm bag, and give them to the recipient to carry in a pocket on their receptive side (opposite their dominant hand) or give them to be placed in the home, office and/or car of the recipient, to continue the healing until completion.

Peaceful Sleep Candles
Candle Color: 1 Black Candle, 1 Light Blue Candle, 1 Deep Blue Candle
Moon or Sun Tide: Waning Sun Tide

Day: Any Day
Hour: Moon, Saturn
Dressing: Chamomile or Lavender Oil
Tools: Cup, Herbal Tea (Chamomile, Passionflower, or Valerian), Mugwort, Frankincense, Incense Burner

This is a spell for when we experience insomnia or are sleeping but not getting rest. Carve your name and the words PEACEFUL SLEEP on the candles. Anoint the three candles with either chamomile oil or lavender oil in a base oil. Charge for exactly that, a peaceful night's sleep, and light the candles. Place them in a triangle formation, with the point of the triangle facing you, ideally in your bedroom or wherever you are going to sleep. Make an incense that is ¼ dried Mugwort herb with ¾ Frankincense resin and burn upon charcoal. Then while the incense and candles are burning, make yourself a simple cup of herbal tea. Chamomile is gentle, though some people with ragweed sensitivity are allergic to it. Passionflower is stronger than chamomile and valerian is stronger than passionflower, though in a small percentage of the population, valerian actually excites rather than sedates. If you have never taken either chamomile or valerian, passionflower or any favorite pre-packaged restful sleep tea will work. Once you've brewed the tea, place the cup between the three candles. Throw some more of the incense blend upon the burning charcoal. Let it soak in the energies of the candles for a bit. About a half-hour before going to bed, drink the tea. Keep the candles burning until you ready to go to bed and then before bed, snuff them out.

With the prepared candles, you can repeat this spell whenever having restless sleep without using new candles. Please don't leave candles burning while you are sleeping.

Inspiration of Awen Candle

Candle Color: 3 White Votive Candles
Moon or Sun Tide: Waxing
Day: Sunday, Monday or Wednesday
Hour: Mercury, Sun, Moon
Dressing: Hazelnut Oil, Dragon's Blood, Bay Leaf, Sage, Yarrow, Skullcap, Angelica
Tools: Tray, Glass Holders for Votives

Awen is a Welsh word indicating magickal inspiration, the poetic power of bards and Druids, and adopted by modern Witches and Wiccans. Modern Druidic orders use a symbol consisting of three dots, for the three drops of wisdom from the Cauldron of Inspiration, with three lines emanating right, left, and center from the three drops, surrounded by three circles for the three worlds. This spell invokes the blessings of Awen, of creative inspiration, through light and herb. The hazelnut, in particular, is the Celtic tree of poetic knowledge and inspiration. The mythic Salmon of Wisdom was said to feed off the nuts from this sacred tree. Use this spell at the start of a big creative project, or if you get stuck in completing the project.

Figure: Awen Symbol

The Lighting of Candles

Upon your tray, place the three votives in the position of the three drops of inspiration. Anoint them with hazelnut oil and sprinkle a pinch of dragon's blood on the left drop, bay leaf on the middle drop, and sage on the right drop. Draw the lines from those three drops with the herbs dragon's blood (left ray), bay leaf (middle ray), and sage (right ray). Then sprinkle three clockwise circles with the herbs yarrow (inner ring), skullcap (middle ring), and angelica (outer ring).

Light the candles left, right and center and let them burn. When the candles are done burning, sweep up the herbs and scatter them to the wind. This scattering will draw the Voice of the Wind, the whispers of secret knowledge, to your mind, and grant you the inspiration for the project. This is a particularly good spell for creative projects and art directly involving magickal themes.

A variation of this theme in the Temple of Witchcraft is to use red, yellow, and blue candles for Will, Wisdom, and Love. You can adapt it to suit your needs, and if you desire, explore these ideas fully in my book, *The Three Rays of Witchcraft.*

Skull Candles to Resolve a Fight

Candles: Two Skull Candles of Different Colors
Moon or Sun Tide: Waning
Day: Friday, Wednesday
Hour: Venus, Sun, Mercury, Jupiter
Dressing: Lavender Essential Oil in Olive Oil
Tools: None

Place two skull candles of different colors on a tray, facing away from each other. Designate each one as a particular person in the conflict. Anoint each with lavender oil in olive oil. Lavender brings peace and relieves tension and the olive branch was traditionally a symbol of peace.

On day 1, light the candles and let them burn for a bit while facing away from each other. Snuff them without letting them burn more than ten minutes.

Day 2, turn the candles so they are both facing you, the practitioner, even if one of the skulls represents "you" in the fight. Light them again. Speak to them both like a good friend wanting to encourage peace and reconciliation. Snuff the candles after ten minutes of burn time on day 2.

On day 3, turn the candles to face each other and light them. Tell the skulls they will get along and all problems will be resolved. Let them burn until they go out. The pattern of the wax on the tray might give clues to how the two will resolve each other. Look at **Chapter Eight** for more guidelines on candle divination.

Candle Vigil for an Ancestor

Candle Color: White Seven-day Jar/Pull-Out
Moon or Sun Tide: Anytime
Day: Anytime
Hour: Anytime
Dressing: Myrrh Oil
Tools: Photo of the Deceased, White Cloth, Myrrh or Sandalwood Incense, Clear Glass of Water, Food Plate, White Stone, Mementos

This is a deceptively "easy" ritual in terms of what to do with a candle, but is a profound act of healing and service to the deceased. It's basic "ritual technology" found in many ancestral craft traditions, but shared with my community by an Ifa priest giving basic instructions on how to work with the recently dead. Essentially you set up a shrine to hold a vigil for the recently dead. This helps their spirit move along, giving them plenty of spiritual energy for the journey, and helps the living with unresolved business detach from their departed loved one more easily.

Place a white cloth out and upon it, place a photo of the deceased, and only the deceased. No living people should be in the photo. Place a clear glass of fresh water, a food plate to place favorite foods and drinks, and a white stone. You can also burn an incense such as myrrh or sandalwood, or anything you feel would be pleasing to the deceased. You can put any other mementos, such as jewelry, upon the altar. Place a candle anointed with myrrh behind it all as a guiding light.

Light the candle. Light the incense. Blow three times upon the water for blessing. Call upon the deceased in whatever fashion is appropriate for your religion and the religion of the departed. Offer the water. Offer the food. If there was a favorite alcohol, you can do a glass of that as well, but always make sure there is water on the altar. This is an offering of blessing and energy for the journey to the next realm.

Then speak to the departed. If you are mad, tell them you are mad. If you are sad, speak of your sadness. If there was something you were not able to say, say it. When you are done, listen. You might receive a message, vision, or feeling. Most won't the first day, but give it time.

Continue this practice for at least three days, and up to a full month, with intervals such as seven, nine, twelve, and fourteen days being common. Ideally, the candle is burning continuously, but in the days of fire safety that is not always advisable, so it can be snuffed when you leave and relit when you return. Some in the modern Ifa traditional also use an electric light candle to keep the illumination all day and all night. When done, the stone becomes a talisman for future contact. Usually, the items are integrated into a multi-person ancestor altar for the household for continued veneration, but some simply take it down, particularly if this person was not a close relative or friend. The stone goes into a bowl of ancestral stones. In either case, the single shrine should be taken down.

There is not always a clear result or message from this work, but be assured it is a tremendous service of love and compassion for all involved.

Healing Karma

Candle Color: White & Black Dual Action Candle
Moon or Sun Tide: Vernal or Autumnal Equinox, or When the Moon is transitioning from 1st to 2nd Quarter or 3rd to 4th Quarter
Day: If you cannot catch a balance Solar or Lunar Tide, then Saturday
Hour: Saturn
Dressing: Holy Oil

Karma is a hard concept to understand, simply because the original idea has undergone many adaptations in the Western world. In an effort to find appropriate words in modern occultism and metaphysics, students and teachers have borrowed liberally from the Eastern teachers who were liberally disseminating their teachings with the infusion of Hinduism, Buddhism, and various forms of Yoga to Europe, the United Kingdom, and the Americas. Karma is probably the most well-known of these terms. In its most basic form, karma means action and has become the word to denote the results from our actions. One could argue that it is the result of an action not visible in this lifetime, but the result in a future lifetime from when the action took place. Karma is talked about in terms of credits or debts meaning what is given and what is owed, but the terms have been translated in the West, erroneously, as "good" and "bad" karma. Good karma being viewed as pleasurable things and bad karma as unpleasant things, reinforcing the Judeo-Christian worldview of reward and punishment in a new form. The ideal from most Eastern teachings is "no karma" or the freedom to step out of a cycle of death and rebirth. As Western occultists explore karma, they look to reclaim words like the Anglo-Saxon *Wyrd*, usually translating as "fate" though the Teutonic concept of fate is often different than the popular ideas of fate being tied to a fatalistic sense of destiny. The idea of ancestral inheritance is also tied with karma, the idea of "family karma" manifesting through a genetic line, rather than from life to life. They also look to Egyptian mythology, and the Scales of Ma'at or divine order.

Regardless of whatever view you have of karma and its related words, this spell is for those who want to heal and transform the energetic burden they feel they are carrying, and manifest a greater sense of freedom. Many occult traditions have the concept of the "Lords of Karma" or the "Lords of Opposition," spiritual beings who help us manage and learn from the results of our actions. Even if we believe this is simply an impersonal force, in the act of magick, if we personalize it to commune with it, we can alter its course and transform a situation.

Usually, White/Black Dual Action Candles have white on top and black upon the bottom. Carve upon the white side the glyph of Saturn. On the line dividing the colors, carve the glyph of Libra. Below the line, on the black side, carve another glyph of Saturn (see page 77). Anoint the whole candle with Holy Oil. Recite the following:

Ladies and Lords of Karma,
Holy Powers of Opposition,
I seek to understand, integrate, and heal
from the karma of this lifetime,
and the Karma of past lifetimes,

with ease, grace, and gentleness
for the good of all involved.
So mote it be!

Light the candle. Let it burn all the way, even if it requires multiple relights. Bury any remains on your property or someplace near your living space. Be open to the guidance of the Ladies and Lord of Karma. Take wise advice. Choose better action and watch your life be transformed. You might find people you have wronged, knowingly or unknowingly, presenting opportunities to ask for forgiveness and create a space for healing. No matter how hard, take every opportunity you can to create healing for yourself and for others.

Boat Lantern Wish Candle Ritual

Candle Color: White Tea Light
Moon or Sun Tide: Waxing
Day: Any
Hour: Any
Dressing: Any
Tools: Tissue Paper, Elmer's Glue, Balloon, Thick Marker, Cheap Paint Brush, Small Orange

This creative, simple, and powerful ritual was taught to me when on retreat in Wales with the Temple of Witchcraft. One of our guides, a very creative and adventuresome gentleman, suggested it and brought the materials. We essentially created a paper mâché boat to carry a small wishing or blessing candle out onto the tide. Our retreat house was near an estuary, and we took the lanterns we spent the week creating down to the bay and floated them upon the outgoing tide, watching them then travel the coast with the current, taking our wishes into the sea. It was a powerful act of fire and sea magick with very little formal ritual yet had a lasting effect. Many of our pilgrims on the retreat were both personally moved and manifested new dreams at the conclusion of the trip.

Start by inflating a balloon, and rather than tying a knot at the end, stick a thick marker into the end, large enough to seal the balloon and prevent air from escaping. While there are a variety of methods to make paper mâché, including using flour and water or liquid starch, we used white "Elmer's" craft glue. It's a safe, non-toxic substance to use for the project and will easily biodegrade in nature.

In a bowl, mix equal parts Elmer's Glue and water. If you'd like to add small pinches of ground herbs or a few drops of an essential oil to match your intention, you can do so. Cut strips of thin tissue paper and wrap them around the balloon. Typically, the tissue paper is white, but you can choose a color or colors attuned to your magickal intention. The candle inside this lantern will shine out through the paper, making a stained glass effect with the paper. Use a cheap paintbrush you don't mind ruining and dip it into the glue-water mixture, and "paint" the tissue paper. The trick is to cover the balloon, connecting all the paper, making it watertight, without laying on the glue too thick, weighing down the lantern so much that it fails to float. Leave an opening in the paper at the neck of the balloon large enough for your hand. Wait at least twenty-four hours to dry, and then see if you need to add any more to fill any gaps or holes as it dries. Once you are satisfied and the outside of the lantern is complete, pull the marker out of the balloon, allowing it to gently deflate. Popping a tied balloon can damage the lantern. Remove the balloon and place the open end up. The lantern may rock a bit, like an egg. You can use non-toxic paint, markers, or food dye to decorate the lantern with specific shapes, images and symbols, all according to your intention.

Peel a small orange, making sure to keep the bottom third of the peel whole, creating a small dish-like shape from the peel. Place that at the bottom of the lantern to be the candleholder. Consecrate your tea light, place it in the orange peel. Take your boat lantern to the water, and when ready, using a long match or long lighter, light the candle, and float it upon the outgoing current. An invocation or blessing can be said, such as:

By the magick of the Water City
Through the People of the Sea
By the blessings of fire and water
May this wish come to be.

True Justice

Candle Color: Black and White, Green
Moon or Sun Tide: New Moon or Full Moon
Day: Friday
Hour: Saturn
Dressing: Frankincense & Myrrh Oil
Tools: Chess Board, Frankincense & Myrrh

Unlike a simple win in a court case, a True Justice spell is one where you are evoking the power of cosmic justice, which always runs the risk of deciding in a way that is not in your favor. This power is not a personal entity that can be supplicated to, but a restoration of balance and will have repercussions, unseen at first, upon all involved. It is often the best course of action when action needs to be taken, but you realize you are unsure of what result would serve the highest good.

The spell is relatively simple, but works best for practitioners who have crafted long-standing relationships with the spirits the

The Lighting of Candles

world and cosmos. Practitioners who have achieved their own sense of inner balance to a certain extent.

Light the frankincense and myrrh incense. Pass the candle through the smoke before doing anything with it. Then simply carve the candle with the hieroglyph of the feather of Ma'at, the Egyptian goddess of justice, balance, and cosmic order.

Figure: Feather Ma'at Hieroglyph

Anoint with equal parts frankincense and myrrh oil, representing the dark and the light. Place the candle upon a black and white chessboard, or simply black and white square grid, 8x8 alternating squares, that you have created from paper. Keep the incense burning.

Light the candle with the situation clearly in mind. State:

I, (name yourself), ask in the name of the Power of Ma'at, for cosmic order to be established in (name the situation). I ask this fulfill true balance and the highest good. So mote it be.

Chant the Word of the Aeon of Ma'at, IPSOS, in its four permutations, as taught by the Thelemic author Nema in her book *Maat Magick: A Guide to Self Initiation:*

IPSOS
IPSOSh
IPShoS
IPShOSh

Do this for as long as you are able to maintain focus, knowing the longer you do, the more energy will gather for this intention. Let the candle burn and allow the cosmic order to re-establish itself. Expect the unexpected as we rarely know what true balance looks like as humans.

Divorce

Candle Color: 2 White Candles (Can be human-shaped of appropriate gender identities)
Moon or Sun Tide: Waning
Day: Tuesday, Wednesday, Saturday
Hour: Mars, Mercury, Saturn
Dressing: Magick Power Anointing Oil, Legal Success Powder, Salt, Stack of Ten Coins (Silver Dimes if possible)

Upon your workspace or tray, create a circle of salt. In the center of the salt, place the stack of coins and the two candles, anointed with oil. Designate one candle as the person you are doing the work for, if not yourself. Sprinkle that one with a little bit of legal success powder. If they are human-shaped figures, have them face each other with the coins between the figures. Charge the candles for a successful, clear, just, and quick divorce. You can add any other disclaimers or qualities to your intention. Light the candles. Then, if human-shaped figures, turn them away from each other. Let them burn for a few moments then break the circle of salt. The seal around their relationship is fully broken.

Start moving the candles away from each other in opposite directions. Based upon the intention of the caster, do you wish to get all of the money, the majority of the money, or divide the money and assets equally? Divide the coins appropriately, and "take" with you the stack you desire, next to your candle, placing the remaining coins, if any, next to the other candle.

When the candles have burned a quarter of the way, move the candles further apart with their coins. Sweep up the salt, and now place the salt between them.

When the candles have burned halfway, move them again further apart, with their coins at their side.

For the last quarter, move them as far apart as you can, to the edge of the tray or altar space, and let them finish burning. Flush the salt remains down the toilet or pour down the sink. Have the recipient of the work pocket the coins by their corresponding candle, and then scatter the coins of the opposing candle. A wishing well or someone asking for change on the street is an excellent way to release the remaining coins of the spell.

Excommunication Candle

Candle Color: White Taper or Pillar Candle (No Glass)
Moon or Sun Tide: Waning, Dark Moon is ideal
Day: Saturday, Tuesday
Hour: Saturn, Moon, Mars
Dressing: Dark Power Oil, Protection Powder No. 2

While I hesitate to use the term "excommunication" because it truly is about excluding particular individuals from participation in a Christian church and its sacraments, the original way I learned this spell from a friend and mentor, formerly Catholic, is excommunication. For many of us, such a term still carries a heavy energetic charge in our consciousness, but the definition for this spell is more excluding someone from participating in your personal life, and would truly be called a personal banishment.

Public pronouncements of banishment never seemed to take in the magickal communities where I traveled, but the few candle spell excommunications I've participated in never seem to fail, so I'm returning to the use of this term as I learned it.

This spell is used in extreme situations, where complete separation is the only solution, and any hope of resolution is not possible. It's to be used after you have exhausted other options. You want to be done with this person in this lifetime, though one teacher cautioned it does not last into other lifetimes, and if there is something to be resolved, you should resolve it, rather than banish if possible. But when that is not possible, this spell works well. If the person is really a teacher disguised as an antagonist, I've found people will immediately draw to themselves a person who is very similar and will fulfill the same role and lesson. So be sure you are truly done and have learned everything you can from the situation to release it fully. While I have banished a few people out of anger or pain over the years, some I've followed up with undoing the banishment, or they have spontaneously returned into my life when the energy between us changed, and I was grateful. None who returned received this specific excommunication treatment.

This is best done outside on the ground with dirt, or you should bring a bowl of sand or dirt inside if doing it inside. Dirt is essential to the practice, though it does not need to be "special" dirt from a holy place. Any dirt will do, though soil from the place you live or own works really well because you have sovereignty on that land. If doing it outside, do it someplace you don't frequent often to help break the connection. If you take the dirt from your land inside, you will deposit that dirt someplace further away.

Carve into the white candle the full legal name, and any nicknames or craft names the person is known by, down the side of the candle. Include any titles, and if possible, the glyph of the person's zodiac Sun sign. Anoint with Dark Power Oil and dust with Protection Powder No. 2. If not available, anoint with simple salt and water or any other protection potion or oil. In my tradition, the Temple of Witchcraft, we use a water-based protection potion with salt, water, herbs, and iron powder, which works well in this spell. The recipe can be found in my books *The Outer Temple of Witchcraft* and *The Witch's Shield*.

Get centered and into your own sacred space. Meditate prior to casting the candle spell, or do anything else that will align you with your highest and deepest power. If you still feel it is the only course of action open, continue. Even if you anointed the candle with other potions and herbs, consecrate salt and water together to make a "holy water" for yourself. Direct your energy through your hands over the salt, then the water, then join them together.

I charge this salt to bring purity and blessedness.
I charge this water to bring cleansing and healing.
I join together this creature of salt and this creature of water to work
    my magick
So mote it be.

"Baptize" the candle sprinkling the top or "head" of the candle, the center or "heart" of the candle and the base or "feet" of the candle, and say, "In the name of the Goddess, God, and Great Spirit, I name you _____." filling in the names and titles of the person you seek to banish. Repeat this naming three times. Light the candle.

Let the candle burn for a few minutes. Pour all your connection, your energy, your thoughts, and your feelings about this person into the flame of the candle. Direct energy from your belly, your heart, and your head into the candle, letting go completely. Some will treat the candle as if it was the person, and explain to the person why you are banishing them, saying goodbye and clearly drawing a boundary why you don't want any further contact.

Recite the spell:

In the name of the Goddess, God, and Great Spirit
I excommunicate you from my life.
We shall no longer cross paths.
Our lives shall no longer mingle.
Our work is complete.
You are banished from my world.
I extinguish your light from my life.
I ask this be for my highest good
And thank the gods for all my blessings.
May I continue to receive blessings and learn in a manner that is with
    ease, grace and gentleness
So mote it be!

Turn the candle one hundred and eighty degrees, so the flame is on the bottom. Let it burn a little bit, and then forcibly snuff the candle into the ground or the bowl of soil. If outdoors, press it in as far as it will go. Know that it is done. Release any sacred space you created. If indoors, go outside and bury the candle with the dirt in an area you don't frequent. If outdoors already at a place you don't frequent, and the soil is loose enough to press the candle all the way into the earth, do so. If not, bury the candle, placing more dirt, or even stones upon it, until it is covered. You can also sprinkle more herbs, salt, oil, and consecrated water on it. When done disposing of the candle, turn around and leave, and don't look back. Don't make contact with this person. If you receive contact, do not respond. If a response is required, legally or socially, use the absolute minimum. Restrict yourself to one word answers or

The Lighting of Candles

simply say, "I don't wish to talk to you further," and walk away. Usually, the magick will take this person out of your life and out of your orbit of contact.

Chakra Candles

Chakras are the Vedic word for energy centers within our bodies, acting like spiritual organs processing energy, as our physical organs process food, drink, and air in our bodily system. While the seven chakra system is most popular in Western occult and New Age traditions, there are several different versions of chakra systems. In the Western world, each chakra is related to one of the seven colors of the rainbow. Traditionally, each chakra is aligned with a body system, physical organ, and physical gland, as the hormones of the endocrine system are the closest to the physical expression we have of these non-tangible energy centers. Their proper balance and movement regulates our spiritual and physical health. Commercial candles aligned with the seven chakras are available, but practitioners can also create their own. You can light a single candle when working with one specific chakra in its area of influence to heal, clear, or balance its energies. You can also work with a single candle to do a complex spell balancing and healing all seven chakras.

Figure: Chakras in the Body

You can carve "simple" versions of the chakra's mandala upon the candle. As each chakra is associated with various planets, you can use an appropriate oil or herb from those planetary associations. The chakra mandalas are shown vertically from the crown to the root in the *Chakras in the Body* figure.

Root Chakra Candle
Hindu Name: Muladhara
Candle Color: Red
Planet: Saturn, Mars
Oil: Patchouli, Myrrh, Oakmoss, Vetiver
Herb: Horsetail, Comfrey, Burdock, Patchouli, Myrrh, Oakmoss, Vetiver
Influence: Basic Needs, Survival, Sustainment

Belly (Sacral) Chakra Candle
Hindu Name: Svadhishthana
Candle Color: Orange
Planet: Jupiter, Moon, Mercury
Oil: Ylang-Ylang, Sandalwood, Spearmint, Bergamont, Clary Sage, Melissa
Herb: Lemon Balm, Burdock, Sandalwood, Gravel Root
Influence: Trust, Pleasure, Intimacy, Gut Intuition, Fear

Solar Plexus Chakra Candle
Hindu Name: Manipura
Candle Color: Yellow
Planet: Mars, Sun
Oil: Frankincense, Cinnamon, Cedar, Coriander, Clove, Ginger, Basil
Herb: St. John's Wort, Sunflower, Marigold, Black Pepper, Turmeric, Ginger, Basil, Clove, Holly
Influence: Power, Will, Anger

Heart Chakra Candle
Hindu Name: Anahata
Candle Color: Green
Planet: Venus, Sun
Oil: Rose, Geranium, Bergamont, Rosewood
Herb: Lady's Mantle, Vervain, Yarrow, Raspberry, Meadowsweet, Rose
Influence: Empathy. Relationships, Love

Throat Chakra Candle
Hindu Name: Vishuddha
Candle Color: Blue
Planet: Mercury, Uranus
Oil: Lavender, Eucalyptus, Peppermint, Cypress, Fennel
Herb: Fennel, Dill, Peppermint, Lavender, Hazel, Marjoram
Influence: Communication, Expression, Thought, Writing, Magickal Power

Brow (Third Eye) Chakra Candle
Hindu Name: Ajna
Candle Color: Indigo/Purple
Planet: Moon, Jupiter, Neptune
Oil: Jasmine, Ylang-Ylang, Mugwort, Lavender, Lemon, Bay Laurel, Vertiver
Herb: Jasmine, Mugwort, Lavender, Chickweed, Passionflower, Poppy, Wild Lettuce, Willow
Influence: Psychic Abilities, Vision, Intuition

Crown Chakra Candle
Hindu Name: Sahasrara
Candle Color: White/Lavender
Planet: Sun, Saturn, Pluto

Oil: Frankincense, Angelica Root, Rosemary, Helichrysm, Elemi, Spikenard, Rosewood

Herb: Chamomile, Angelica Root, Frankincense, St. John's Wort,

Influence: Spiritual Union, Enlightenment, Connection

So, for example, if I wanted to work on my issues around anger and the appropriate expression of power, I might make a solar plexus candle to help rebalance my chakra of personal power. I would take a cleared bright yellow candle and carve the symbol of Manipura in it, and perhaps my own name or initials beneath it. Then I would anoint the candle with ginger essential oil, diluted with base oil, and sprinkle it with turmeric powder. I would charge it with the intention of balancing my power issues and light it over a trivet, tray, or plate.

Zodiac Candles

Candles can be created for the twelve zodiac signs to bring their influence into your life or otherwise evoke their energy. They are most popular to bolster the energy of a practitioner's sun sign, and can be done when the Moon is the birth sign over the course of the year, or annually, on their birthday, or the Full Moon when the Sun is in the recipient's birth sign, as the Moon sign will be in the opposite zodiac sign. It's a powerful way to align with your vital energy and basic purpose here in the world. Complex astrological spells can use more than one zodiac candle, or balance the powers of all twelve signs by making all 12 and burning them upon the full or new Moon. When arranged in a circle, in astrology the signs go counterclockwise, usually with Aries to the far left, at the nine o'clock position if it were a clock face.

Like the chakra candles, you can carve the appropriate colored candle with the corresponding symbol, known as an astrological glyph and anoint it with the appropriate oil. Listed are single oils, though occult shops often carry blended zodiac perfumes that can also be used. The Zodiac Glyphs figure shows the symbols for Aries through Pisces, from left to right.

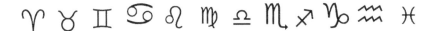

Figure: Zodiac Glyphs

Aries Candle
Candle Color: Red
Oils: Black Pepper, Allspice, Mace
Key Phrase: I Am
Influence: Leaders, Warriors, Facing Fears, Taking Action

Taurus Candle
Candle Color: Red-Orange, Green
Oils: Benzoin, Storax, Rose, Thyme
Key Phrase: I Have
Influence: Stewards, Gardeners, Artists, Sensuality, Pleasure, Riches

Gemini Candle
Candle Color: Orange
Oils: Lavender, Fennel, Peppermint, Lemongrass, Grapefruit, Neroli
Key Phrase: I Think
Influence: Speakers, Siblings, Communication, Story Telling

Cancer Candle
Candle Color: Yellow-Orange, Silver
Oils: Jasmine, Camphor, Mugwort, Chamomile
Key Phrase: I Feel
Influence: Motherhood, Family, Food, Creation, Empathy, Magick

Leo Candle

Candle Color: Yellow, Gold
Oils: Frankincense, Ginger, Amber, Rosemary
Key Phrase: I Create
Influence: Artists, Performers, Creativity, Sensitivity, Ego

Virgo Candle

Candle Color: Yellow-Green, Grey-Green
Oils: Dill, Sandalwood
Key Phrase: I Process
Influence: Healing, Service, Discernment, Analysis, Reaping Results from Past Actions

Libra Candle

Candle Color: Green, Pastel Green
Oils: Rose, Geranium, Palma Rosa, Catnip
Key Phrase: I Balance
Influence: Relationship, Marriage, Partnerships, Justice, Harmony, Art

Scorpio Candle

Candle Color: Green-Blue, Black, Deep Red
Oils: Wormwood, Garlic, Clary Sage, Patchouli, Basil
Key Phrase: I Desire
Influence: Power, Secrets, Psychic Ability, Occultism, Obsessions, Intensity

Sagittarius Candle

Candle Color: Blue
Oils: Cedar, Nutmeg, Juniper
Key Phrase: I Understand
Influence: Exploration, Sports, Travel, Philosophy, Education

Capricorn Candle
Candle Color: Blue-Violet, Indigo, Dark Purple, Black
Oils: Patchouli, Cypress, Ambrette
Key Phrase: I Use
Influence: Business, Organization, Tools, Administration, Career, Discipline

Aquarius Candle
Candle Color: Violet, Light Purple, Electric Blue, White
Oils: Spikenard, Neroli
Key Phrase: I Know
Influence: Unorthodoxy, Innovation, Technology, Revolutions, Social Justice, Unexpected Changes

Pisces Candle
Candle Color: Red-Violet, Lavender
Oils: Ylang-Ylang, Elemi
Key Phrase: I Believe
Influence: Art, Dance, Dreams, Addition, Religion, Merging

So, for example, if I wanted to evoke the power of Capricorn for business success, I would ideally look for when the Moon is waxing in Capricorn, and carve the Capricorn glyph, a symbol that is supposed to look like a "fish-goat" onto a dark purple candle. Anointing it with Patchouli oil, I'd focus my intention on evoking all the beneficial qualities of Capricorn to help me with my work. I can light the candle and let it burn all the way, or snuff and relight it when I need Capricorn's energy, and the Moon or Sun is nowhere near it. With this technique, you can "save" astrological energies for times when you need them.

Another method is to help mitigate when an energy is too strong. Personally, I know due to my own astrological birth chart I have difficulties when the Moon is in Cancer. While I can't, and shouldn't, try to avoid the experience of the Moon in Cancer, I can be more aware of its effect upon me. I might make a Cancer candle when the Moon is waning in Cancer, and light it during the days when I feel overwhelmed by the emotions of the Moon in Cancer. I'm still working with the energy, but I'm looking to "bleed off" some of the intensity, even if currently the Moon is waxing in Cancer.

Elemental Quarter Candles for a Temple

Many traditions of magick that formally honor and work with the four classical elements of fire, air, water, and earth create altars to the elements with various tools, incense, and images corresponding with the element. There are various ways to "build" a Temple spiritually. One of the most simple is the Witch's Circle, which can be created almost anywhere through ritual and intention, but those actively meeting in a dedicated space, solitary or group, will establish their powers in regular patterns through the use of altars and shrines.

Among the tools for anchoring the elements in a sacred space are the elemental candles. While, in general, we think of candles as a symbol of fire, we have to remember that the candle contains the principles of all the elements. Candles can be tuned and charged, by correspondences, to specifically hold and radiate an elemental energy. Those who create sacred space in a temple room will arrange the candles to anchor those energies in the space. With pre-prepared candles, the energy is activated in lighting, and the energetic dynamic of the space is easier to "hold" requiring less concentration on the part of the magician or Witch. Over time the energy builds, making the place a natural sacred space, but the candles serve as energetic portals and thresholds to the powers they are dedicated to. The same principle can be used for deities, spirits, and the "group" soul of the tradition (See Votive Candle Offerings for Gods and Deity Specific Candles later this chapter), but most often starting practitioners will begin the process of temple building with the elemental energies, as basic spiritual "building blocks."

While any candle can be used, I prefer colored jar candles, pull-outs if possible, so the symbols can be carved upon them. If not using pull-outs, images can be drawn or adhered onto the glass. Some use other candles, such as tapers and votives, and place them in a lantern dedicated to the element, with the appropriate corresponding decorations on the lantern, so only the candle itself would have to be replaced and re-prepared.

Fire Candle
Color: Red, Orange
Oil: Ginger, Black Pepper, Cinnamon, Frankincense
Traditional Time: Noon
Zodiac Signs: Aries, Leo, Sagittarius
Magickal Intentions: Passion, Creativity, Sexuality, Art, Career, Protection

Air Candle
Color: Yellow, Light Blue
Oil: Peppermint, Lavender, Eucalyptus, Melissa (Lemon Balm)
Traditional Time: Dawn
Zodiac Signs: Gemini, Libra, Aquarius
Magickal Intentions: Communication, Study, Memory, Logic, Perception, Truth

Water Candle
Color: Blue, Aqua

Oil: Jasmine, Ylang-Ylang, Mugwort, Lemon
Traditional Time: Sunset
Zodiac Signs: Cancer, Scorpio, Pisces
Magickal Intentions: Emotion, Relationships, Dreams, Healing, Love, Compassion

Earth Candle
Color: Green, Black, Brown
Oil: Patchouli, Myrrh, Vetiver, Oakmoss, Cedar
Traditional Time: Midnight
Zodiac Signs: Taurus, Virgo, Capricorn
Magickal Intentions: Prosperity, Health, Security, Pleasure, Grounding, Business

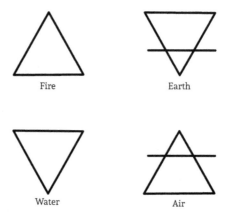

Figure: Elemental Triangle Symbols

To make an elemental candle, take a candle of the appropriate color and either carve the triangle for the element upon it or affix it to the glass case. You can also use the images of all three zodiac glyphs of the element. Anoint with one of the appropriate oils and then consecrate. Ideally, do it when the Sun or Moon is in one of the elemental signs, as determined by an astrological almanac, ephemeris, or computer program. To simplify timing matters, each

The Lighting of Candles

element has a traditional time of day, dividing the day into four quarters. You can consecrate the candle at the elementally appropriate time of the day.

To further attune to the elements, you can place the candleholder in vessels that are elementally appropriate. For earth, place the jar or candleholder in a clay, stone, or ceramic bowl filled with soil, stones, or crystals. For fire, place the jar or candleholder in an iron cauldron or pot. For air, place the jar or candleholder in a clear bowl with feathers, or a brass bowl filled with sand that you can also use as an incense burner for incense sticks. For water, place the jar or candleholder in a glass or crystal bowl filled with water. If looking for uniformity, you can place them in lanterns.

Recite one of the elemental invocations, or one in your own words. In the Temple of Witchcraft, we use certain vowel sounds to evoke the primal spirit of the elements. Different systems use different vowels, so if you know a different system, as long as you're consistent and use what works for you, the primal calls will help empower your candle. These charges use the classic occult imagery of the elements, their kings, and the archangels. They can be adapted as needed for your own traditions.

Fire Candle Consecration
By the sacred flame
I call to the element of fire
I call to the Staff and to Victory
and to the Light of the One
By the blessings of the Salamanders, the Fire Elementals
And by their rulers, King Djin and Queen Litha
By the stars of Aries, Leo and Sagittarius
and the power of archangel Michael
I consecrate this candle as a vessel for Elemental Fire
as a portal to the realm of True Will

Intone: I as in "eye"

May blessings of Fire be here and flow between us.
So mote it be!

Air Candle Consecration

By the sacred breath
I call to the element of air
I call to the Sword and to Truth
and to the Life of the One
By the blessings of the Sylphs, the Air Elementals
and by their rulers, King Paralda and Queen Eostar
By the stars of Gemini, Libra and Aquarius
and the power of archangel Raphael
I consecrate this candle as a vessel for Elemental Air
as a portal to the realm of Clear Truth

Intone: E as in "me"

May blessings of Air be here and flow between us.
So mote it be!

Water Candle Consecration

By the sacred flow
I call to the element of water
I call to the Cup and to Compassion
and to the Love of the One
By the blessings of the Undines, the Water Elementals
and by their rulers, King Niksa and Queen Mara
By the stars of Cancer, Scorpio and Pisces
and the power of archangel Gabriel
I consecrate this candle as a vessel for Elemental Water
as a portal to the realm of Perfect Love

Intone: O as in "so"

May blessings of Water be here and flow between us.
So mote it be!

Earth Candle Consecration

By the sacred land
I call to the element of earth
I call to the Stone and to Sovereignty
And to the Law of the One
By the blessings of the Gnomes, the Earth Elementals
And by their rulers, King Ghob and Queen Tanu
By the stars of Taurus, Virgo and Capricorn
And the power of archangel Uriel
I consecrate this candle as a vessel for Elemental Earth
As a portal to the realm of Deep Wisdom

Intone: A as in "day"

May blessings of Earth be here and flow between us.
So mote it be!

Those working in a Temple tradition might start with just one element. Various meditations and pathworkings will help you commune with the elemental spirits, rulers, kings, queens, angels, archangels, demons, and deities of the elements. Other techniques ask the spirits of the elements to come to you in your ritual space for deeper communication. By lighting a prepared candle before doing such spirit contact or journey, and facing the direction of the element for your tradition, you hold open a gateway between human consciousness and elemental energy, making the whole process much easier. Once conscious contact is established with all four elements, one can more easily and clearly evoke all four elements at the same time, lighting all four candles. A psychically aware practitioner might perceive it as four streams of energy gently flowing through the four candle flames, through the dark arch of the flame that looks like a doorway. Some would use a center candle for spirit, created in a similar way, or the Working Candle for the current ritual, a Master Candle (further in this chapter), or a general central temple candle (see **Chapter Ten**) to anchor the four streams in the center.

While evoking the elements for a temple is a powerful and uplifting practice, elemental candles can also be used for practical purposes. You can use the power of a single element as the focus for a specific spell or intention. For personal development, you can meditate before it to simply attune to its principles, or you can charge it for a specific outcome. A water candle can be used in love magick. An air candle can be created to pass a test at school. A fire candle can be used to have the energy to complete a project and keep your creativity during it. An earth candle can be used for money magick, or to obtain some physical item. When you work heavily with a single element, it can be really immediate and effective, but sometimes it will also be heavily skewed towards the element. For example, the water candle love spell gets you a very emotional and intense partner. The fire candle for energy helps you accomplish the task effectively but leaves you feeling burned out. The air candle for a test allows you to pass, but you don't retain the information. It floats away like a breeze. The earth candle money magick buys you just what you asked for, but it turns out to not be exactly what you wanted. To mitigate these effects people will sometimes mix several elemental candles together with one intention, to make sure the magick is working on all levels.

Once you master the basic technique, it can be applied in a number of creative ways. As one who has hosted many outdoor backyard sabbats for groups, we marked the circle in kerosene-filled "tiki" torches. We added a few drops of essential oil to the lamp fuel, and decorated the torches with appropriately colored feathers and ribbons, and hug small slate stone signs with the elemental symbols painted upon them. Depending on the magickal tradition, if you have another symbol, or specific entities for the elements, you can use them on the candles, such as the Vedic tattva symbols or the seals of the elemental archangels. A wide variety of sigils and glyphs are available in the ceremonial traditions, but I think the elemental triangles and the zodiac glyphs are the best place to start.

Sabbat Candles

The Sabbats are the eight major holidays of the Neopagan Year, celebrated in many forms of Witchcraft and Wicca. These holidays are a fairly modern union of the cycle of the equinoxes and solstices, known as the solar holidays because they are based upon the Sun, with the Celtic fire festivals, agricultural and fertility celebrations traditionally celebrated between the solar holidays. Collectively, the Wheel of the Year sabbats are a story of the Goddess and God, and their changing faces and worlds through the seasons of the year. For many, the tale beings at Yule, or the Winter Solstice, with the birth of the god of light. He grows in strength and power, awakening the goddess of the earth from her slumber. The two assume their role as queen and king of the land in the summer tide until he is challenged and defeated by his nemesis, and the waning year of darkness is ushered in. The goddess mourns her lover's death at Samhain, opening the gates between worlds, and prepares for his rebirth to renew the land again. Different traditions interpret the same basic story with cultural and regional differences, but a body of lore has developed among Pagans and Witches to celebrate the sabbats of Yule, Imbolc, Ostara, Beltane, Litha, Lammas, Mabon, and Samhain.

Sabbat candles are candles that evoke and mediate the energy of the seasonal sabbat. They can be used in the home to prepare for the tide of energy that is building for the holiday. They can be used as the working candle for a traditional sabbat celebration or created and lit as a simple ritual of celebration on their own. The Sabbat Symbols figure shows the traditional glyph for each sabbat, starting with Samhain and moving through to Mabon, left to right.

Figure: Sabbat Symbols

Samhain Candle

Date: Usually Oct 31
Ritual Theme: Death and Rebirth, Celtic New Year, God and Goddess in the Underworld, Honoring the Ancestors, Third Harvest – Meat
Candle Colors: Black, Orange, Scarlet, Brown
Oils: Myrrh, Patchouli, Garlic, Tarragon, Vetiver, Parsley, Cypress

Yule Candle

Date: Near Dec 21
Ritual Theme: Rebirth of the Sun God
Candle Colors: Red, Green, White, Black
Oils: Wintergreen, Pine, Fir, Frankincense, Myrrh, Spruce

Imbolc Candle

Date: Usually Feb 2
Ritual Theme: Awakening the Goddess through a Festival of Lights, Home and Child Blessing
Candle Colors: Orange, White, Aqua, Lavender, Magenta
Oils: Cinnamon, Clove, Nutmeg, Benzoin, Camphor, Birch

The Lighting of Candles

Ostara (Vernal Equinox) Candle

Date: Near March 22
Ritual Theme: Resurrection of the land through the awakening of the Earth Maiden
Candle Colors: Red, White, Black
Oils: Narcissus, Marjoram, Grapefruit, Violet Leaf, Ylang-Ylang

Beltane Candle

Date: Usually May 1, Beltane Eve sometimes celebrated the day before
Ritual Theme: Fertility of the Land through the joining of the young Goddess and God, Sexual Passion, Handfastings
Candle Colors: Green, White, Black
Oils: Rose, Geranium, Yarrow, Juniper, Melissa, Sandalwood

Litha (Summer Solstice or Midsummer) Candle

Date: Usually June 21
Ritual Theme: God and Goddess preside as King and Queen of the Land, Defeat of the Light God, Opening to the Faery Realm
Candle Colors: Gold, Yellow, Green, Brown
Oils: Rosemary, Frankincense, Cedar, Juniper, Thyme, Chamomile, Elecampane, Ginger

Lammas (Lughnassadh) Candle

Date: Usually August 1
Ritual Theme: Sacrifice of the Grain God, Funeral Feast, First Harvest – Grain
Candle Colors: Gold, Green, Gray, Black
Oils: Frankincense, Rosemary, Fennel, Sage, Ginger, Hyssop

Mabon (Autumnal Equinox) Candle

Date: Usually Sept 21

Ritual Theme: Journey to the Underworld, Balance of Light and Dark, Second Harvest – Fruit, Thanksgiving
Candle Colors: Orange, Bronze, Gold, Red, Green, Black, Wine, Purple, Pastels
Oils: Myrrh, Sage, Valerian

Candle Circle for Ritual & Meditation

One of the traditional training methods of magick that seems to have been abandoned by most teachers today is the use of an actual physical circle, either drawn in chalk or on a mat that can be rolled out for ritual and meditation. Some reproduce the circles of the Medieval grimoires, and others are simply a circle of contiguous rocks and stones. A few of us learned to trace a nine foot circle in the ground using our cord, wand, or athame. I learned to create a circle of salt and candles.

Using a string or cord and a paper funnel, or salt container with a spout, a ring of salt was created upon a hardwood or stone floor, traced from a central point. The circle would be nine, ten, twelve, or thirteen feet in diameter, depending on the size of the space and if it was to be used solitary or in a group. Upon the salt would be placed a variety of candles, marking spots and creating both the atmosphere and energy for deeper work.

While I've seen tapers, votives, and tea lights used, my safety recommendation and preference is to use pillar jar candles contained in glass. You can use either poured jar candles, or pull-outs. The reason is that if you accidentally knock over a taper, votive or tea light, the exposed flame could easily catch something on fire and create a safety hazard. With the glass contained candle, knocking it over will make a mess with the wax but usually extinguishes the candle.

The most basic candle circle took the four quarter candles, as described above, in their appropriate directions in the north, east, south, and west. The practitioner would work or meditate in the center of an elementally balanced circle. Other variations would essentially create the candle grid or mandala, in a size in which one could stand, sit and work magick. Most popular was an eight candle circle, like the Neopagan Wheel of the Year, or twelve candles, for the zodiac. You can use the techniques above for the elements, sabbats, and zodiac to craft jar candles to make a ritual circle. Try meditating by the lit circle and see if you notice a difference in your experience. The energies should be more easily stabilized for you, and aid you in learning how to hold a sacred space in ritual, but one doesn't need to know how to create a ritual circle sacred space to take part in the sacred space created by a ring of properly charged candles.

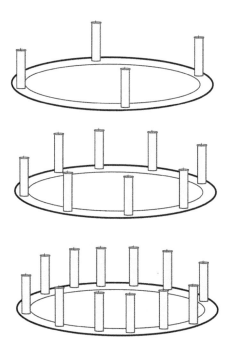

Figure: Four, Eight, and Twelve Candle Circles

Obviously, this can be effectively completed with the four elemental candles previously discussed.

Moon Goddess Candle Ritual

This Moon Goddess Candle Spell is not to manifest any specific power associated with the Moon, but to align you with the cycle of the Moon for greater wisdom and understanding of its patterns and flow.

White Taper Candle
Red Taper Candle
Black Taper Candle
3 Candleholders
Camphor Oil
Rose Oil
Myrrh Oil

The Moon cycle takes roughly a month, thirty days, from new Moon to new Moon. The Moon waxes, or grows in light, peaking at the full moon about sixteen days into the cycle, and then diminishes, or wanes, until it goes dark, starting the cycle again with the new Moon. These are the rhythms of our lives, and the Moon's cycle, often ignored by most people, plays a strong role in our own inner cycles and season for the month. A wise magickal practitioner learns to attune to it.

Create a space to do this work for a month. If you don't have a dedicated altar, this can be left out on a table, disguised as simple décor. You might also find a Moon calendar to track this helpful. Have all three candles out, with the white, red, and black from right to left as you face them. At the start of the cycle, at the next new Moon, carve the waxing crescent upon the white candle. Anoint it with three drops of camphor essential oil. Let it burn while meditating before it for a few minutes every day, for about nine days. By the ninth day, let the white candle burn down completely. Each day recite this incantation:

By the crescent white
I call upon the Lady of the Night
Waxing Moon, Bow of the Maiden
Show me the waxing of all that lives
Under the sway of the Goddess.
Blessed be.

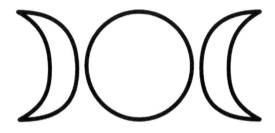

Figure: Waxing – Full – Waning Crescent Symbols

Leave out the empty candleholder of the white candle. On the tenth day, carve the red candle with the full Moon symbol. Anoint it with rose oil. Rose absolute is often difficult to obtain, so anything reminiscent of rose for you, such as rose geranium, will also work. Let it burn a small amount while meditating before it for nine days. On the fifteenth day, the day of the full Moon, or with the slight variations in the cycle, if the full Moon falls on a day before or after, let it burn the longest and dwell the most time with it. Leave a little of the red candle remaining to burn on the seventeenth and eighteenth days. Each day of the red candle, recite this incantation:

By the Circle Round
I call upon the Lady Star Crowned
Full Moon, Belly of the Mother
Show me the potential of all that lives
In the realm of the Goddess.
Blessed be.

On the nineteenth day, take the black candle and carve the waning Moon symbol. Anoint it with myrrh oil. Burn it until the new Moon, reciting this incantation and reflecting in meditation for a little while each day:

By the crescent dark
I call upon the Lady of the Mark
Waning Moon, Sickle of the Crone
Show me the withering of all that lives
Under the sway of the Goddess
Blessed be.

On the last day, let it burn down completely. Reflect upon the whole cycle. What did you feel? What did you learn? What did you experience? Journal upon the mysteries of the Moon.

The Pillar Gates of the Temple

A traditional use of candles in Western Magick, particularly those influenced by Qabalah and Hermeticism, is the use of a black and white candles representing the pillars of the sacred temple. While some might have elaborate temple spaces with actual pillars, most of us make do with a small workspace, so the candles serve many purposes functionally and for esoteric symbolism.

If you are passingly familiar with the Rider-Waite-Smith tarot deck, which encodes many magickal concepts within its pictures, you'll see that pillars show up in a few of the cards, and most notably in the High Priestess card. She sits between a black and a white pillar, with the letters "B" and "J" on them, respectively. The B is for Boaz, which refers to ending or negation, while the J is Jachin, to denote a beginning. They are a historic reference to the gates of the Temple of Solomon, and behind her is the Temple veiled. Some consider them the Pillars of Tubal Cain, lost after the Great Flood. If one looks at the Tree of Life glyph, also known as the Etz Chaim, with its ten spheres and twenty-two lines, the left side is depicted as a dark pillar, known as the Pillar of Severity, while the right side is white, the Pillar of Mercy. They are considered akin to the catabolic and anabolic, breaking down and building up forces of creation. The center pillar is gray and called the Pillar of Equilibrium. Depending on the artistic rendition, the pillars repeat in the Hierophant and Moon cards.

Figure: Priestess Tarot Card

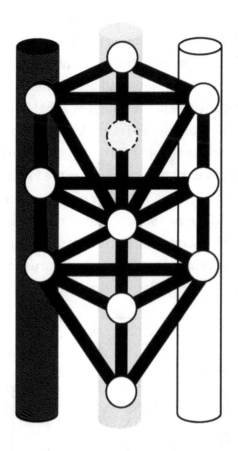

Figure: Etz Chaim Tree of Life with Pillars

If you place a black candle to your left and a white candle to your right when doing ritual magick and meditation; it is as if you are facing the entrance to the temple, and alignment with the Tree of Life as a portal to the mysteries. From it, you can enter any sacred space or temple. Lighting the candles opens the gates. Extinguishing the candles closes the gates. It serves as a portal to journey, as well as to invite spirit allies and guardians. Just be careful to be clear in your intentions regarding who you are opening the door to enter.

To reverse them is to symbolically place yourself on the reverse of the Tree of Life, the Nightside of Eden, and is ill-advised unless you are a deeply experienced magician, and even then should not be entered into lightly without a clear plan of magickal development.

Most importantly, functionally, as I've learned in Hermetically inspired Witchcraft traditions, these two candles serve like statues for the divine as feminine and masculine, Goddess and God, and even more importantly, serve as a psychic way station. The black candle, for the Goddess, has the nature of absorbing things. Black draws light, and therefore energy, into it. A black candle will draw forth the psychic energies you need for your magick and meditations. The "work" can happen at the altar, which is really the space between. If you are using a working candle, it will often go between the two pillars. Then the white candle transmits the intentions from the work, as white will send forth and reflect light. Together they act as a psychic station to absorb, transform, and redirect your intentions.

If not using a working candle, some will adapt these pillars to be two shades of what would be the working candle, either the same color but light and dark shades or two colors from the same elemental or planetary alignment. For example, a peace spell using blue candles can use a navy blue candle for the black candle and a light turquoise blue for the white candle. If you are doing a Venusian love spell, you can use a green candle for the black candle and a pink candle for the white.

To use the temple pillar candles, cleanse and consecrate them. They can be simple tapers, seven-day jar candles, or larger pillars. If you have a Goddess Oil, Lunar Oil, or Saturn Oil, use it on the Black Candle. Dark Power Oil would work well too. If you have God Oil, Solar Oil, or Jupiter Oil, use it on the White Candle. Likewise,

Blessing Oil could be used. Dressing the candle is excellent but not required for it to be effective in this magick.

Charge the prepared black candle, holding it with intention to absorb energy and function as the black pillar of your personal magickal temple, with these words:

I charge this black candle in honor of the Goddess, the Moon, and the
Night
I name you Severity and Mystery
May you draw all the perfect and balanced forces for my magick.
So mote it be.

Charge the prepared white candle, holding it with intention to send energy and function as the white pillar of your personal magickal temple, with these words:

I charge this white candle in honor of the God, the Sun, and the Day.
I name you Mercy and Resolution
May you send all the perfect and balanced intentions for my magick.
So mote it be.

Light the candles black and then white, and when you extinguish, some insist it should be white then black, while others say repeat black and then white. I tend to do white, then black, but follow your best judgement in these matters. Neither will harm you nor make your magick ineffective in my experience. Or you can use fresh pillars each time you do the ceremony. While I tend to extinguish them, I also recite the blessings each time I relight them to reinforce the magick.

If you have a particular calling to Solomon's Temple, you can replace Severity with Boaz and Mercy with Jachin if you desire. Some even ritually carve in the B and J into their respective pillars.

In the seven principles found in the modern Hermetic traditions, these candles embody the Principle of Polarity, being light and dark, and the Principle of Gender, named male and female. They are really simple but powerful tools in the hands of an aspiring magician, and connect you symbolically to a thread of wisdom from the ancient days and occult tradition.

The Master Candle and Temple Light

For those magicians who keep a working ritual room, chapel, shrine, or temple, there is a variation upon the ritual Working Candle that can be used for empowering such a space. A single candle, usually in the form of a glass seven-day jar candle, is used, though a taper or smaller pillar candle is not out of the question.

In Hoodoo and Conjure candle chapels, it is referred to as the Master Candle, as it can be anointed with High John the Conqueror Oil, Power Oil, or Master Oil. It is the source of fire for all the other candles used in the work. Ideally, once lit, it is burned continuously, though if it must be snuffed, along with the other lights of the chapel, then it is the first light rekindled, and all other candles are relit from it.

The candle embodies two main principles, that of the mastery of magick and occult forces and the source of such forces as represented by the primal flame. It is the embodiment of the source of divine power; however the magician sees the source: God, Goddess, Great Spirit, The Light of God, the Holy Spirit, The Trinity, the Unknowable, the Divine Mind, the Sun, the Stars, the Secret Fire or Holy Formless Flame.

From the Master Candle, a practitioner will prepare and light subsidiary "master" candles for specific intentions with different colors, markings, and dressings. When doing work, the appropriate subsidiary candle will be used to light working candles. For example, there could be Master Love, Master Healing, Master Prosperity, and Master Protection candles lit from the main Master Candle. A love spell candle would be lit from the Master Love Candle, while a healing candle would be lit from the Master Healing Candle. If sending the candle to a client, rather than burning it in the chapel or temple, the client candle will be snuffed and sealed off with a bit of wax to seal in the magick for travel. Such subsidiary candles are like the "working candles" described in the previous chapter, a candle of general intention rather than specific outcome. Traditionally such specific secondary Master Candles are long-term works, dressed with seals from The Greater Key of Solomon or other grimoires, or other detailed sigils and markings along with oils and herbs, while a simple working candle from a ritual usually is not. If there is not a specific subsidiary candle, or if the practitioner does away with the concept of such candles all together, then all candles are lit from the Master Candle.

In Hoodoo lore, John the Conqueror is the source of the power, and his oil brings the magickal presence to empower the work, along with your own. John the Conqueror mediates the "mojo" between the Creator and the worker. Candle magicians working in other spiritual traditions might adapt the concept to suit their own understanding of magick and the source.

Ceremonial magicians could be empowered by their own Holy Guardian Angel, or Bornless Self, looking at the regular relighting of the Master Candle as a reaffirmation to their own divine selves. They can also look beyond it to the Tetragrammaton, the divine source as YHVH often pronounced in exoteric lore as Yahweh or Jehovah, and not by the letter names Yod Heh Vau Heh for it is the unpronounceable name of God.

A Witch might see the first source of magick as the First Witch or First Sorcerer, or the Goddess as the Earth Mother or Star Goddess. Sabbatic-styled Witches might look to the light of the

Fallen Angels known as the Watchers who brought the gifts of civilization to Earth, including fire.

Rituals to empower the Master Candle can include purifications, offerings to the spirits, prayers, and ceremonial lighting, usually from a simple white taper candle, and not a match or lighter. Along with the magickal oil, a drop of blood can also be used, to merge your personal power with that of the divine to empower the candle work. Often the altar of the Master Candle has two crossed keys, skeleton keys, to represent the crossroads, and the ability to open and close ways, as needed. Hoodoo tradition will often recite the Twenty-third Psalm as a part of the empowerment.

Psalm 23 (KJV)

The Lord is my shepherd; I shall not want.
He maketh me to lie down in green pastures:
he leadeth me beside the still waters.
He restoreth my soul:
he leadeth me in the paths of righteousness for his name's sake.
Yea, though I walk through the valley of the shadow of death,
I will fear no evil: for thou art with me;
thy rod and thy staff they comfort me.
Thou preparest a table before me in the presence of mine enemies:
thou anointest my head with oil; my cup runneth over.
Surely goodness and mercy shall follow me all the days of my life:
and I will dwell in the house of the Lord forever.
Amen.

Master candles can be burned as a spell unto themselves, for personal control and self-mastery, discipline and to increase psychic or magickal power, but more often than not, they are part of a larger candle burning setting.

While "setting the lights" refers to setting candles for personal or client work in Hoodoo, in the occult temple traditions, setting the lights refers to a different process. In an occult temple, setting was to create an energy field or vortex in a Witch's covenstead or in the magician lodge's temple, to attract the people who are correct and in harmony with the purpose of the group conscious, as well as to repel those who were not appropriate. It uses candle magick to flow with the power of a tradition's egregore, as well as the group mind of an individual group within that tradition. It's a magickal act that conjoins the outer manifestation of the temple space with the group's inner astral temple. A high priestess of the Alexandrian tradition with ceremonial magick training was kind enough to share the details of these practices with me without giving away specifics to her tradition.

Such temple lights can be through a candle or lamp and is often encased in a lantern for both the image of the seeking Hermit from the Tarot, and safety, as the light can be left burning for as long as you want to attract members or kept going as a sacred illumination of the mysteries, and a lantern addresses many safety concerns involving leaving a burning candle unattended.

The enactment of the ritual is done in both the inner worlds through vision work and the outer world through actually preparing and lighting a candle. The candle or lamp can use any oil or dressing that would be particularly associated with the tradition. Through meditation in the group's "astral" temple, one gathers the energy of the inner temple flame and through will, intention, and imagination, transfers it to the flame used to light the Temple candle. If the tradition has a temple flame already established, a teacher or master in the temple will pass it to one whom they have authorized to "set the lights" for a newly chartered group.

In accordance with occult tradition, the original flame must be kindled naturally, without use of chemicals. Either a flame produced from the friction of rubbing wood, stones, or from sunlight passed through a crystal or glass. This is known today in candle magick as "Drawing Down the Sun" but should not be confused with Wiccan invocations of solar energy into a sacramental cup or bodily invocations of the Sun god into the High Priest. Through the use of a magnifying glass or crystal, the fire is kindled. I've seen some Hoodoo books suggest the use of saltpeter upon sandalwood chips to kindle a sacred fire more easily, though other traditions forbid any such chemicals.

While most of us are not members of esoteric orders, or even if we are, are not the Keeper of the Flame in such a group, solitary practitioners keeping a temple at home can use this idea, along with the more Hoodoo inspired Master Candle, to create a shrine to the mysteries of the divine embodied by flame. A simple ritual to create a Master Candle could include:

✦ White Master Candle (Seven-Day Jar Candle or Beeswax Pillar)
✦ Candleholder or Stand (Lantern, Bowl or Cauldron)
✦ Sacred Oil (High John the Conqueror, Master Oil, Mandrake Oil, Altar Oil or Abramelin Oil)
✦ White Taper Candle
✦ Bowl of Water
✦ Bowl of Salt
✦ Incense Burner with Charcoal
✦ Loose Incense (Equal Parts Frankincense, Myrrh, and Benzoin or other Holy Incense)
✦ Offering Bowl

- ✦ Offerings (Honey, Milk, Wine, Mead, Bread, Fruits, Grains, or Nuts)
- ✦ Cauldron of Fire – Fire Cleansing Materials (Cauldron, Alcohol, Salt). See **Fire Cleansing** later in this chapter for details.

Set up all of the tools before you on a clear altar cloth, ideally black or white cotton or silk. Take a small handful of the salt in and place the intention of cleansing into the salt by thinking deeply about the ability of salt to absorb unwanted energy. Place the salt into the water, and put your hands over the water, infusing the water with your intention of blessing. Dip your fingers into the salt water and sprinkle drops upon yourself, upon your tools, and most specifically upon the candles. Light the charcoal in a flameproof vessel. It can be another small cauldron, like the one used for the Cauldron of Fire, or a metal bowl filled with sand to absorb the heat. Sprinkle your loose resin incense upon the charcoal and let the smoke waft upward. Fan some smoke towards your body. Then pass the candles, offering bowl, and offerings through the smoke.

On the center of your altar space, place the candleholder or stand. Some will use a bowl or cauldron and fill it with water, blending the primal image of the fire and water, envisioning the fire floating above the waters of creation. The water can then be used as a fount or source of holy water in the temple. Behind it, place a prepared Cauldron of Fire for both cleansing and to represent the holy primal fire of mystery. Place the offering bowl in front of the candleholder. Some magicians have a personal sigil or symbol, or one from their tradition. If you do, carve it upon the candle if you desire.

If you come from any spiritual tradition that creates sacred space or opens to an "astral temple," then do so now in a simple and heartfelt way. If not, you can recite any special prayers for yourself, or simply acknowledge the four directions and center. Call upon any spirits, ancestors, angels, or deities.

Light the cauldron fire and gaze into it. Know this is the same as the fire that dwells in the heart of the universe, in the heart of the mystery. This is the magick fire of all things. Take your offerings to the spirits and powers and bless each one with heartfelt intent. Offer it by placing it into the offering bowl.

Take your main candle, and anoint it with the sacred oil of your choosing. If none of the blends are available to you, simple olive oil is more than sufficient to invoke the holy in Christian, Jewish, and Pagan traditions. Hold that candle and infuse the blessing of the divine, in any form you imagine, guiding the pattern of your life and granting you the flow and power of magick. Also, know that with that magick comes the responsibility to master yourself, or the magick will master you. Place it in the holder between the cauldron and the offerings.

Take your taper candle, and light it from the cauldron fire of divinity. As you do, pause and really imagine you are drawing upon the fires of creation, of the divine, from the source. Imagination will be the key to unlocking deep magick within you. Imagine it, and it is so. Become a light-bearer. Then use that flame from the taper to light your Master Candle, with these or similar words:

By the fires of creation
I bear this light
I light the flame of the mastery
May I know the source of all life and light
all love and law guiding my path
And may I know my own responsibility for self-mastery
To bear the power of magick in the world.
So be it!

Gaze upon the cauldron flame and the candle flame until the cauldron fire burns out, and all that remains is the candle flame. Use this flame to light your other candles in the temple and in your magick. Keep it burning when you can as a part of your candle magick work. Snuff it when unattended and relight as you would other candles unless you have the type of temple space to keep a candle burning continuously. You can prepare a second Master Candle, and rather than go through this entire ceremony each time, simply light the newly prepared Master Candle from the old before the old runs out. At least once a year, repeat this ritual to renew your Master Candle flame, or redo it whenever you feel there is a spiritual miasma or impurity in your life or temple that needs to be regenerated.

For more information and ideas on doing this work for the good of the community and the world, as a light-bearer, look to **Chapter Ten**, specifically in the Temple Keepers section, to learn about keeping a temple flame even as a solitary practitioner and magician.

Votive Candle Offerings for Gods and Deity Specific Candles

While today the term votive refers to the small candles, the original meaning was an offering relating to a promise or vow. Usually, votive offerings were given to deities and then later saints, in return for a boon, blessing, or wish fulfilled. The type of votive would relate to the entity being asked or the type of request. The supplicant would either vow to do something in return, or vow to offer something to the spirit. Votive offerings could include traditional offerings and sacrifices of foodstuff but were often creative, such as a garland of flowers and herbs, handmade clothing, sculpture, or a carving of the injured limb or afflicted organ the supplicant was seeking to heal. Votive offerings could also be a specific ritual done as a gift or a song performed. The idea was popularized in a church setting where parishioners would make a private request to a saint and burn the familiar small cylindrical candles as the promised offering, though the offerings were really more about the light than the wax. The promise was often to be a "better" or more moral person in the eyes of the Church's moral code and rules.

Today modern Pagans and magickal practitioners will use the same idea as an offering to their gods. Lamps and candles belong to no one religion. And in the same vein, the candles can be used as gifts and promises to the gods, given before asking for favors and after giving thanks for fulfilled requests. The candle will be chosen in a color suitable to the god, and dressed with symbols and oils that are in harmony with the deity's nature. Some systems of magick believe the more attention you give a god, the more powerful they become, and therefore, the more strongly and quickly they will be able to act upon your behalf. The cycle of "worship" create a reciprocal relationship between the gods and the people, and can explain why some of the older gods, without continuous organized worship throughout history can sometimes seem more difficult to contact than deities and spirits with continuous worship. From a purely practical level, from the polytheistic pantheons, the Hindu gods and African spirits seem more readily available, with their continual offerings and strong iconography, when compared to cultural religions that have died out and been reconstructed in the modern era. Yet those with surviving temples and strong iconography seem to fall between the two, such as the Egyptians and Greco-Romans. These cultures have held sway a bit more strongly in our overall Western culture and art than those of say, the Irish or Finnish.

Modern magicians can shy away from the concept of worship or subservience to the gods, but talk about "working with" and "active partnership" with the gods. We venerate, and while we serve, our service is freely given and not a form of fearful slavery or mindless devotion. Through the magickal "technology" of ritual and altars, we realize that candles can serve a few functions. Along with "feeding" a god with intention and energy, from the attention and energy placed in the candle by the practitioner, things like fire and water can create portals upon a well-constructed shrine or altar to facilitate the presence, energy, and communication of the deity in your space, and the clear rapport between the two of you. The living presence of a deity in a temple or home can influence that home. The deity can guide, protect, and teach the magician and others in the home, but it must be important to have the appropriate matching deity that suits the home. For example, a death deity can be detrimental to a home with small children or the elderly. That is not to say a death deity is evil on any level, but the energy would not be an appropriate mix for those living there, as the strong energy could expose the vulnerable to greater difficulties, causing more problems than solving.

If you would like to work with a deity through candles, in either a religious sense of votive offering, or a magickal connection, the initial steps are the same. Usually, you start with a deity with who you have some kinship. You will feel as if the deity has reached out to you in some way, or you are enticed by its story and iconography. Set up a small shrine in a part of your home that you feel is appropriate. If you have a dedicated magickal space, that can be great, but also realize some deities don't like to be only in that space. If you are in no danger to have your beliefs in the open, or if you can disguise a shrine as "art," then certain deities might be more comfortable elsewhere. A shrine to Hestia/Vesta, a

Greek/Roman hearth and home goddess is appropriate either in the kitchen or on the mantle of the fireplace. An information-based deity, such as the Egyptian Thoth, is appropriate in your library. Ganesha likes to be wherever there are children present.

A shrine would include an image of the deity, ideally a statue. While modern renditions are lovely, magickally more traditional images, if available, seem to work better. The deity is more familiar with them, unless the "new" image was crafted by a magician with a relationship to that deity. If the deity has any historic symbols or traditional offerings, they can be incorporated into the shrine. Sometimes specific incense, oils, flowers, or foods will be known from history.

Others will use systems of magickal correspondence, such as those found in the Hermetic Qabalah, to find appropriate colors, symbols, and offerings. Before the image, make a space to place a votive candle. If the deity has no specific oils, anoint it with a basic blessing oil. If they do, use that oil if you can obtain it. Say a prayer to the deity, inviting that deity in love and trust into this space for mutual benefit and no harm to anyone. Light the candle. If you keep a master or temple candle, you can light your deity candle from that flame. The candle will be a portal to the deity's presence and attention. When starting out, and being new to deity work, you might find it takes many offerings to get the attention of the deity, to know you are serious. Those with established ritual magick skills might have an easier time. I know some seekers who will make offerings daily for over a month before they start to feel the presence of the deity in their practice, dreams, or life. Once you feel you have established contact, the deity might "mind touch" with you, and communicate in simple ways, or visiting you in meditations or dreams. If you are accepted by the deity, usually something fortunate involving the deity's sphere of influence will occur in your life, or rejected, something unfortunate in that sphere of influence.

Deities are nonhuman entities, can be capricious, and do not always operate in ways we understand. There is always a level of risk and danger in inviting the attention of the ancient gods to you. Don't choose them haphazardly, particularly if you have no experience with deities. If you are just starting, start with a kinder, more benevolent goddess from whatever culture or pantheon you feel a connection with and then develop more complex deity relationships. Remember, like all relationships, it requires attention to prosper and will wither with neglect. Don't set yourself up to have multiple daily rituals to multiple deities. Magicians develop relationships with deities that are for specific work, personally, communally, or for the "greater good" but are usually not engaged in regular active worship, unless deeply dedicated to a god or pantheon. Deity shrines will be established as needed for the work.

For those who are not magickal priestesses and priests, with their own altars and shrines, candle magick practitioners will prepare deity candles. These candles, usually seven-day candles, can act as the shrine and the spell, with the spell being an act of magick to invite the blessings of a particular deity into your life through the offering of light and attention, or to ask that deity to manifest a specific prayer or spell. Such candles can either have commercial or makeshift art printed and adhered to the outside of a glass candle, or be carved in a pull-out candle. Such deity candles do not represent a long-standing partnership with a divinity, but a one time "can you do me a favor if I honor you" kind of arrangement. Some priests and priestesses shy away from such work, feeling it's disrespectful, but I've found that for dabblers and seekers, it can be the key that opens a deeper gate for serious study and true discipline. People need a catalyst, and if a god sees potential, they might really help to serve as that catalyst for deeper spiritual exploration.

Ganesha Candle

One of the most beneficent and welcoming deities is from the Hindu Pantheon. Known as Ganesh or Ganesha, he is the elephant-headed lord who is the remover of obstacles and bringer of blessings. His is called Ganapati, meaning Lord of the People, and unlike many other gods, is not fickle and never displays malice or anger. He is often honored first in ceremonies to "open" the way, not unlike other gatekeeper gods.

He is associated with the color red and red flowers and red sandalwood traditionally, though western magicians often associate him with orange, relating his powers to the realm of Mercury, or because of some myths associating him with the Moon, purple or lavender. So Ganesha candles can be red, orange, or purple. If using a pull-out, you can carve this simple image of Ganesha on it.

Figure: Ganesha

Anoint with peanut oil, and sprinkle red sandalwood and powdered marigold/calendula flowers upon it. Light the candle with these words:

Om Gam Ganapataye Namaha
Lord Ganesha
Lord of the People
Please bring your blessings to me.
Please remove the obstacle of _____
In a manner that is for my highest good.
Thank you.
Namaste.

The first line is a popular mantra hailing Ganesha to get his attention. If you do mala work, you can recite it 108 times to really attune with Ganesha. If you don't have a specific obstacle to remove, you can simply leave that part out and focus on blessings or just getting to "know" him.

He loves sweets, so placing sweet fruit, particularly bananas or coconuts, near the candle is an excellent offering. He also likes candies, and many American devotees offer him peanuts or hard candy. The offering can be removed and disposed of after a day or two.

When buying my first house, at the last minute, there was a mixup with the credit check, and it looked like the deal would fall through. A friend taught me a Ganesha offering and mantra with a candle. We let the candle burn all night, and the next day, the mortgage company said there was no problem and didn't even know there had been a problem. We followed up the candle with more offerings and thanks and have occasionally called upon Ganesha with a great success in our lives and now keep a small permanent shrine to him.

Macha Candle

Macha is a Celtic goddess, specifically from the Irish myths. She is depicted as one of the three goddesses comprising the triple goddess known as the Morrighan (also Morrigan or Morrigu), along with either Anu and Badb or Badb and Nemain. Popularly seen as war goddesses, for they appear on battlefields urging warriors onward, they are also goddesses of death, prophecy and sorcery, as well as sexuality, fertility, and the land. All of these goddesses are associated with crows and ravens, and Macha has further myths relating her to horses and the fields.

In her Ulster myth, her human husband Crunnchu betrays his oath and reveals her nature to others, claiming she can outrace the king's fastest horses. The unjust king forces her to race his fastest horses or her husband will lose his life, all while she is pregnant with twins. She succeeds and immediately gives birth to her children and curses the men of Ulster to know the pain of labor in their hour of greatest need, a curse that comes true many generations later in the tale of the hero Cu Cuchulain, who also has associations with the Morrighan as both teacher and antagonist.

Macha is called upon for aid when facing injustice, particularly injustice that normal channels of law are not addressing. Crow is considered the bringer of sacred law, not human law and regulation, to tell us to restore natural order and sovereignty. In the Cabot Tradition of Witchcraft, black feathers are sent to the perpetrator of injustice to draw Macha's eye to their wrongdoing. You can't ask her for specific punishments, but simply ask her to address the situation in divine order.

A candle for Macha can deepen your relationship with her, help with courage, activism, sexuality, and deepening sorcerous skills. I use a black glass jar candle, and upon it affix an image of a crow or horse, or another suitable image of this goddess specifically, or the Morrighan in general.

Anoint the candle with hazelnut oil, as hazels are supremely sacred to the Celts. If you have access to blackthorn leaves, sprinkle powdered leaves upon the candle. If not, the blackthorn berry, known as the sloe, is used in making Sloe Gin, and a few drops of Sloe Gin can be sprinkled upon the candle. If possible, place three acorns around the candle. Charge it for the blessing of Macha, light it and recite this evocation to Macha:

Macha of the Red Fire Mane
Macha of the Black Feathered Cloak
Macha of the Green Burial Field
Be with us.

Daughter of the Sea
Tender of Dreadful Acorns
Faery Queen
Be with us.

Macha, Mother of Twins
Macha, Seer of the Future
Macha, Lady of the Red Tresses
Be with us.

Grant us your blessings.
May we heed your warnings
And always honor you as Goddess and Queen
Blessed be.

Inviting Macha into your life, if she has not already chosen you, can bring some potent changes. Many believe the goddesses of the Morrighan choose their own, and if she doesn't want to work with you, all the candles in the world won't make a difference. Others have found that with some persistence and patience, you can start a relationship even if she is not your main goddess or ally. If your petitions intersect with her work, she will work with you when you show enough commitment and respect.

Bridget Candle

The Irish Celtic goddess Brid, also Bride or Brig, is so popular she has undergone many incarnations and interpretations. Originally the goddess associated with the fire festival of Imbolc, or early spring, she appeared in myth with her two sisters, and collectively held sway over healing, poetry, and smith-craft. She was later called Bridget along with her two sisters, also named Bridget. Bridget is a goddess of holy fire and sacred wells and the daughter of the good god, the Dagda. She is also a patron of beekeepers, midwives, nursemaids, shepherds, herbalists, and teachers.

With the rise of Catholicism, she could not be banished, so she was adopted as St. Bridget holding similar blessings in a different religious theology. In some folklore, she was nursemaid to Jesus. Kildare, her Pagan holy site, soon became the center of her Christian veneration. Imbolc soon became St. Bridget's Day. Many modern Pagans believe her priestesses later evolved into the nuns of Kildare. Many Christians would insist that Bridget was a physical human, a devout Christian who was later canonized, or possibly a Druid dedicated to Bridget who converted to Christianity. However, most magickal folk don't believe the idea of a goddess becoming a saint and a woman named for her becoming a saint are mutually exclusive ideas. Today many Pagans and Witches gather light from the perpetual flame kept in Kildare in her honor and water from her sacred wells with no spiritual dissonance about the current Catholic custodians.

In some myths, she is described, as are many of the Irish gods, as a faery being, resonating deep within the land rather than becoming a human saint. As in other Faery traditions, cloth strips, known as clooties, would be tied to the trees near her sacred wells. In folklore she is paired with the old crone Callieach, as the two exchange places for summer and winter, bringing life and death. Reimagining of her tales casts her as a creatrix, making the Earth from her green mantle.

Even most peculiarly, with the influence of the Irish upon the Vodoun traditions, she was transformed into Mama Brigette, the lady of cemeteries and wife to Baron Samedi, lwa to the dead. She shares the distinction of being the only traditional lwa depicted as caucasian, usually with red hair and green eyes. In some ways, her Vodoun manifestations are more like the Callieach.

Due to her wide range of traditions, I've found the spirit responding to the call of Bridget in her many forms to be very friendly and welcoming to the seeker. In my community, we call upon Bridget particularly for healing on physical as well as mental-emotional-spiritual levels, and keep a shrine to her on our larger community healing altar.

Her colors are white, for the purity of the flame; red for the forge of the blacksmith; and green for the growing things of the Earth. A candle in any of these colors would be appropriate, depending on the aspect you wish to call. I like to use a seven-day glass jar candle, and apply an image on paper to the outside of the candle. Images can include a Bridget's Cross, a cradle, or any of her associated animals, including ewes, lambs, cows, swans, geese, bees, and other hibernating animals.

The Lighting of Candles

Figure: Bridget's Cross

To deepen the connection, place a small bowl of milk before the candle and possibly some honey. Small bells are also a wonderful way of drawing her attention, being a part of both Pagan and Christian traditions. A traditional prayer from the *Carmina Gadelica* is called "Bride the Aid-Woman," used for healing work in folkloric Christian tradition. Despite my own Witchcraft path, I've used this prayer with Christian clients as a good "meeting in the middle" theologically for both our paths to work together.

Bride the Aid-Woman

There came to me assistance,
Mary fair and Bride;
As Anna bore Mary,
As Mary bore Christ,
As Eile bore John the Baptist
Without flaw in him,
Aid thou me in mine unbearing,
*   Aid me, O Bride!*
As Christ was conceived of Mary
Full perfect on every hand,
Assist thou me, foster-mother,
The conception to bring from the bone;
And as thou didst aid the Virgin of joy,
Without gold, without corn, without kine,

Aid thou me, great is my sickness,
 Aid me, O Bride!

One of my favorite calls to Bridget is from *The Dream of Mary
MacArthur*, as recounted by the poet Fiona MacLeod. Mary was
gathering driftwood when she encountered a beautiful woman
who said to her:

I am older than Brighid of the Mantle, Mary,
and it is you that should know that.
I put songs and music on the wind
before ever the bells of the chapels were rung in the West
or heard in the East.

I am Brighid-nam-Bratta (Brighid of the Mantle),
but I am also Brighid-Muirghin-na-tuinne (Brighid of the conception of
 the waves),
and Brighid-sluagh (Brighid of the immortal host),
Brighid-nan-sitheach seang (Brighid of the slim faery folk),
Brighid-Binne- Bheullbuchd-nan-trusganan-uaine (Brighid of sweet
 songs and melodious mouth),

and I am older than Aona (Friday)
and am as old as Luan (Monday).

And in Tir-na-h'oige (Land of the Ever Young)
my name is Suibhal-bheann (Mountain traveler);
in Tir-fo-thuinn (Country of the Waves)
it is Cù-gorm (Grey Hound);
and in Tir-nah'oise (Country of Ancient Years)
it is Sireadh-thall (Seek-beyond).

And I have been a breath in your heart.

And the day has its feet to it that will see me
coming into the hearts of men and women
like a flame upon dry grass,

like a flame of wind in a great wood.

For the time of change is at hand, Mairi nic Ruaridh Donn—
though not for you, old withered leaf on the dry branch,
though for you, too, when you come to us and see all things in the pools
of life yonder.

Recite a prayer to Bridget, a traditional prayer, or one from your own heart. Call upon her. Light the candle. Honor her. Ask for her aid if needed. Be open to how that aid comes, as it is usually subtle, and always remember to thank her.

Thor Candle

Due to popular media in comics and movies, Thor is one of the most well-known gods, though much of the media depiction is at odds with his traditional lore. But one theme they both share is that Thor is a god for the ordinary person. While a strong warrior, he was a patron and protector of the average villager or farmer. His control over the weather helped with the growth and harvest of the crops. In his myths, he protected people from the dangerous forces embodied as giants and trolls. He is a god of honesty and honor as well as strength and skill.

In modern magick, Thor carries all the correspondences of Jupiter, for Jupiter's day is Thursday in English, being "Thor's day." Colors would be blue, both sky blue and dark stormy blue and gray. He is also associated with yellow-gold for lightning and red for the traditional color of his hair and beard.

As with the Greek Zeus, Thor is also associated with oak. Oak is a poor conductor and tends to explode when hit by lightning. The pieces fly off burning, looking like the god is giving fire to people to take and use, hence why oak would be sacred. Thor was associated with giving humans fire, unlike the stories of Zeus with Prometheus, who was trying to keep fire from humanity.

Thor is associated with mead, a honey wine, for an offering, as most Norse gods are, and his main symbol is his hammer, Mjölnir, which has been made into jewelry and votive offerings.

Carve a candle with Thor's Hammer image upon it. Anoint with Hazel or Sunflower Oil and sprinkle powdered oak bark upon it. Place a glass (or even better, a drinking horn with a stand) of mead out as an offering. Light the candle with these words or something similar:

Figure: Thor's Hammer

Oh Great Thor
Lord of Thunder
Wielder of Lightning
Bringer of the Rain and Storm
Bless me

I am honest and true
A keeper of oaths
And a hard worker
Guide me.

Slayer of Giants
Protector of Midgard
Grant me the strength of the Storms

The Lighting of Candles

The truth of the clear skies
and the courage of a warrior
May my belly be satisfied
And my glass be filled.
May I be surrounded by loving friends and family
For all of my days.
So be it!

Allow the blessings of Thor to enter into your life. Be prepared to rise to any challenges in your life with honor and fortitude.

Candlelight Vigils

A powerful form of magick for when situations are critical, usually around protection or healing a life-threatening illness, is the process of a magickal vigil. Vigils begin much like any other candle spell, where the candles are dressed, set, and charged for a specific intention. Vigils are usually created with a powerful religious or spiritual component. Like a votive offering, they are dedicated to either the "Creator" in general or a specific deity, angel, or saint. Unlike a traditional candle spell, where the candle is lit and the left alone to do the work, the vigil rituals have you stay with the candle, repeatedly focusing and/or praying for the outcome. Vigils I've participated in have been performed from about dusk to dawn. The candle itself was a simple smaller candle. A typical taper candle will burn one hour for every inch, so a twelve-inch taper will burn roughly for twelve hours, though in all practicality, I've had them burn out just after ten hours. It all depends on quality of wax, thickness of wick, and thickness of the candle. The trick is to make the candle burn a time period that would be reasonable, if difficult, for a vigil and not longer. If you enter too deeply into exhaustion and lose your focus, the vigil will be for nothing.

General Guide to Candle Burn Times

Tea light	4-6 Hours
8 Inch Taper	6-8 Hours
10 Inch Taper	8-10 Hours
12 Inch Taper	10-12 Hours
Votive (2 Oz)	13-15 Hours
Jar Candle (5-6.5 Oz)	35-40 Hours
Jar Candle (10 Oz)	60-80 Hours
Jar Candle (14 Oz)	80-90 Hours
3'x3' Pillars	30-35 Hours
3'x5' Pillars	65-70 Hours
3'x7' Pillars	90-95 Hours
Large Glass Pillars	75-80 Hours
Pull-Out Pillars	120 Hours

The difficulty with this task is that it takes a tremendous amount of focus and stamina; it can be draining on your personal energy. I have observed that it works better for those who follow a path of religious devotion rather than esoteric science, but if the need is great, it can work for anyone. The greater difficulty is because it's usually used in dire situations, not to get too drawn into fear or hopelessness, and really marshal all your will into the candle magick. I have found having a form of repeated prayer or mantra to be very helpful.

An example of candle vigil magick that I would share is one devoted to Archangel Michael, beloved of Jews, Christians, and even Pagans. While in occult ceremonial lore, Archangel Raphael is strongly associated with healing, in both Christian folklore and modern New Age tradition, Michael has a strong reputation as a healer. In Qabalistic lore, he has mixed associations with Raphael, as each has been assigned to the Sun and to Mercury in various

The Lighting of Candles

systems. Along with the traditional warrior's sword or spear for fire, he has also been known to carry the scepter or scales. He has been an archangel of death, and it is in that role he can also stop someone gravely ill from crossing into the land of the dead.

For this healing magick, prepare a candle with either simple olive oil or a St. Michael Oil. I use this oil recipe as one of many Michael oils in my practice.

St. Michael Oil

6 Drops of Frankincense Essential Oil

2 Drops of Cinnamon Essential Oil

1 Drop of Bay Essential Oil

1 Drop of Myrrh Essential Oil

1 Pinch of Angelica Root

1 Pinch of Dragon's Blood

1/8 Oz of Base Oil (Grapeseed, Apricot Kernel, etc.)

1 Pinch of Salt

Place the seal of Archangel Michael (see the Candle Art figure in **Chapter Four**) beneath the candle. Prepare it as a healing spell for whoever is gravely ill. If you can carve upon the candle, as I suggest a tea light or taper, carve the name of Michael, the name of the recipient, and Michael's seal. If you have a photo of the recipient, you can place the photo next to or beneath the seal. Light the candle and for a focus, recite a prayer to St. Michael repeatedly.

You could use the novena to St. Michael:

Saint Michael the Archangel,
loyal champion of God and His People.
I turn to you with confidence
and seek your powerful intercession.
For the love of God,
Who made you so glorious in grace and power,

and for the love of the Mother of Jesus, the Queen of the Angels,
be pleased to hear our prayer.
You know the value of our souls in the eyes of God.
May no stain of evil ever disfigure its beauty.
Help us to conquer the evil spirit who tempts us.
We desire to imitate your loyalty to God and Holy Mother
and your great love for God and people.
And since you are God's messenger for the care of His people,
we entrust to you these special intentions:

(specific intentions for healing or other purposes here)

Lord, hear and grant our special intentions for this Novena.
Amen.

There is also the Act of Consecration to Saint Michael the
Archangel, from the text of *The Opus Sanctorum Angelorum:*

Oh most noble Prince of the Angelic Hierarchies, valorous warrior of
Almighty God and zealous lover of His glory, terror of the rebellious
angels, and love and delight of all the just angels, my beloved
Archangel Saint Michael, desiring to be numbered among your devoted
servants, I, today offer and consecrate myself to you, and place myself,
my family, and all I possess under your most powerful protection.

I entreat you not to look at how little, I, as your servant have to offer,
being only a wretched sinner, but to gaze, rather, with favorable eye at
the heartfelt affection with which this offering is made, and remember
that if from this day onward I am under your patronage, you must
during all my life assist me, and procure for me the pardon of my
many grievous offenses, and sins, the grace to love with all my heart
my God, my dear Savior Jesus, and my Sweet Mother Mary, and to
obtain for me all the help necessary to arrive to my crown of glory.

Defend me always from my spiritual enemies, particularly in the last
moments of my life.

The Lighting of Candles

Come then, oh Glorious Prince, and succor me in my last struggle, and with your powerful weapon cast far from me into the infernal abysses that prevaricator and proud angel that one day you prostrated in the celestial battle. Amen.

Obviously, there are very Catholic prayers, looking to Michael as St. Michael from the Catholic traditions, and the wording might not suit the modern ceremonial magician, Neopagan, or even dabbler in candle magick. I know they don't sit well with me as a Witch, but I endeavor to show you many forms of magick and repeat the idea that candle magick belongs to all traditions and people.

A simpler, more mantra-like focus that could be used in conjunction with mala beads or another form of prayer beads while keep vigil would be:

St. Michael the Archangel
Prince of the Sun
Bring complete healing now
To this loved one.

Inevitably you should take breaks throughout the night if you need to use the restroom, but no food or drink except pure water should be taken. Once the candle is burned out, the vigil is done, and the spell is complete. Rest. Relax and allow the magick to take place before checking in with the one in need.

Oil Lamp Magick

Lamp magick is a similar method to candle magick with rich traditions in western and folk magick. We sometimes forget that candles were not as common or cheap as they are today until we look at the history of the candle (**Chapter Nine**). Lamps were a more common form of illumination until the 18th century. Lamps of various forms were far more common in ancient temples and for folk magick practitioners. We can trace the history of the most primitive lamps back to our Stone Age ancestors, who used hollowed rocks and shells filled with animal fat and most likely simple moss or grasses as a "wick" to illuminate their surroundings. The technique was safer than a torch and portable, unlike a campfire. As ancient civilizations developed, we have the evolution of the container to include clay, stone, and metal vessels, along with more advanced woven wicks that would last longer. Olive oil and fish oil were used, and while producing both soot and scent, their scent can be modified with the addition of aromatic herbs and oils to lamp oil. Beyond the Stone Age people, we find evidence of oil lamps in Bronze and Iron Age people, and specifically with the Hindu, Egyptian, Greeks, Persians, Africans, Hebrews, Romans, Christians, and Muslims, with religious significance. Oil lamps can also be found among the Chinese, and even in the Arctic, with the native people of the north using seal oil primarily. Today, remaining oil lamps usually use kerosine, and are primarily lit for atmosphere and ambiance, as artificial electrical light covers their traditional use. In magick, oil lamps have been reintroduced to the Western magickal traditions through the African diasporic traditions and those seeking to reconstruct temple traditions from the ancient world. Most popular are oil lamp spells in Hoodoo, Rootwork, and Conjure traditions from American folk magick.

Any talk on magickal lamps would be remiss without a mention to the "magic lamp" that would contain a wish-granting genie, more traditionally spelled "djinn." When taken out of fanciful fiction, such magick is more in alignment with spirit servitors, bottle imps, and artificial elemental constructs and beyond the scope of a book focusing on candle magick.

For functional purposes, a lamp usually has several features:

✦ **Chamber** – A place to hold the fuel. Sometimes open to the air, in bowl style lamps, and other times sealed in a chamber in more advanced lamps.

✦ **Wick Hole** – The wick hole is simply a hole for the wick to reach the fuel and extend outwards from it to be lit and illuminate, fulfilling the function of the lamp. Some wick holes are simply a "lip" from the open style chamber to rest the wick upon, while others are more of a nozzle.

✦ **Disc and Shoulder** – The opening to the chamber is often referred to as the "disc" while the chamber, or more specifically, the top of it, is the "shoulder." Many simpler bowl-type lamps don't really have these parts, but it's more common in what most of us think of as traditional oil lamps.

✦ **Handle** – Most, but not all lamps, have a handle to carry the lamp from place to place. The more simple the lamp, the less likely it will have a handle.

Lamps can be simple or complex. Some have multiple wicks, while others just a single one. When looking at the history of oil lamps, they are often decorated with religious and cultural iconography, indicating the purpose of that particular lamp.

Most common in magick today are lamps that use the "hurricane" oil lamp style, particularly in Hoodoo and New Orleans Voodoo spells. Those produced for sale by practitioners often have the clear glass oil container, in which the ingredients for the spell are artfully displayed and filled with oil. The wick mechanism and wick are placed on top, sealing it and the hurricane glass around the wick to shield it from both breezes and to more safely contain the fire. The wick can be adjusted with a simple "key" mechanism that lowers or raises the wick, depending on the desired size of the flame. The higher the flame, the faster the oil burns. They now make such mechanisms that can easily be added to a mason jar rather than a decorative lamp. When you want the effects of the spell, you light it, and let the lamp burn until the original oil is used up, completing a specific spell.

I learned lamp magick using items more common to Hindu temples, particularly a simple brass container etched in Sanskrit. Lamps such as this are called diyas or deepaks and use vegetable oil or ghee (clarified butter) as the fuel. Found in India and Nepal, they are used in Hindu, Buddhist, Sikh, Jain, and Zoroastrian rituals. Along with festivals and holy days, they are used in pujas or devotional prayer rituals. Many home shrines include these lamps. Due to the popularity of Indian imports, they can be easily found in the western world now too, and have been adopted by many Neopagans devoted to such figures as Kali or Ganesha, and that is how I was introduced to them.

The first lamp I used looked much like a brass candleholder, but the opening for the candle was more of an open bowl. There were two "lips" for where the wicks would go, making it a double lamp. Since then I've seen brass versions with a mechanism to center the wick or having multiple "lips" for up to seven wicks in a vessel. My mentor taught me to add pinches of herbs and drops of essential oil to a base of vegetable oil, speak my intention as a petition directed to a specific divinity, and then light the wick. Sometimes the wick would have to be adjusted as the fuel burned, and she would do that carefully with tongs or tweezers. The longer base handle made moving the lamp easier, though some modern lamps are simply bowls, not meant to be moved when lit. As with everything pertaining to fire, use caution and common sense.

I later learned traditions and found materials in Jewish and Christian religious lamp supply shops. Their containers were often glass votive holders, and most used a specially crafted cork "floater" that would hold the wick. They would use either prepared wicks or twist cotton balls into a makeshift wick. I later found what they called "Old Believer" or "Russian Old Believer" style wick holders made from metal to sit on the rim of the glass and maintain the height of the flame at the same height, rather than float with the level of fuel. This required a longer wick to reach deeper into the fuel container. I've found that Eastern Christian church supply shops to be particularly helpful with supplies, ranging from the easy and cheap to finely crafted and very expensive. Olive oil is the oil of choice in these traditions.

Various other containers that can be used for lamp magick include shells, heat-resistant ceramic bowls, crystal bowls, metal bowls, hollowed-out pineapples, cupped orange rinds, coffee cans, tin cans, and coconut shells which have been halved and hollowed out. Depending on the material, make sure that it is sitting upon something heat-resistant, as metal containers can easily scorch a wooden table and have safety precautions prepared. I keep a bowl of sand near my oil magick, and in our greater temple, we have fire extinguishers. With most vegetable base oils, you can maintain a flame and not have a great risk of causing a fire, which is one of the reasons why we don't usually use petroleum products like kerosene, but base oils like olive oil, vegetable oil, and in some forms of Hoodoo, even palm oil. Lampante is a form of inedible olive oil often used for oil lamps. Some practitioners use lamp oil that is a form of liquid paraffin, which is more combustible than natural oils, being a petroleum product. There are still those who do use kerosene, though it has both an odor and emits more chemicals than any of the other forms of lamp oil.

You can color your oil if placing it in a glass container for added magick, but you can only do this with vegetable oils like olive and corn oil but not any petroleum products. Put the oil in a dish in the microwave and heat it on high for ninety seconds. When you take it out, add a few drops of food dye and stir it in. Unlike with water, it won't dissolve, but it will diffuse through the oil, though it works best for solid colors unless you mix colors with the dye first before adding it to the oil. Adding red and blue to make purple first, rather than red and blue to the oil, would work best, as you might get patches of red and patches of blue. The lighter the oil, the more color it will take.

While water-based food coloring is more accessible to practitioners being found in easily in kitchen products, if you can find oil based food dye, also known as candy coloring used for candy coating and chocolate, you can have a much better mix with the oil and not require the heat. Soap dye also mixes well with oil.

My preferred oil lamp magick style is to use a colored glass or colored votive with an Old Believer holder, bent, so the flame is deep enough to illuminate the glass, rather than be above the glass. The cotton wick is dipped in oil and set in the holder, and various oils and herbs can be added to the fuel in the cup, usually olive oil. Then, like a candle spell, it is held, charged with intention and a spoken spell, and lit.

Lamp magick can be used just like candle magick in general, but the items are added to the base oil. There are lamp spells for love, lust, healing, fertility, protection, money, and peace. Some are used for specific intentions with immediate results, while others are for long-term work, such as general protection of a home, or creating a happy and harmonious dwelling. Lamps can be lit to increase psychic ability when doing readings, or for healing when seeing clients for spiritual cleansing or energetic healing. A general magick power lamp can be lit when doing rituals and circles, and lamps can be created to enhance and evoke the blessings of a particular sabbat or moon. Many devotees of specific deities or spirits will dedicate a lamp in a shrine to that entity, filling the chamber with the correspondences of the spirit. When working with the entity, or simply doing devotion or giving thanks, the lamp is lit to tune into the spirit and to let the spirit tune into the shrine and practitioner.

For all of these spells, like most forms of magick I teach, I recommend you cleanse all the items with either a purifying smoke, cleanse them with a sprinkling of blessed salt water, or use energy and intention to clear them of unwanted intentions and vibrations. As you use each cleared item, you charge it with your intention, giving it "instructions" on what you wish it to do as a part of the spell, along with the overall intention of the spell.

In Hoodoo and Conjure, the hurricane style or mason jar lamps are often "awoken" first by breathing life into the vessel before adding ingredients and pouring the oil. Sometimes a Biblical prayer is recited. I haven't seen a similar thing in the Hindu or traditional Judeo-Christian forms of magick, though they are cleansed and blessed.

Lamp for a Happy Home
Brass Bowl or Open Oil Lamp and Stand
Cotton Wick
Cork Floater (if the brass vessel doesn't have a "lip" for the wick)
Corn Oil
Honey
10 Drops of St. John's Wort Infused Oil or Pinch of Ground St. John's Wort
8 Drops of Lavender Essential Oil or Pinch of Ground Lavender
4 Drops of Cinnamon Essential Oil or Pinch of Ground Cinnamon
1 Drop of Rosemary Essential Oil or Pinch of Ground Rosemary
Blue Lace Agate Polished Stone

Pinch of Salt

Place the Blue Lace Agate or another stone that means peace and happiness for you (Citrine, Rose Quartz, or Amethyst could be used as well), at the bottom of the vessel. Charge it for peace and happiness as you do. Drizzle a little honey upon it for sweetness among members of the home. Fill the vessel more than halfway with corn oil as you bless it, so all in the home will have enough to eat and enough money to prosper. Add the oils or herbs with these blessings:

I add St. John's Wort to protect this home, and bring health and blessings to us all.
I add Lavender to heal this home, and bring peace and rest to us all.
I add Cinnamon to warm this home, and bring love and success to us all.
I add Rosemary to bless this home, and so we always remember and rekindle our love.
I add this pinch of salt, so we are grounded to the Earth and remember our place here with Her.

Prepare the wick by dipping it in the oil. Place it in the cork floater. Float the cork upon the oil. Light the lamp with the words:

I light this lamp for happiness, health, peace, and prosperity for all who live in this home. May there be peace and love between us together, and between us and the land and spirits here. So mote it be!

Lamp for a Healing Altar
Blue or Green Glass Votive Vessel
Cotton Wick
Russian Old Believer Wick Holder
Olive Oil
6 Drops of Frankincense Essential Oil
4 Drops of Amber Essential Oil

3 Drops of Rose Essential Oil
1 Drop of Lavender Essential Oil
Tumbled Clear Quartz

Pour the oil a bit more than halfway into the votive vessel. Prepare the wick by dipping it in the oil. Add your essential oils or other oils specific to the healing needs in general, or if dedicating the candle to a specific person or situation, oils appropriate for the individual need. For example, you might use ginger oil for those with stomach problems, or eucalyptus for a cold. Float the cork on the oil. Place the entire thing between your hands and recite this or something similar to set the intention of the lamp:

I charge this light for Healing
May (name a specific person or situation, or say "all those whose names
    are placed upon the altar") receive healing
To bring resolution to their illness or injury
For their highest good in a manner acceptable to them.
So mote it be.

Light the wick. You can dedicate your healing altar for a specific healing deity or spirit, such as Bridget, Asclepius, Apollo, Hygia, Isis, Imhotep, Yemaya, or any others you feel appropriate. Place the names of people in need of healing upon a list or on slips of paper in a decorative, ritually cleansed, and consecrated bowl. I place the lamp in the bowl, with the names around the base of the votive glass. Every month we burn the names and start again at the new Moon.

Lamp Devoted to Hecate
Hurricane Oil Lamp
Olive Oil
13 Drops of Myrrh Essential Oil
Pinch of Saffron

3 Small Pieces of Dragon's Blood
9 Garlic Cloves
1 Piece of Jet
Horse Hair
Snake Skin
Black Dog Hair
Baneful Herbs – Belladonna, Datura, Aconite, Henbane, Yew

If you work with Hecate, you might already grow herbs sacred to her, baneful herbs that are often difficult to procure otherwise. If you have them fresh, place the leaves, stalks, roots, berries and flowers decoratively in the oil container. You can do the same with the dog and horse hair, and the snake skin. As you do so, bless them and offer them to the Goddess of Witches. Fill the vessel about halfway with oil. Then add the other ingredients one by one, each charged and offered to her. Top-off the chamber with oil and place the wick mechanism with a primed wick. Say this or something similar:

I dedicate this lamp of light to She who is Queen of Witches
May the Lady of the Crossroads watch over me.
May the Lady of the Crossroads guide me in my craft.
May the Lady who brings the light to the darkness guide me upon the
    Crooked Path
And through her may I understand and be united with the Cosmos.
So mote it be!

Light in a Hecate shrine to call upon and to thank the goddess of magick and mystery.

With these examples, you can surely adapt other candle spells for lamp magick, and be even more creative in the process. When using hurricane lamps, you can put rolled-up petition spells, or if using a smaller vessel than a hurricane lamp, you can put the

The Lighting of Candles

ashes of a petition spell into the oil, linking the magick with a specific phrasing of the spell for more precise results.

Unlike with candles, you can add coins, shredded money, real or symbolic, for prosperity and cash spells. Seeds, acorns, and corn can all be used. A spell to commune with the ancestors can have graveyard dirt, twigs from a graveyard tree, funeral flowers, or Mercury dimes. A protection spell can have nails, thorns, and twisted red thread. For a lamp for a specific person, use personal concerns or "tag locks" to link it to a specific person, such as hair, nails, small amounts of bodily fluids, or a scrap of clothing. Usually this will be your own, unless doing magick for another. Many spells can be adapted to lamp use.

There are deeper teachings beyond spellcraft on the temple lamp. While some temples today keep the perpetual fire going in the form of a candle, easier for the modern world, the oil lamp was traditional to set the intention, and group "soul" of a temple and tradition.

Patricia Crowther, in her book, *Lid Off the Cauldron,* writes about the Babylonian Lamp, and the goddess of the lamp, Aruru. Modern mythologists relate Aruru, as a goddess of creation, to the Sumerian Ninhursag, a goddess of the Earth and fertility. Interestingly an arura, rather than aruru, is an ancient Greek word for fertile lands or measurement of lands, similar to an acre today. Crowther states that Aruru is a secret name of Aphrodite. She equated the lamp as a fertility symbol represented by the images of a vagina as the opening of the lamp. The lamp symbolized life, and the moths attracted to it were death. The image is a warning of attempting sexual magick "without *wisdom* and *instruction.*"[2]

I learned from a mentor Witch who was enchanted with the works of the British Traditional lines, and probably familiar with

---

[2] Crowther, Patricia. *Lid Off the Cauldron: A Wicca Handbook,* p. 128

the work of Patricia Crowther, though I don't think had any legitimate claim of initiatory link to her or any British group that the Arurus were the Witches, a secret name of priestesses and priests of the Old Craft, and later when I learned that the term for Witches, Venefica, could refer to Venus rather than venom; I gave her and Crowther's ideas some serious thought. It paints a portrait of all Witches as lamps, as lights, in the world. That light-bearer image also relates to the figures of Hecate and Lucifer as light-bearers.

The lamp is also a symbol of our energy bodies, of our souls. Practitioners often simplify the model into three cauldrons, as found both in Celtic and Taoist traditions, with a cauldron of the belly, heart, and head. In many forms of Witchcraft, the three centers relate to a Lower, Middle, and Higher Soul. In alchemy, we relate them to Mercury, Sulfur, and Salt, three spiritual principles using those chemicals as symbols. In Chinese medicine, there are three "treasures" known as the Jing, Shen, and Qi, three forms of energy working in our bodily vessel.

Three Souls

Cauldron	Soul	Alchemy	Treasure	Lamp
Belly	Lower Soul – Shaper	Mercury	Jing (Essence)	Chamber & Oil
Heart	Middle – Namer	Salt	Qi (Vitality)	Wick & Flame
Head	Higher Self – Watcher	Sulfur	Shen (Soul/ Deity)	Light

The Lighting of Candles

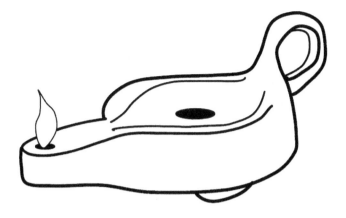

Figure: Babylonian Lamp

In *The Casting of Spells*, we reviewed the role of the three souls in the practice of magick. The middle self is the conscious, personal self, the part of us that identifies with the "I" of "I am." It is the self that perceives desire and wants and often starts the journey of magick. The lower soul is the primal self, filled with instincts. This soul houses our needs, starting with food and shelter to basic needs for intimacy, kindness, and friendship. It often manifests as pre-verbal and takes qualities like a child or animal. The higher soul is the true soul, the infinite and immortal self beyond space and time. It holds our True Will, our soul's purpose. It is the "I am that I am" presence. Magick, for many, is the alignment of the personal self, primal self, and higher self, bringing together desires, needs, and purpose into proper alignment.

We fashion our lamp as we practice our craft. The lamp itself, being made of clay, stone, or metal, is the body. Our work dedicates and "decorates" it towards a particular tradition. The chamber and the fuel it contains relates to our lower soul. The fuel is our life force. In Chinese medicine, this manifestation of the life force is Jing, known as the essence, meaning the fluid essence of our qi.

Jing is dense. Jing is also equated with spirit and described like sperm, making connections to alchemical mercury. Likewise it has connections to our ancestry, and many consider the lower soul, what is known as the Shaper in the Temple of Witchcraft, as the blood soul or ancestral soul, as it draws from the ancestry of our parents' lineage. While there is a predetermined amount of pre-natal jing, upon which consuming results in death, non-prenatal jing can be replenished through diet and exercise, as well as martial and mystical practices, and resides in the lower body, in the kidneys primarily.

The middle soul corresponds with that which is visible in the world, the human self, personality, and identity, as well as the middle of the lamp, the oil-soaked wick and that which is most visible, the flame. The jing is converted into the flowing vital qi through the wick, and illuminates, feeding the flame. Despite being soft, the "solidness" of the wick, like the solidness of the spine corresponding to the primary energy channel, relates to the solid alchemical principle of salt, the pattern or matrix which holds the whole process together. The qi also relates to the breath and the vitality carried on the breath, and of course, air feeds the flame as much as the oil. Without both, the flame will soon give way.

The higher soul is considered ineffable, outside of time and space, untouchable. It is the light, not the flame, of the lamp, which radiates out in all directions. The third treasure of the shen. The shen, the divine, meaning both the divine self and various gods and spirits, is what oversees this entire process, but appears to be in the lamp, the end product. But it is the invocation of the primal light, our desire for illumination on all levels, that leads to the making of a lamp at all, so in many ways the principle of the light occurs before the lamp, fuel, or flame is ever developed. In alchemy, sulfur is the rock that burns, albeit with an unpleasant odor. In plant alchemy, the sulfur is the unique essential oils identifying a plant and its medicine by its chemical composition. Mercury is the plant-based alcohol extracted from the gross plant matter through fermentation and the salt is the trace elements. Sulfur is really the volatile principle, producing light. In the Celtic cauldrons, the upper cauldron is one of awen, of divine inspiration, the illumination but not the fire. It leads the druid, bard, or poet to having "fire in the head" and poetic inspiration, but the origin of this awen is from beyond.

In the process of study, dedication and initiation, we fashion our lamp through the body, making our body and corresponding energetic body the appropriate vessel for the magickal work we are fusing in the light of our lamp, down to the fuel and very structure of the lamp. Our rituals, disciplines, and daily practice fashion the lamp, the earth element, and our understanding of the symbols, images and functions, the air element, shape and "decorate" the spiritual bodies. The life force in its various forms flows like liquid, akin to the water element, and we work on the free flowing of that energy through the spine, the wick, and our other natural channels. Devotion, aspiration, experimentation, and initiation can serve as ignition, lighting the lamp, at least in a way that is spiritually visible, and bringing the attention of the higher self, known as the Holy Guardian Angel or Watcher, who is the true initiator upon our personal path.

Fire Cleansing

Fire itself is a powerful, spiritually-cleansing force. Our work with candle flame has the additional benefit of revivifying the aura. When we meditate before a candle or focus our gaze upon the candle, the fire itself can naturally help clear the unwanted energy. This effect is strongest in simple consecrated altar candles, rather than a spell candle, but a side effect of spell candles is if you spend some time before them in meditation while they are "doing the work" the flame can help attune your own auric energy to the results of the spell, preventing subconscious blocks to your stated intention.

When meditating with a candle, if you find that meditation is difficult, and really, even the most experienced meditators do from time-to-time, you can intend and direct all distracting thoughts and feelings from our daily life to go into the fire. You can visualize images, or an internal statement directing them, or simply a non-verbal and non-visual sense of will directing the distractions into the flame. Unlike just telling your mind to stop thinking or to just relax, your consciousness works in harmony with the living flame. Regular meditation practice not only alters our brain and body chemistry for the better, as science is discovering, but it also shifts our energetic health, and the meditation candle can help us in this purification process, burning away over time all that doesn't serve.

Cauldron of Fire

While not a candle spell, there is a powerful method of cleansing that involves fire. While Witches use it quite often these days, and you see it among some modern shamanic practitioners, I first learned a simple version of it from a spiritualist, who uses it to cleanse her home after seances where she is speaking with the dead.

Small Cauldron
Epsom Salt
Sea or Table Salt
High Proof Rubbing Alcohol or Grain Alcohol
Cleansing Essential Oils

Alcohol fires create a hot, fast flame that tends to "eat" up unwanted psychic energies. It creates a type of spiritual "vacuum," sucking it up and automatically transmuting it in the transformative nature of fire. The way to steady the flame is to fill a small flame-proof vessel with an equal measure of Epsom salt (magnesium sulfate) and sea or table salt (sodium chloride) in the vessel. This can be done with metal bowls, as I first learned, but I like to use a small cauldron, around 3-4" opening. They are often used for burning incense charcoal and loose incense. The advantage is they are less likely to spill, can be easily and safely doused with the lid, and if you need to move them right away after they are extinguished but while still hot, you can place a spoon through the handle and lift it up and out of the way if necessary. The handle itself will still be quite hot.

Set the vessel on a heat-proof surface that won't char if the cauldron or its legs get too hot. Place it somewhere in the center of the space you wish to cleanse. I have a small square of marble I put in the center of the room, placing the cauldron on top of it.

Pour the alcohol into the vessel, soaking the salts. Fill it about halfway. It will create a salt sludge at the bottom of the cauldron.

Add any cleansing oils, just a few drops at most, to the alcohol. I would choose from grapefruit, orange, lemon, lavender, sage, eucalyptus, or frankincense.

Throw a lit match in, or use a long match for fireplaces and furnaces. If not, use a long mechanical lighter. As the alcohol burns, the fire, alcohol, and salt will "suck in" all the unwanted energies floating around. I usually step away from the flame and put my back to the wall, watching it, so I don't leave it unattended, but not to be in the path of what is getting sucked up.

When done, you'll notice the energy of the environment around you is much different. It's a heavy-duty fire cleanse that I wouldn't often do but perhaps seasonally in a psychically busy space. It will leave things feeling fresh and clear. The cauldron itself will have to be washed out. Sometimes the layer of salt gets crusty and thick and needs to dissolve. Iron cauldrons used for this purpose can be "cured" or "seasoned" like a cast-iron skillet. Scrub clean with soap and water, scraping off any rust. Cover inside and out with fat, such as vegetable oil or lard, and gently heat it in an oven for fifteen minutes at 200-250 degrees. Let it cool and take it out. With the salt, you might have to re-season your cauldron every time you do this particular cleanse.

If you don't feel safe using a flaming cauldron, you can do a candle spell with a similar intention. A simple taper candle anointed with cleansing oils and charged to suck up and transmute unwanted and harmful energy can work quite well, though its results are not quite as spectacular as the cauldron fire.

Offerings to the Fire

Making offerings to a sacred fire is a time-honored tradition found all over the world. Two prevailing thoughts occur on the nature of fire offerings. The first is that fire is purifying, and that what is placed into the fire is purified and transformed. So things offered to the fire are burdens and difficulties, things you no longer want and for the good of yourself, and the world, need to be transformed by the flames.

The second is that the fire is a conduit to the gods, and to give something to the fire is to give it to the gods in sacrifice and offering. The fire is the gods' way of "eating" it. In Hindu traditions, Agni is the divine fire and takes the role of elemental fire as part of creation and cosmology, a directional temple deity of the southeast and the primary Vedic deity of fire. In rituals, he is the means by which the gods receive offerings, for he is the "mouth" of the gods and relays the appropriate offerings to the gods once they are consumed in his fire. Agni is a part of home shrines, similar to the goddess Hestia or Vesta in the west, and honored in rites of passages such as weddings and funerals. Agni is also the fire of metabolism in Vedic healing, not unlike the similar sounding principle of igni in ancient Greek medicine. Likewise, the Greeks and many ancient Middle Eastern cultures, including the early Jewish Temples, used similar fires for offerings to the divine, placed just outside the temples since animal offerings were common. Sweeter resinous incense offerings were reserved for inside of the temple.

Other cultures have their own fire ceremonies with a similar nature. In the Peruvian shamanic traditions of the Q'ero, popularized due to great interest from modern shamanic practitioners, there is a ceremony known as a despacho. A ceremonial bundle with a spiritual intention is artistically created with various substances as an offering, starting with a paper to serve as a wrapping for the offering. Grains, flowers, leaves, oils, candy, and sometimes even llama fat, depending on the intention, are arranged like a mandala, then wrapped up. Often this is accompanied by song, music, and prayer. Sometimes the bundle is used to cleanse and bless the participants, and sometimes it is simply offered, to a deity, most often to Pacha Mama, Mother Earth, in an act of ayni, or reciprocity, by placing it into a ceremonial fire.

Mayan fire ceremonies are deeply aligned to the traditions of the Calendar Keepers. Fire pits are dug, with three stones to align with the stars of the belt of Orion, and a mandala of offerings is built in the circular pit. I was honored to attend a Mayan fire ceremony that involved a mandala of candles arranged in what looked like a "medicine wheel" of the four directions, various concentric circles, large rolled balls of copal incense, various grains and seeds, and high-grade alcohol, used to ignite the whole thing. It became a pool of burning melted wax, and participants were encouraged to bring their own colored candles. We would be instructed to raise a candle, recite the prayer with the celebrant, involving the sacred counts of the calendar system, and then throw our candle into the fiery pool, extending its fuel. This was repeated several times until the power built and the counting and recitations gained fervor. The intention was to "turn the calendar" and return us to spirit, though that was through translators, for our celebrant spoke no English during the rite.

Here is a fire ceremony that is appropriate for those of a Pagan, Wiccan, or Witch background:

The Ritual of Nine Woods

In modern Wiccan lore is an often forgotten section of the long form of the Wiccan Rede, referencing the Nine Woods.

Nine woods in the Cauldron go,
burn them quick a' burn them slow.
Elder be ye Lady's tree;
burn it not or cursed ye'll be.
When the Wheel begins to turn,
let the Beltane fires burn.
When the Wheel has turned at Yule,
light the log and let Pan rule.

Along with the long form of the Wiccan Rede, there is the Poem of Nine Woods, describing the nine woods in detail. Sometimes it's included in the Rede, and other times made into a separate work since it uses the first four lines in the Rede to start and finish it.

Poem of Nine Woods

Nine woods into the cauldron go,

burn them fast and burn them slow.
Birch into the fire goes,
to represent what the Lady knows.
Oak gives the forest might,
in the fire brings the God's insight.
Rowan is the tree of power,
causing life and magick to flower.
Willows at the waterside stand,
to aid the journey to summerland.
Hawthorn is burned to purify,
and draw faery to your eye.
Hazel, the tree of wisdom and learning,
adds its strength to the bright fire burning.
white are the flowers of the apple tree,
that bring us the fruits of fertility.
Grapes that grow upon the vine,
giving us both joy and wine.
Fir does mark the evergreen,
to represent immortality unseen.
Elder is the Lady's Tree,
burn it not, or cursed you'll be.

The trees named in the poem are part of the Celtic Ogham system of wisdom and divination, represented by certain symbols named after tree associations, similar to Norse runes.

The Nine Woods

	Tree	Poem	Ogham	Magick
1	Birch	What the Lady Knows	Beithe	Renewed Life, Youth, Regeneration, Hope, New Beginnings, Growth, Purity

	Tree	Poem	Ogham	Magick
2	Oak	Forrest Might, God's Insight	Duir	Strength, Stability, Health, Truth, Endurance, Nobility, Honesty
3	Rowan	Power, Life, Magick	Luis	Protection, Courage, Healing, Insight, Foresight, Inner Vitality, Inspiration, Spiritual Strength
4	Willow	Journey to Summerland	Saille	Psychic Power, Visions, Spirit Contact, Intuition, Prophecy, Enchantment, Healing, Emotion, Cunning
5	Hawthorn	Purify, Faery to your Eye	Huath	Protection, Purification, Faerie Magick, Disruption, Obstacles, Release, Self-Control, Pleasure, Sexuality, Love, Marriage
6	Hazel	Wisdom, Learning, Strength	Colle	Wisdom, Inspiration, Knowledge, Divination, Creativity, Science, Meditation, Communication
7	Apple	Fertility	Quert	Rejuvenation, Immortality, Faeries, Goddess, Love, Beauty, Perfection, Wholeness, Eternal Youth, Gratitude, Wonder
8	Grape	Joy and Wine	Muin	Healing, Happiness, Protection, Wealth, Introspection, Speaking Truth, Liberation, Fruition, Harvest

The Lighting of Candles

Tree	Poem	Ogham	Magick
9 Fir	Immortality	Ailm	Purification, Protection, Health, Strength, Discretion, Objectivity, Perspective, Higher Road, Joy, Elation
0 Elder	Lady's Tree, Burn it not or Cursed You'll be	Ruis	Blessing, Cursing, Protection, Healing, Change, Fate, Transition, Flow, Retribution, New Paths, Regeneration

Today, many modern Witches and Wiccans light cauldron fires of magick and blessing, or ritual fires for Beltane, with these nine woods. It can be challenging to find all the woods and realizing that some, like grape, are woody, but not technically trees despite being part of the "Celtic tree alphabet" of Ogham. Some metaphysical stores sell small bundles of all nine woods, making sure to omit the elder tree as it must never be burned. Elder is associated with faery lore, and its medicine makes it much more valuable as a healing tree. The flowers and berries are used in cures for the flu and respiratory illnesses. Years that have abundant elderberries are usually followed by harsh winters, as nature knows what we will need in the wintertime.

The ritual of nine woods can be done as a community ritual, as part of a sabbat with a fire, or a ritual of fire blessing. It is not necessarily an offering to the gods nor a transformative release. It is more about evoking the tree spirits and their blessings. The fire releases their blessings to all present. You will need:

Large Cauldron for the Fire
Second Cauldron with Drinkable Water
Sword
Kindling

Firewood
9 Twigs of the Trees
Various Herbs and Resins

Start with a large cauldron. Take one of the more abundant woods as the main firewood, if possible, such as the oak or birch, and with kindling, start the fire in the cauldron. Create a simple sacred space. If you practice Witchcraft, cast a circle and call the quarters. Give everyone an opportunity to invite their own gods, guides, and ancestors in love and trust.

Add each of the woods in the order of the poem, reciting the poem. Different participants can take turns adding the woods and reciting the appropriate lines of the poem.

If it was a Beltane ritual, participants would often jump over the fire. Depending on how big your cauldron is or how tall the fire is burning; this can be pretty dangerous. If you are planning this, some might forego the cauldron and build a fire pit, or dig a hole in the ground for the cauldron. For many, the older traditions of Beltane have a practical lesson in them. In the often-quoted original version of the film *The Wicker Man*, Sergeant Howie expresses outrage observing a fire jumping ritual dance, as all the participants are naked! Lord Summerisle replies, "Naturally! It's much too dangerous to jump through the fire with your clothes on!"

Along with the nine woods, other aromatic herbs and resins can be added to the fire. I have a personal preference for frankincense and myrrh, though pine pitch and dragon's blood can also do well. Herbs such as mugwort, wormwood, St. John's wort, and tansy also work well.

If not pertaining to a Beltane or other sabbat rite, I like to perform a blessing with the sword and a second cauldron filled with water. A larger sword is used rather than the smaller knife-sized athame blade for both the drama of a larger group ritual, and for safety. If worked as a smaller solitary rite, with a smaller cauldron and only twigs, I would use the athame and a chalice with water.

Place the blade into the fire and say this or something similar:

By Birch, Oak, and Rowan
And the herbs that we have thrown in
By Willow, Hawthorn, and Hazel
To dispel the forces of harm and ill
By Apple, Grape, and Fir
The fires of this cauldron I do stir
And bring their blessings to us, one and all.
So mote it be!

Place the warmed blade in the water-filled cauldron three times, performing a form of the Great Rite in token, a symbolic union of the Goddess and God coming together in ritual. The words used often in the Temple of Witchcraft tradition are:

As the sword is the to the grail,
the blade is to the chalice,
truth is to love.
I draw together the power of the Goddess and God,
and drink it in.
May all paradox be resolved.
Blessed be.

With a chalice, or if the group is large, with several chalices, scoop out the water and pass the chalice so all may drink the blessings of the nine woods. When done, perform any other magick for the gathering, though this act of sacrament is a huge act of magick in itself. Release your ritual space and celebrate together in community.

The Needfire

The needfire is a magickal fire said to be kindled in times of great need. Today we associate the needfire with Samhain, opposite of the more joyous baelfire of Beltane or other summer celebrations. At the time of Samhain, known as Halloween to popular culture, traditional Celtic people were preparing for the harsh time of winter. One was seeking protection from the gods from the dangers of winter – cold, famine, pestilence, and natural disaster. Likewise, the dark time of the year brought spiritual dangers with the veil being thin, and creatures from the otherworld roaming about. While we modern people tend to associate the winter seasons with the coziness of modern convenience, it was truly a time of physical and spiritual danger for our ancestors, and the reason why the blessings of the needfire would be required.

Needfires were struck in times of distress, particularly illness and plague facing the people or livestock. All fires within the community would be extinguished, extinguishing any parasitical miasmas living on the flame. The new, clear, and clean fire was kindled by hand. Torches would be lit from this fire and used to go throughout the community, rekindling hearth fires with this new blessing. Often two fires would be kindled, and as in many of the traditions around Beltane, the cattle and people would be driven between the two for purification. While it was a precaution at Beltane, with a needfire, it became a necessity. In Germanic Heathen traditions, the ceremonial dousing and relighting was more likely near Yuletide. There is some cross over with the customs of the yule log. We see in church prohibitions of Pagan customs making the kindling of the needfire illegal under religious law.

The needfire, like some temple fires, could not be kindled with any modern convenience. It requires no chemical and no iron. Rubbing sticks together or using a rope and stick kindling would be acceptable. Folklore indicates gathering embers from a lightning-struck tree would also be not only acceptable, but divinely preferable, yet you can't really count on a lighting struck oak when you need one. Various cultures have other requirements or prohibitions to the fire, including Bulgaria, where the kindlers of the fire must be two naked men, and in Halberstadt, Germany, the two must be chaste boys. Other requirements included they needed to be brothers or married with children. Since matches were not available during the origin of these customs, some modern practitioners believe striking a wooden match can be a modern equivalent of striking a fire through friction, since the spark is created through the friction of striking the match to the grainy side.

Witchcraft elder Raven Grimassi offered an adaptation for a needfire ritual in an article on *The Witch's Voice* community website entitled *A Call for Needfire* in 2004. His teaching speaks of the need of the people to renew the relationship between the land and the people and the mysteries of sacred kingship. He suggests a ritual using the names of trees on slips of paper if one cannot obtain the trees themselves to evoke their light in the cauldron fire, and uses candles as well. His list of trees is different than the nine woods poem and includes birch, elm, hazel, holly, oak, pine, rowan, willow, and yew. Though I prefer the traditional nine woods, you could easily adapt it to include whatever woods are important and sacred to you. In this article, Raven offers the use of a black candle to embody the fire that is afflicted and the problems with the land and the people. At the time he was suggesting it for healing the political strife in the United States and in the world. A white candle would hold the renewed fire. Other candles, if this was used in community rather than solitary practice, would be lit from the white candle. The needfire would be shared in community, signaling a renewal of life and the bonds between the people and the land for a just cause.

To perform your own version of his ritual, prepare two candles, black and white, a small cauldron and either nine twigs from sacred trees, or nine slips of paper with tree names on them. The trees should have qualities you feel you wish to kindle into the fire and pass onto the world.

One would light the black candle and then focus upon all that is afflicted and all that needs healing. All the lights in the home or area would be extinguished, one by one, until only the black candle would be left. All present would focus upon this flame as the source and root of the energy causing the affliction. Then the candle would be snuffed. In the darkness, reflect on the stillness of the void, releasing and renewing all.

The twigs or paper would be placed in the cauldron and set on fire. With each one, a ritual invocation of its plant spirit and the qualities it brings to the fire. The fire is seen as renewing and blessing. A white candle is lit from the fire, containing the virtues of that light. The candles are lit from this white candle, and other lights in the area are renewed with this newfound light. The light and candles can be shared with others. Let the main white candle burn. Bury the remains of the black candle and scatter the cold ashes of the twigs or paper to the winds, to carry the blessings to the world.

CHAPTER EIGHT: SPELL DIVINATION

One can divine the potential results of the spell from the action of the candle itself, and sometimes candle workings can give us signs to not go forward with the magick, that to do so is to invite failure or even harm. Fire is a living thing, and out of all the forms of magick, fire magick, including candle magick, seems to communicate the most to the practitioner. The sacred languages of the ancients were said to be composed of flames. Hebrew letters themselves look like flames, so spells, magick, and incantations already have both a fiery quality to them, and a communicative quality. Listening to the crackle of a fire can be as illuminating, spiritually, as scrying into the flame.

The Three Match Rule

I'm not certain it should be called a "rule" but it has become a tradition amongst students in the Temple of Witchcraft due to past experiences of many. The teaching is simple: If it takes more than three matches to light something in magick, don't do it. The universe, the spirit of fire, your guides, someone is giving you a sign not to go forward. This counts for lighting a candle, burning a petition, making a fire offering, or kindling any other magickal burning. Three tries allows room for error, inexperience, faulty matches or lighter, poor angle to the match or any other technical reason.

The question arises if one should use matches in magick, or lighters. Strong opinions on both sides can be found in manuals of magick and among practitioners, both with sound reasons. In the end, only you can decide. While I believe magick can be effectively done with both and have participated in effective magick with both, my teachers emphasized matches, so in my heart, I feel more magickal when using matches. But for reaching high candles on my altar, or into jars, I do enjoy having a long mechanical lighter with an easy-grip handle.

Those who favor matches believe they are more "natural," creating fire with friction and chemical reaction, rather than mechanical parts and lighter fluid. They burn wood and sulfur, two magickal ingredients, and are closer to the action of light sparking flames. Natural flint, or a magnifying glass, are technically the two most magickal ways of starting a temple hearth flame, but not so practical to light a candle flame. Lighter fluid, made from petroleum products, is not as pure being so synthesized. Hopefully, practitioners using matches for that reason also don't use petroleum-based candles.

Those who favor lighters believe they are cleaner than matches. Sulfur has a tendency to "banish" spirits with its foul smell, or is associated by Christian mystics with the fires and brimstone of Hell. To use it invokes those associations and banishes the spirits who want to help your magick. A lighter poses no such risk. Though the advocates of matches say that sulfur only banishes harmful spirits, so if you are doing "good" magick then matches gives you an extra benefit of clearing your ritual space. With a lighter, you are not wasting wood, and the chance of failure is less than most matches. Those concerned about the use of plastic lighters can get refillable metallic mechanical lighters.

One helpful technique to lower the chance of technical difficulties is to have a taper on the altar as your source of flame instead of a match. We use a white taper with no specific intention, a red candle for fire, or the working candle itself. With a simple, non-charged white taper, you can lift it, turn it and use it instead of a long-lasting matchstick without fear that you'll ruin a magickal intention as is possible with a more ritualized candle for elemental fire or the working. You can reach into glass jar candleholders with it. If such a taper goes out, then that is truly a sign to not move forward with the intention.

Those who continue to the fourth try report the spell operates, but not in the intended way, creating greater complications and issues in the spellcaster's life. Likewise, the spell can work as asked, but the requested result was really not what the person needed, and gaining what was desired was also problematic. Or simply the spell does not work at all, and a lot of time and energy was put into it when more introspection was needed first.

Divination by Candle Flame

Divination by flame occurs by gazing at the candle flame. The first lighting will give you a lot of information. Does it burn immediately and quickly, forming a strong flame? Or does it struggle? If immediate, then your spell could be fast and strong. If there is a struggle to burn, then it could indicate a struggle to succeed. If the flame is low and burns long, the spell can occur over a long period of time. If the flame burns large and fast, then the manifestation is more immediate. It might be too quick and need to be repeated later. Sometimes soot will gather, or a bit of herb will catch fire, and there will be two flames when you only intended one. This can mean the candle is having a double effect, or affecting someone who was not originally part of the spell, for good or ill. If the soot forms a blossom on the wick, your work is blessed!

Some look to the movement of the flame. If the flame leans towards a particular direction on the altar, in terms of north, south, east, west, then what does that direction mean for the practitioner, or the established altar? Different traditions place the elements in different directions. The most popular places earth in the north, air in the east, fire in the south and water in the west, though I practice a tradition that has multiple placements, with the traditional fire and air being switched as a popular alignment. As long as you have determined in your mind what element goes to which direction, you can add the leaning of the flame to your divination.

✦ **Earth Direction** – If the flame leans towards the earth direction, usually north, then the spell result will be solid, tangible and long-lasting. If burning poorly and leaning towards the earth direction, any blocks to it will be practical in nature, and require practical solutions.

✦ **Fire Direction** – If the flame leans towards the fire direction, usually south or east, then the spell will manifest quickly and with a lot of energy. If burning poorly and leaning towards the fire direction, the spell might be too energetic or manifest in passion or anger.

✦ **Air Direction** – If the flame leans towards the air direction, usually the east or south, then the spell will manifest clearly and peacefully. If burning poorly and leaning towards the air direction, the spell might have blocks in communication, written or oral, or have administrative road blocks if working with a company or agency in the spell.

✦ **Water Direction** – If the flame leans towards the water direction, usually the west, then the spell will manifest with love and affection, or in friendship and good feelings. If burning poorly and leaning towards the water direction, the spell might have blocks of an emotional nature. Do you really want it? What unresolved feelings are stopping you? Or someone else's emotional response in the situation might cause the spell to fail.

A candle that stops burning before it is consumed, particularly before it's halfway burned, usually indicates a failed spell, and one should contemplate and meditate about trying again, looking to see what obstacles you have both internally and externally, or consider abandoning the goal for a time.

If you continually have failed candles, you should contemplate if candle magick is the path for you; however, you might also want to reflect on the source of your candles. Perhaps the candles are low quality or defective; try a higher quality candle and compare results. Sometimes you can have a bad batch.

Divination by Wax

Divination by wax is to gaze at the remaining wax of a candle for insights and shapes that are suggestive of information. One might consider it ceromancy or wax scrying, though ceromancy is usually done by dripping melting wax into cool water and gazing at the shapes formed as you ask a question. And such a technique is perfectly valid, but for this work, we mean gazing at the wax remains, usually in a dish or inside a glass jar. The shapes suggested give clues to the psychic mind about the success, style, and method of manifestation for the spell.

For example, wax reminding you of a dragon might indicate a powerful and fierce spell result, while a mouse could be smaller and more subtle. In light of your intention, which would be preferable? It will differ depending on the spell. A good omen for one intention can be an ill omen for another intention. A shape of a question mark might indicate the result is not clear. A complete ring of wax can indicate the results will come full circle. No wax at all can indicate a powerful and complete spell, though a lot of dripping wax from a candle that burns all the way can indicate a fast and powerful, but messy, result.

While wax divination, assuming there is any wax left from the spell, can prove insightful, it requires a basic knowledge of understanding symbols as omens. Resources helping one with scrying, particularly tea leaf reading, can be helpful in learning to read wax remains. Here is a basic list of symbols that might take shape in the wax, or any other fluid system of divination like tea leaf or coffee ground reading.

Wax Divination Shapes

Shape	Associations
Angel	Divine Aid, Receiving Messages, Pay Attention to the Help Others Offer to You.
Arrows	Movement, Changing Directions. Arrows to the Left Mean Going Backward, to the Right, Going Forward.
Arrow, Down	Defeat, Loss, Need of a Break, Grounding
Arrow, Up	Success, Ascension, Assuming Power, or Higher Vision
Baby	Conception, Child Birth
Bird	Message, Spirituality
Bull	Stubbornness, Planning for the Future, Being Rooted
Bumblebee	Hard Work, Group Work, Sweetness of Life
Cat	Mystery, Fickleness, Sleep and Dreams
Coin	Money, Job, Pay Increase, Financial Concerns
Crab	Retreating into Your Shell, Motherhood, Listening to Your Intuition
Crow	Message, Wisdom, Times are Changing, Listening to Sacred Law and the Inner Voice, Inability to do Things for Yourself
Crown	Success, Promotion, New Job, Assuming a Position of Power, Responsibility
Cup	Family, Love Between Family
Dagger	Communication Issues, Argument, Betrayal

The Lighting of Candles

Shape	Associations
Diamond	Money, Possessions, Valuables, Clear Sight or Being Blinded
Dog	Loyalty, Protection, Friendship
Dollar Sign	Money, Investment, Financial Concerns
Dolphin	Aid, Kindness, Hearing, Breath, Benevolence
Dragon	Power, Wealth, Influence, Magick, Land
Egg	New Things to Come, Incubation, Rebirth
Feathers	Wisdom, Writing, Change
Fish	Religion, Spiritual Journey, Inner Talents
Flag	Honor, Pride
Flower	Love, Spirituality, Awakening
Goat	Stubbornness, Nagging, Social Climber
Heart	Love, Relationship, Romance
Horse	Travel, Freedom, Need to Escape
Infinity Loop	Never Ending, Power, Magick
Lightning	Inspiration, Illumination, Reflection, Destruction
Lion	Father, Pride, Humility, Arrogance, Sensitivity
Moon	Womanhood, Intuition, Emotions
N	No
Owl	Secrets Revealed, Witchcraft, Feminine Power, Wisdom, Deception
Mountain	Climbing Ahead, Journey, Far to Go
Pen	Communications, Creativity
Pyramid	Spiritual Focus, Protection
Ram	Leadership, Headstrong
Ring	Marriage, Fidelity, Cycles
Rose	Love, Spirituality
Scales	Justice, Balance, Legal Issues
Shamrock	Luck, Good Fortune, Elemental Blessings

Shape	Associations
Snake	Change, New Beginnings, Shedding Old Identity
Star	Guidance, Balance, Humanity
Square	Building a Foundation, Balance of the Four Elements
Sun	Manhood, Success, Good Marriage, Good Health, Going Forward
Sword	Argument, Fights, Communication Issues
Torch	Light, New Way, Passion, Vitality
Twins	Balance, Two Sides to the Story, Something Hidden
Y	Yes

Other times the symbolism is more direct. If using a seven-day glass jar candle, and it all turns black with soot, I would expect a "dark" result. Not necessarily a failure from the intention, but perhaps a difficult and unexpected manifestation, unless that was your original intention. A glass that cracks can be a very powerful spell; or backfiring on the sender. Usually, cracking at the end means a good result, but cracking before the spell is done is not a good omen.

For a free-standing candle, if the wax gets messy spilling beyond the expected space allotted for it, such as a dish or tray, that can mean the results will be messy or unexpected. No wax left can indicate a really clean outcome, but means there is little to "divine" beyond that.

Accidents and Undoing Candle Magick

Accidents in fire magick are always a possibility. We can burn ourselves, others, ritual items, altar cloths, or even our working area and home. We must be careful and vigilant with fire safety. But from an oracular point of view, accidents indicate unexpected, unintended, and unwanted consequences.

If you experience an accident with your candle spell and feel it is an ill omen for your results; you cannot "un-cast" a spell, but you can cast a second spell to neutralize the first. While you might be a little shy to try another candle spell on the heels of a fire mishap, the best advice would be to cast a second spell, using the opposite color of the candle used initially, if possible, on the opposite Moon cycle (Waxing/Waning). If you feel you cannot wait, simply use the opposite color candle with a clear and strong intention of neutralization. Opposite colors, via the color wheel, are:

Red – Green
Red Orange – Turquoise
Orange – Blue
Yellow – Purple
Yellow Gold – Indigo
Lime – Violet
Metallic Gold – Metallic Silver
Brown – Gray
Black – White

For other specialty colors, use your best guess and intuition in finding a color that resonates with the opposite vibration to neutralize the spell.

Divination Prior to Spell Casting

Many traditions of magick suggest learning a divinatory tool, even sometimes as simple as the yes/no response of a pendulum, and ask for higher guidance through divination before working any spell, to see if A) the request, B) the method of spell casting, C) the timing of the spell and D) the people involved are all appropriate to the success of the spell.

Obtain or make a pendulum, a weighted device upon a string or chain. A simple handmade pendulum can be a metal washer tied to a length of cotton thread. Many use a necklace or crystal on a chain. Serious pendulum enthusiasts have specially balanced and weighted pendulums, fearing that homemade ones are not sufficiently balanced for an accurate response.

Clear the pendulum as you would any tool, over an open flame, through sacred smoke or running it under cool water for a few moments. Bless the pendulum with the intention of higher guidance and true, accurate answers. Most importantly, a step most people don't learn, ask for higher guidance out loud or silently, before beginning each session. Simply asking to connect to your higher self, and for the higher self to respond through the pendulum is enough.

Ask to see a yes response. Hold the pendulum out and steady. Close your eyes for a few moments. Open them. How is it moving? Repeat and ask the same for a no response. Traditionally yes is clockwise and no is counterclockwise, but many people have different personal responses, and it sometimes varies with different pendulums, or if they use the pendulum to speak to other spirits or spirit groups, so it's good to start each session establishing yes and no.

Use the pendulum and higher guidance to get answers about points A-D. For example, your questions can be worded like this:

A) Should I do a spell for a new job right now?
B) Should I use this green candle with success oil on it?
C) Should I do it on Friday night at 7 PM as I planned?
D) Should I involve my mother to help me with it?

When you get a "no" response, you can refine your question further. If you get a no response to question B, you could then ask

about a blue candle. You could separate the question into two –
one about the color and one about the oil. If you get a no to
question C, try asking first if the day is correct, and then narrow
down the time once you've established the day. Often your first
intuition about this work will be correct, and a pendulum can help
confirm it. But be open to conflicting information from what you
already think, as we can blind our own intuition with strong
desire.

Fire Scrying

Fire scrying is a powerful form of divination. Also known as
pyromancy, it can be used beyond scrying for the results of a
particular candle spell and used as a divination technique in its
own right. Fire scrying can certainly include gazing into a candle
flame, though I've found it most effective with either a cauldron
fire or a more traditional campfire.

Scrying as a form of divination means to gaze into a substance
as a medium in which we project our "inner sight" or "mind's eye."
Most common is a crystal or dark mirror, but once the technique
is really understood, almost any substance or surface can be used.
Generally, mediums that are considered to be portals to a spiritual
dimension are used, such as crystals both transparent and
reflective, mirrors, pools of water, and, of course, fire.

At the first stage of scrying, we often catch shapes of
something in the medium, much like what was described above in
the wax reading. The shape the substance takes, even for a
moment, reminds us of a symbol, and that symbol resonates with
a chain of meanings that gives us psychic information. The process
can be facilitated with a number of techniques to gain new and
meaningful shapes or generating particular sounds from the fire.

- **Salt** – One can look at the shapes salt sprinkled into the fire makes, and when the fire goes out, the residue of the salt among the ash can create shapes. Salt and fire divination is known as alomancy, though many other forms of salt divination are also considered alomancy.
- **Plants** – Casting plant matter, particularly twigs and branches of sacred trees, into the fire, is known as botanomancy, and believed to be associated particularly with Druidic magick, calling upon the spirit of the tree for wisdom as well as that of the fire. The shapes the burning branches take will conjure the symbols. Divination can also be made from the smoke of the fire. Daphnomancy is a specific form using bay laurel leaves which can make quite a bit of crackling noise, indicating success, while silence indicates a less fortunate outcome.
- **Smoke** – The smoke of the fire can contain shapes to be read, and in general, the pattern in which it wafts is considered to be divinatory. Generally, smoke going straight up is a good sign, and anything else indicates problems. Smoke divination, or capnomancy, is known across the world in a variety of cultures, including Mesopotamian, Greek, Celtic, and Asian.
- **Bones** – Bones would be thrown into a fire or heated, and the resulting cracks in the bones would be read. Various bones, particularly animal "knuckle" bones and scapulae would be used, and in China, turtle plastrons were heated. Bone oracles are found all across the world, not always using fire, and are technically known as osteomancy for bones in general, scapulimancy when using scapulae, or plastromancy when using turtle shell.

At later stages of skill, one projects the "screen of the mind" upon the substance, and can see a fuller vision in the medium. Sometimes the medium is a portal for speaking with spirits and deities. The visions are more like guided journeys, yet there is no conscious guide, or a lucid dream projected into the scrying medium, not unlike watching a movie or television show.

You can use any form of candle for scrying, though as I've said, I prefer the larger flames of a cauldron fire or campfire. For larger fires, adapt the pervious fire spells. Adapt the cleansing Cauldron of Fire for fire scrying by adding Bay, Cedar, Mugwort, Jasmine, Vetiver, Lemongrass, or Ylang-Ylang essential oils to it. You can adapt the format of The Ritual of Nine Woods, but use woods that would be appropriate for psychic power. Specifically, Willow, Ash, Beech, Yew, Oak. Hazel, Rowan, Cedar, Linden, and Witch Hazel, though feel free to use a base of whatever common wood you can easily obtain. You can throw twigs or bay leaves into the fire to add to the psychic magick. Recite this or something similar to set the intention of the fire for scrying:

By the Spark of Light
And the Soul of Flame
By the Secret Fire
and the Hidden Name
I call upon this Living Blaze
To open my sight beyond
To hear my call into the night
To hear and to respond.
So mote it be.

If you wish to scry with just a single flame, then work with this scrying candle spell and formula for a fire scrying lamp.

Scrying Candle
Purple Pillar Candle
1 Amethyst
1 Clear Quartz

1 Obsidian Stone

Yellow Paper Equilateral Triangle

3 Drops of Bay Essential Oil in 1/8 Oz of Base Oil

Cleanse the candle and carve into it the symbol known as the Eye of Horus. It is both protective and opens mystical sight. It might be difficult to do on a taper candle, so a purple pillar might be best.

Figure Eye of Horus

Anoint the candle with the bay oil in the base, charging it for accurate fire scrying, and place it upon the triangle with the point facing you. Anoint all three stones with the remainder of the oil. Place the amethyst on the point closest to you, with the obsidian to the left point and the quartz to the right point. Light the candle and recite this charm:

By this light I seek to scry the flame
By the blessings of the candle true
I ask questions from beyond this time
and the answers shall come into view.
So mote it be.

Gaze into the flame, asking your questions aloud and let the images in the fire guide you.

The Lighting of Candles

Fire Scrying Lamp

Hurricane Oil Lamp

Olive Oil

Jasmine Flowers

Mugwort Stalks and Flowers or Dried Mugwort

6 Bay Leaves

5 Whole Star Anise Seed

Flecks of Silver Leaf

9 Moonstones

2 Amethyst

1 Clear Quartz

Cleanse and place the stones at the bottom of the oil vessel. If you have fresh or dried stalks of mugwort, place them into the vessel. If not, add a few pinches of the dry herb. Then add the bay leaves, star anise, and jasmine flowers. Fill the vessel with oil and prepare the wick by dipping it in the oil. Then replace the wick and mechanism. Charge the whole thing with these or similar words:

I charge this light to safely open my psychic sight
By the blessings of the lamp may I see clear
May my answers be understood and create no fear
I ask this for the highest good
So mote it be.

Light the lamp and place the hurricane glass on it. Gaze both into the fire and into the reflections of the light off of the glass case for your divination. Ask your questions and let the images arise from the fire and play of light.

The candle and lamp spells can also be used when doing any type of psychic work, such as card or rune readings. Having it lit when doing this work will give an added boost to your psychic ability.

Exercise: Divination

Perform an act of candle or fire divination. Ideally, perform two, one prior to casting a spell, to determine if this is the correct time and intention, or if there is another better possibility, and then perform a divination by the remains of the spell, if any. Note both in your journal or magickal record and review after sufficient time has passed. Was the divination successful and helpful? Did you interpret the signs correctly? Use this knowledge for future divination work.

Chapter Nine:
Making Your Own Candles

Making your own candles is both a difficult and worthy endeavor. I must admit that while I've enjoyed making them in the past, it's not something I do often. The process has made me appreciate the availability of candles whenever and wherever I want them. I'm not sure if I would do candle magick as frequently as I do if I had to make my own, but I did go on a phase of candle-making earlier in my magickal career.

The History of Magickal Illumination

In the process of making candles, it can be helpful to appreciate their evolution, both as sources of light and as tools of magick. Technically what makes a candle a true candle is a wick, but most credit the start of the candle, to our knowledge, with the Egyptians, who used the inside of reeds dipped in melted animal fat. The Egyptians began using true wicked candles by 3000 B.C.E. The simple lamps preceded them.

Many ancient civilizations used variations of the wicked candles with waxes from plants, animals, and insects. The Chinese used rice paper wicks and formed candles in paper tubes, filling the tubes with a wax from an insect and combining that wax with seeds. The Japanese used a seed wax in their early candles. The Romans created wicks from rolled papyrus dipped in beeswax, while those in India used the wax of the cinnamon fruit. Yak butter was the source of fat for candles in Tibet. Candles in all of these cultures played roles in religious ceremonies and household lighting.

The most popular ancient images we have of candles come from Jewish religious ceremonies, such as the candle lighting rites of Hanukkah, starting near 165 B.C.E. This Festival of Lights celebrates the miracle of the lamp oil that would only last for one day, lasting eight days until more oil could be made, and due to the time of the year, works with the general theme of light in a time of darkness near the Winter Solstice. The seven-branched menorah is used in the temple and usually uses oil for fuel. Jewish synagogues have a sanctuary light or lamp before their ark and, may or may not, have a seven-branched menorah. Since the seven-branched menorah can only be used in the Temple, the more modern Hanukkah candleholders are for nine candles, eight for the eight days of Hanukkah and a central candle as the "servant" to light the rest during the holiday. This nine-branched candelabrum can be used in homes or in public outside of a Jewish temple. Today, planetary-based ceremonial magicians will often use a form of the menorah for candles devoted to the seven planets, and in the case of nine branches, include either the Earth and the Stars, or the Zodiac and the Aethyr.

Figure: Menorah

The Lighting of Candles

Lamps and candles also played an important role in Christian worship services, being drawn from the Jewish, since there are several Biblical references to candles. Emperor Constantine used candles for Easter celebrations. Candles were gifts given during the Pagan Roman celebration of Saturnalia, one of the main sources of our modern-day Yuletide and Christmas celebrations.

Lamp oil was made from olives and was a primary source of illumination in homes and temples in much of Africa, the Middle East, and parts of Europe. The fall of the Roman Empire made the trade of olive oil more difficult, increasing the popularity of candles in Europe.

While there are many sources of wax, historically, in Western Christian civilization, candles were primarily made from tallow, which is simply animal fat. Animal fat burns smoky and can be unpleasant. Later, by the Middle Ages, beeswax candles became more popular, particularly religiously, in Europe. Beeswax burns cleanly and smells sweeter than tallow. Beeswax was much more expensive than tallow, and subsequently out of reach of most people for home use unless they were very rich. Tallow candles remained the candles for average households if they were to be used. The art of the chandler, or candle maker, grew, and by the 13th century, a guild formed in England and France. Candlemakers would collect the excess fat from households to make candles.

In America, the colonials learned the wax of the bayberry would burn with a sweet smell, yet it is not easy to extract bayberry wax. One must boil the gray-green berries to extract the oil. Today, bayberry candles are a lingering tradition to burn on Christmas Eve or New Year's, but they are not practical for every day candles.

Those involved with the whaling industry learned that spermaceti, a wax made from sperm whale oil, clearly burned in candles. Spermaceti burned bright and did not smell bad at all. It also remained quite hard, being a crystalized form of oil, and wouldn't soften or distort in the summer heat. Despite most people thinking whale fat was of European origin, whale fat candles can be found back in the Qin Dynasty, 206 B.C.E., in China.

With the advance of modern chemistry in the nineteenth century, stearic acid was applied to animal fat to extract stearin wax. Like spermaceti, stearin wax remained hard in the summer heat and burned clearly. The French chemist Eugene Chevreul was credited with the discovery.

The candle industry developed, changing from an artisan craft with a guild to mechanical mass production. This mass production made the cost of candles affordable to the general public. Further advances in chemistry led to the use of paraffin. Paraffin is a waxy substance that is a byproduct produced from the refinement of petroleum. The major disadvantage of paraffin was that it had a very low melting point which was later managed by mixing it with stearic acid.

The art of candle-making saw a decline with the invention of the electric light bulb in 1879. Candles have retained their uses as decoration and gifts, and of course, in occultism. More shapes, sizes, colors, and waxes became available in the 1980s and onward. Modern innovations include soybean wax and palm oil wax.

While that covers the orthodox candle history, there is the undercurrent of magickal practitioners in the development of candles, particularly in America. In the United States the availability of paraffin candles came after the Civil War. General stores all over the states carried them. In her book, *The Art of Hoodoo Candle Magic*, Catherine Yronwode gives a more extensive history of candles in Hoodoo specifically, noting that the folklorist Newbell Niles Puckett stated that candle magick originated in New

Orleans. New Orleans was and still is a rich melting pot of magick where the folk traditions of Voodoo, Roman Catholicism, and Spiritualism cross-pollinated. A variety of occultists and Witches have been added to the pot, and today quite a number of eclectic Neopagans studying folk magick and Voodoo reside in the city; thus the innovations will continue. Puckett believed the African American ritual practices mixed with the candle work of the Catholics started American candle magick as a form of folk practice. He wrote about the origins of candle magick in 1926, though it obviously must have started much earlier for a folklorist to then take notice of it as a common practice.

Legends of Incense, Herb, and Oil Magic by Lewis De Claremont, the first book addressing candle magick, was printed in 1936 and available nationally via mail order. It was distributed by Oracle Products Company, the first company to supply magickal oils and candles through mail-order, along with other Jewish religious goods.

Mikhail Strabo wrote a series of three small booklets particularly on candle work in Black Spiritualists churches found in New York City. They were entitled *A Candle to Light Your Way, How to Conduct a Candle Light Service*, and *The Guiding Light to Power and Success*, published during the years of 1941-1943.

Probably the most famous book cited by practitioners today, and still available in many stores, is *The Master Book of Candle Burning* by Henri Gamache in 1942. His work mixed a wide range of imagery, drawing from Creole and Hoodoo, African teachers by way of Jamaica, Jewish Kaballah, Christianity, and Spiritualism.

Dorothy Spencer, began writing occult books in the 1960s, under the pen name Anna Riva, and her books contained quite a bit of candle magick. She gathered information from Wicca, Witchcraft, Paganism, European Occultism, Grimoires, African

Folk magick, and Voodoo, often in a sensationalized form. Her *Candle Burning Magic* was quite popular, published in 1980. She created a line of oils, incenses, and other products in addition to her books. In the 1990s, her company was bought by Indio Products, and while they continue to keep her books in print and manufacture her products, many believe now the products are not entirely true to her original formulas.

Less well known than Anna Riva, but beating her publication by a year in 1979 was *The Magic Candle* by Charmine Dey. Dey mixed the products of a Hoodoo practitioner with a lot of traditional Western occult, Theosophical, Wiccan, and ceremonial symbolism and images, including planetary hours, Solomonic seals, and pentagrams. Both Riva and Dey opened the candle-burning world more to the general market and not just practitioners of African American folk magick, but to seekers of the occult in general, and here is where we start to have popular crossovers with today's forms of Witchcraft and Wicca.

In the oldest forms of modern Witchcraft and Wicca, candle magick is not what we know today. The advent of Hoodoo in America made colored candles and a variety of candle shapes available in ways they never were. Those who were trained in groups before the public revival talk about all the candles being white. When we look at available photos from Gardnerian and Alexandrian Wicca's first days, the taper candles seen upon the staged altars were almost always white. Sometimes a red candle would be used as well, but there were not a lot of other varieties and certainly not a lot of shapes. Color would be added from the glass, most often gotten from a Church supply shop or antique store in red or blue. Sometimes a fancier candle, spiraled and perhaps in a color, would be used for a dinner party setting, but on whole, white was used. Laurie Cabot recounted that her teacher used only white candles because that was all they had, and any writing or color went on paper placed beneath the candleholder.

Candles were not available because there were no metaphysical supply shops. Before the day of modern, clean and welcoming shops catering to every spiritual pursuit and culture, we had occult shops in the 1970s and '80s. Some still survive to this day. Some shops, known as botanicas for their botanical products of various herbs and oils, specifically serve the minority communities of the African diasporic traditions of Santeria and Vodou. Much of the product crossed over into some traditional Christian iconography – saint statues and medals, holy water, and prayer cards, so they mixed their business with serious practitioners and seekers. They have in-house practitioners to serve the clientele with custom work or offer professional shopping advice and divination services. In some cities, there was cross-over with the occult shops and the botanicas. Some places served all the esoteric community, and there would be a mix between those in Vodou, Santeria, Hoodoo, and Conjure with traditional Wiccans, Ceremonial Magicians, Satanists, and a wide variety of weird and wonderful folk practitioners with less famous and more personal systems. In these places, a lot of the iconography and techniques started to blend together, and through it, often Western magickal practitioners would seek out botanicas for speciality products if the occult shop or mail order catalog did not carry them. It can be hard to understand for today's practitioner, but much of this work was still very secret and passed word of mouth in person. You could meet and somewhat trust a person in such a shop as they were just as much in danger of being exposed as you.

From this time, Witches in the United States started to use seven-day jar and pull-out candles, carving them with their symbols and decorating them with oil, glitter, and paint. They learned new herbs not found in the traditional European lore and native to the America's, and mixed them with their own. The figure candles of Hoodoo made it into forms of Western magick. Incense and oil blends were traded. The books and products of Anna Riva, and those following in her footsteps, were now widely available. While they are still different traditions, the lines of demarcation were not as solid as they might seem now for some purists, for magick was magick. Granted, the flow was more from the folk traditions to the Western European practices, though previously Hoodoo and Rootwork absorbed a lot from some of the grimoire traditions and some of the basic techniques, such as poppets, have a root in European folk magick as well.

Notable Wiccan author and High Priest, Raymond Buckland, who brought the Gardnerian Tradition to the United States, released *Practical Candleburning Rituals* in 1970. It incorporated a lot of what was going on in American Witchcraft and occult scene at the time. It was followed by *Advanced Candle Magick* in 1996. *Buckland's Complete Book of Witchcraft* was a staple for self-taught Witches, and he later went on to form a more liberal tradition of Wicca known as Seax Wicca. Buckland divided the same rituals into Old Religion Rituals format for Pagans and Witches, and Christian Religion Rituals for Christians seeking magick but not wanting to invoke anything non-Christian, basically repeating the same candle spells in two different styles. From this point, colored candles and a variety of candle spell techniques became ubiquitous in Wicca and Witchcraft across the United States and soon the world.

Author and Hoodoo worker Ray T. Malbrough was an associate of Raymond Buckland, graduating from his Seax Wicca Seminary in 1982. He went onto write *Charms, Spells, and Formulas* in 1986 and *The Magical Power of the Saints: Evocation* and *Candle Rituals* in 1998. Due to his publishing with Llewellyn Publications and his associations with Raymond Buckland, his books were popular among American Wiccans and Witches, and more Hoodoo techniques found their way into what was once a primarily European craft. American magick continued to grow and expand in its identity and popularity.

One of the most successful and well-known of the Witch shops, crossing lines and practices with the local botanica, is Enchantments in the East Village of New York City. In 1982, Lady Rhea and Carol Bulzone, both initiated Witches, created a shop for local occultists, Witches seeking supplies, and those simply looking to get a candle carved and set, a magickal oil, or a special spell kit. Rhea's work with carved pull-out candles at Enchantments was well received, and she wrote *The Enchanted Candle* in 2004, documenting her spells and candle carving designs. While Enchantments has new owners, Lady Rhea continues her tradition of candle magick.

Enchantments carried on the traditions of The Warlock Shop, which later moved and became The Magickal Childe, a shop founded by Herman Slater and Eddy Buczynski, which also became a center of the Wiccan and Neopagan community and general occultism, and seemed to encourage the crossing and blending with African Folk traditions. Slater wrote the *Hoodoo Bible*.

The Candle Magick Workbook by Kala & Ketz Pajeon became a classic for modern occultists mixing old and new ways, including the three selves (souls), occult principles, and Eastern concepts of karma. Though drawing its candle magick most likely from the styles represented by Ana Riva and Charmine Dey, it was firmly rooted in an occult and somewhat New Age theology, yet retained all the old charm. Published in 1991 and available through the bigger chain book stores, it became the candle burning "bible" for the next generation of practitioners, myself included.

Since then, there continues to be a cross-over between magickal traditions, particularly in America, and those traditions have also been exported back to Europe. As the New Age metaphysical movement has grown and eclipsed the occult stores of yesteryear, we find a wider variety of candles and magickal products everywhere. Products and traditions from India, Japan, and China make their way into our practices. Teachings from Central and South America, in harmony with a lot of what was already going on at botanicas, continue to spread across the country where there is strong Latin population, often mixing Latin and African traditions. Mexican folk traditions come up from border towns and enter into esoterica circles. Techniques are widely shared and traded among practitioners, and as new innovations in light, lamps, and candles grow, they will continue to be shared and cross-pollinate.

Candle Crafting

Candle-making processes range from the simple to the complex, and the time, money, and effort they take range accordingly. It all depends on what you want to do to make an effective magickal candle. Some prefer lots of professional or semiprofessional equipment. Others want to do it with the tools of their kitchen, and luckily, both options are available to you.

While candle-making is an art in itself that goes way beyond the scope of one chapter in a book, these basic techniques can get you started if you want to explore the art of the chandler.

✦ **Rolled Beeswax Candles** – The simplest way to make your own candles is to purchase flat sheets of beeswax made for this purpose. Kits from hobby and craft stores come with a wick, and you simply lay the wick down and roll the sheet around the wick and instantly you have a taper. The advantage of this type of candle-making is that you can very easily put oils or herbs on the sheet as you roll to customize your candle. The instructions below for melting and pouring wax don't apply to this type of candle-making, so if it intimidates you, start with rolled sheets of beeswax.

✦ **Jar Candles** – Jar candles are some of the easiest to make as they require no molds or dipping. The melted wax is poured into a jar with a prepared wick and burned in the jar. The basic instructions below work best for this type of candle.

✦ **Molded Candles** – Molded candles are like jar candles, but the jar is a specially prepared candle mold that can be opened, and the candle popped out to be free-standing. They are a little more complex than the simple jar candles, but once you understand the basics, they only have a few extra steps. Most commercial pillar, votive, and taper candles are cast from molds, though on a mass production scale.

✦ **Hand-dipped Candles** – Hand-dipped candles are the most artfully created, usually resulting in lovingly made tapers of various lengths, but go beyond what we can explain in this candle magick book and beyond my own experience and interest in magickal candle-making.

One can consider tea lights to be a form of "jar" candle but the jar is a metal tin rather than a glass jar, yet due to the flexibility of the metal, then can easily be popped out as if the metal was a simple, cheap mold.

To create basic candles of the jar or mold type, you need:

Wax
Wicks
Essential Oils
Wax Color
Double Boiler
Jar Container or Molds
Spatula
Oven Gloves
Thermometer
Scissors for Trimming Wicks
Old Pens/Pencils
Drop cloth, Towels or Newspaper to Cover Surface

First, you need to decide on your source of candle wax. The raw waxes most easily available for the amateur candlemaker are paraffin, soy, and beeswax. For beginning candlemakers, I often suggest paraffin. It's cheap to purchase, and easy to add color and scent. Many Witches and magicians dislike paraffin as it is a petroleum product. When you are learning what to do, it can be a more forgiving medium. If you made mistakes in the candle-making process, you can simply remelt the wax.

Beeswax is the way to go for all-natural candles and a favorite for Witches, but with the threats to bees today, it is not always the cheapest, and many feel any bee products should not be wasted. Beeswax has a natural golden color that can make adding color difficult. Likewise, it can be difficult to add scent due to its natural sweet smell. Beeswax, out of all of the available options, is both the most magickal in terms of history and the most expensive. Soy wax is natural, but sometimes has other waxes blended into it, including paraffin; just make sure to read your labels carefully.

If you have the option to purchase your wax in small pellet form, I encourage you to do so. Big blocks of wax will have to be cut up into small pieces with a sharp knife, and it's not as easy as that sounds. Blocks of solid wax can be quite hard.

Wicks are the next main component of a candle. Wick sizes are the width of the wick. Larger wicks are better for jar candles and smaller wicks for tapers. If the diameter of the candle is less than an inch, go for a smaller wick, if it's two inches, a medium wick would work nicely and, three inches or more, use a large wick. Some wicks are pre-trimmed for the type of candle you'll be making, such as a votive size, and a few have pre-fastened ends to sink the wick in the wax.

The essential oils to scent a candle are not always necessary. You'll have to decide if you are making a candle from the start for a specific intention, such as love, money, or healing. You don't necessarily have to set the candle in its creation process for a specific person, but the overall intention of the magick. Many would suggest just keeping them scentless and based upon color to be used for any purpose. The candle can then be dressed with appropriate oils and potions when consecrating for a specific magickal working. Many would argue the specially formulated fragrance oils for candle-making are superior in scent and strength to essential oils, but if you are doing magick and you are adding scent, I think the connection to the living plant is important. Along with scent, some will add chips of crystals or sprinklings of dried herbs to the mix.

Candle-making suppliers also have tablets of color dye that can be added to wax to color it. Paraffin, being white, tends to color best. Some have home tricks such as adding crayons, colored ink, and food dye, but I've found the dye manufactured for candles works best in a home setting.

A simple double boiler is necessary to melt the wax. Direct flame to wax will not work in the candle-making process. While you can use a true double boiler; you can also use a heat-resistant Pyrex measuring cup in a stove pot partially filled with water. As the water heats, the wax in the Pyrex measuring cup will melt quite nicely. There are also forms of "universal" double boiler attachments that can sit on top of a saucepan or pot.

Figure: Double Boiler Melting Wax

For a container, I suggest starting with glass container candles. Smaller glass votives are ideal and then moving on to the taller seven-day style glass candles. If things go well for you, you can work with candle molds that allow free-standing candles to pop out and then try your hand at tapers. Glass contained candles are quite effective as magickal tools. Small, cheap, heat-resistant glass works best. You can even save containers from previously purchased candles and reuse them.

Start by setting up your work area, covering the surfaces with newspaper, towels, or any other cloth you don't mind getting wax on. I would suggest wearing clothes that you don't mind getting wax on either, as until you get pretty proficient with it, wax can splatter in the most inopportune ways. Have all your tools and materials easily accessible.

First, melt the wax into a pourable liquid. Place the wax in the double boiler with water in the bottom pan, surrounding the inner container. I would start with enough for a few candles, depending on your container size, before working with larger amounts of wax. If working with wax pellets, fill your container with solid pellets and add a little more to account for the volume in between, and use that as a measurement for all the containers you wish to fill on the first round. Gently heat the water until it's brought up to melting temperature. You can use a thermometer and aim for a temperature of 160 to 170 degrees Fahrenheit. If it gets higher, or the wax smells like it is burning, reduce the heat.

Next, place the wick in the container, to prepare the container while the wax is melting. You can also do this before you begin if you like to watch the wax melt. Usually, people adhere the wick's end to the bottom of the container. Some wicks have a built-in sticker, but most are just simple wick threads. Some use glue. A traditional technique is to dip the end in wax and use the wax to adhere it to the bottom of the container. It's not that hard if you move quickly. For larger containers, particularly if there is no metal end to the wick, a small weight, like a metal washer, can be used. Try to center the wick as much as you can. Learning to center is the real challenge of this step. Once the wax or glue hardens, it will be set.

Figure: Adhering Wick Before Wax Pour

If you are adding color or scent to the wax, now is the time to do it. Some waxes will tell you the temperature to get the wax to before adding scent or color. For this, use your thermometer to measure the wax temperature. Some are a little more intuitive, and add the color when the wax melts, and add the scent just near the end, before pouring, to not have the heat burn off the delicate chemicals in the essential oil. Add color until the melted wax is a bit darker than what you wish the dry solid color to be, as wax will harden and cool to a slightly lighter color. While personal preference, the type of wax, and the type of oil, as some scents are stronger and last longer than others, the general rule of thumb

The Lighting of Candles

when working with essentials oils is ½ oz of pure scented oil, essential or fragrance, to ten ounces of wax.

Figure: Adding Color and Scent

Now it is time to pour the wax. Turn off the heat and let it cool for just a few minutes, yet not so long that it gets hard. More experienced candlemakers than I will say the optimal pouring temperature is between 130-140 degrees Fahrenheit. Hotter does not actually make it better and can create more divots in the surface when it cools. That was a problem with my early candles, as the wax would sink around the wick. Once it's cooled, pour it into the container, keeping the wick in the center as much as possible. Don't pull hard on the wick, or it will disconnect from the bottom. Just hold and guide it. The hot wax can disconnect the wax or glue used to adhere, but as long as it's in the right place, it doesn't matter too much. Leave some wax in the container, as you'll top off the candles again to fill in any sinkholes around the wick or other divots that appear in the surface as it cools and contracts.

Figure: Pouring Wax

Take two pencils or pens, and lay them parallel to each other over the opening of the container, with the wick in between, and bring them together to keep the wick in the center of the container. Or use one pencil with the wick firmly wrapped around it prior to pouring the wax, as shown in the figures.

Figure: Pencils Surrounding Wick

As the wax cools, take some of the remaining wax and "top off" the container to fill the spaces now that the wick is secure. If it's taken too long, you might have to reheat the wax, which is okay. Some who like really strong initial scents might add a few more drops of essential oil at the top. Add enough to create a new "surface" to the top of the wax, so it will be even. Don't add too much, as you can just create another sinkhole if the top layer is too thick.

Figure: Trimming the Wick

The last step in creating your candle, besides clean-up, is trimming your wick. Traditionally wicks are about ¼" from the surface to get the best burn. Once the candle is cool and hard, trim the wick. Most modern wicks are "self-trimming" as they burn, but some are not, so you might find, particularly with homemade candles, that you have to trim them more between lightings if you snuff them.

If you can, wipe melted wax up while it's liquid with a paper towel, which is the easiest clean up. You don't want to rinse wax down the drain as it will clog your pipes and destroy garbage disposal units or dish washers. If you can dispose of the paper towels and rags, let the wax harden, pick or scrape off the hardened wax, and place it into the solid waste container. Some people save waste wax for future candles, but if I've "fought" with wax to clean it up, I don't like that kind of energy in my magickal candles.

The Lighting of Candles

While I have focused this section on the mechanics of making the candles, to keep a complex process as simple as possible, you can also ritualize the process. Create sacred space in your kitchen or workspace. Call upon the elements and the deities. Make invocations to the power of light and magick at each step. Cleanse all items ritually in purifying smoke and charge them in general for future clear, good magick. When done, thank and release all the powers.

CHAPTER TEN:
KEEPERS OF THE INNER LIGHT

Light is the fundamental mechanism behind our candle and fire magick, but there is a reason why it is considered a universal symbol of divinity. The image of light as consciousness is timeless. Temples all around the world use lit candles, lamps, and controlled flames to both illuminate and remind us of divinity. Earlier traditions, and still in tribal and neopagan traditions, we have the sacred campfire. These could all be attempts to bring down to our level the essence of the first divine lights and fires – the stars, Sun, and Moon. Light is one of our oldest experiences of divinity. Imagine the power of light to those with no control over fire yet, living by the rise and fall of these celestial powers. They grant life, death, and protection by their virtue or lack thereof.

Almost as old as the idea of divine light is the concept that humanity has an inner light. Our consciousness, expressed in various terms such as the soul, spirit, atman, or astral (star) body implies light. To the alchemists, the three parts of the self are sulfur, mercury, and salt. Sulfur is the stone that burns, while both mercury and crystalline salt reflect light. We refer to the process of spiritual empowerment and self-realization as "en-light-enment," meaning becoming full of light. Saints are said to ascend into the light body. They are described, East and West, as "illuminated," with halos and shining auras visible to the naked eye. Darkness is equated with a lack of consciousness, as in the dark, we cannot see. While darkness holds its own wisdom, this rationale makes sense. With light, we have guidance and some safety.

We find inspiration in our spiritual traditions and philosophies regarding light. Popular among many, but attributed most often to Gautama Siddhartha, or better known as the historical Buddha, is:

There isn't enough darkness in all the world to snuff out the light of one little candle.

Another very popular one paraphrased by many, but usually attributed to 20th Century Catholic priest and television personality, James Keller.

A candle loses nothing by lighting another candle.

Both demonstrate the absolute hope that is conveyed by the light of the candle. Darkness is intangible. While there is the holy darkness of the womb, the deep Earth, and the places of mystery, here darkness is a metaphor for the lack of consciousness. Even in the deep places of holy darkness, we must bear our own torch. This shows us that the darkness is nothing to fear, as it cannot take action against us. We can respond to it. Darkness will not snuff the light by itself. In a world where many people believe, Witches and magicians included, that power shared is power lost, this second bit of wisdom shows us how powerful we are when we do share our light with others and receive light in times of need from those willing to share with us.

The Light-Bearers

Some of the seemingly darkest, scariest gods of the ancient world, associated with mystery and sometimes even evil, are deities of light. Hecate, the dark mother of Witches, appearing as both maiden and crone and associated with crossroads, ghosts, and priestesses who poison and murder, is in truth, a goddess of light obscured by misunderstandings. One of her titles is Hecate

The Lighting of Candles

Phosphorus, Hecate illuminated with light. Her primary symbol is the torch, as she carries a torch as a psychopomp, a guide leading the spirits in and out of the underworld through the process of death and birth. She leads the goddess Persephone into and out of the realm of Hades in her seasonal journey, being her handmaiden. Traditionally she has been a goddess of birth and life as much as one of death and darkness. Her knife can cut the cord of life, but also the umbilical cord, granting our first freedom in the world of the incarnate.

Another popular yet scary ancient title is Lucifer or Lucifera. Usually, the name is equated with the source of evil in Christian traditions, the Devil. Yet both history and etymology show another side to the Roman name. Often considered a title, it was first associated with the "star of Venus," usually at dawn, for Venus' rise often preceded the sunrise. As a planet orbiting close to the Sun, inside Earth's own orbit, Venus always has to be somewhere close to the Sun from our perception on Earth. The idea of light in darkness also became associated with the Moon.

As Hecate was considered a triple goddess with three different Goddess "selves," one aspect of Hecate is the moon goddess. Known as Diana to the Romans, she was sometimes called Diana Lucifera, or Diana, the Bringer of the Light. In *The Gospel of Aradia,* an Italian Witchcraft document, the goddess Diana, queen of the faeries and the Moon, mates with her brother, Lucifer, or Lucifero. Lucifer is a Roman god of light associated with the star of Venus and had nothing to do with Jewish or Christian lore until a misunderstanding regarding his title. The name Lucifer is not "adversary" even though it is equated with Satan, which does mean adversary or prosecutor. It means light-bearer, and many traditions that are in opposition to the status quo of mindlessness can be considered Luciferian. Another adjective with similar intent but less scary for some is Promethean, referring to the Titan Prometheus who steals the fire of the gods, their very light, from Olympus and shares it with humans. It's a story of both the technology of fire, starting a new level of civilization, but also the fires of free thinking, or personal illumination, or direct gnosis.

Figure: Diana

Light is also associated with the liberating gods, the savior figures like Mithras, Christ, and even some similarities to the Norse Balder. Their original intent is to illuminate. Christ was later co-opted by a massive hierarchy of the early Christian church, but his true stories have nothing to do with worldly hierarchy, but personal freedom and liberation. Ironically, Hecate was also considered a personal savior of sorts, a soteira as the Queen of

The Lighting of Candles

Heaven and Cosmic World Soul. Many of her titles and epitaphs got equated with both Jesus Christ and Mother Mary

Light is something we bear in the darkness, by our very nature as conscious beings. Not necessarily a gift from the gods, but something gained, or perhaps stolen and liberated from the more controlling deities and institutions. All humans seek the light in some way and carry this illumination. Our subtle anatomy, our chakras, meridians, and aura, are described in terms of colors of light. Many say our true nature is a luminous body, the body of light. Some New Age traditions have been describing our "evolutionary leap" of consciousness in this new aeon with the term *Homo luminous* rather than *Homo sapiens*, as popularized in the work of modern Peruvian shamanic practitioner and author Alberto Villoldo. We make the light body stronger with our spiritual work and actions, a vessel worthy to carry our consciousness towards enlightenment and understanding.

When we work with fire, with candles and lamps, we are reminded of the inner light we carry. That is the true source of magick. From that light, we shine and manifest our true purpose in the world. Candle magick is but a catalyst on a greater magickal journey.

LVX

LVX is both Latin and a ritual spelling for light, referring in ritual to the divine light of creation. Pronounced lux, as in Latin, "U" is written as a "V." Fiat Lux refers to the Christian creation of the Lord, saying "let there be light" to create the world. While it refers to actual visible light, it is referring ideally to the spiritual principle of light and its role in creation.

In Qabalistic mysticism and magick, creation begins with the "Three Negative Veils of Existence," which are Ain, Ain Soph, and

Ain Soph Aur, usually translated as either Nothing, Limitless Nothing, and Limitless Light; or Light, Limitless Light, and Limitless Light in Extension. The first step of creation, Kether, what we perceive as the godhead and source actually comes after these three veils of negative light. Negative here should not be equated with evil or harm, but the absence or paradox of creation before there is comprehensible creation. Some equate the veils with the true void, or the ground of being, the limitless potential of creation before creation was brought into being.

Modern ceremonial magicians equate LVX as a ritual formula in their planetary hexagram rituals, embodying the magical formula of life-death-rebirth. L stands for Isis, specifically Isis mourning, the wife-sister goddess of the god Osiris, who is slain by his brother Set. V stands for Apophis Triumphant, the god of death and destruction. In this formula, Apophis is equated with Set, as both are manifestations of death and chaos. While it's tempting to think of them as evil, they are also the destruction that is necessary in the creation cycle. If all things lived, rampant life would be synonymous with cancer. Death is needed to break down and make space for new life, and continue the cycles of creation. X represents Osiris Risen, like a mummy with arms, crossed-over the chest in an "X." Osiris is regenerated nature, reborn as a god of life and death. The life of the goddess Isis and the death in the god Apophis is synthesized into the mystery of the ages in Osiris. Parallels are found in all sorts of death and rebirth gods. Ceremonial magicians say the Age of Osiris is ending, but culminated in the teachings and stories of Jesus Christ, who has some obvious parallels to other death and resurrection gods like Osiris, Tammuz, Adonis, Dionysus, and Balder. Ritual motions and evocations of LVX are done as part of a series of complex rituals

The Lighting of Candles

known as hexagram rituals, also using the gnostic chant of IAO, understood in the modern age as Isis–Apophis–Osiris.

So as you can see, LVX or Light, has a huge spiritual role in the powers of creation, divinity, and the sustainment of our world. We equate light with the fifth element of spirit in its primal radiance. When that light manifests as flame, we see it as a part of the world, as part of the four elements, though it's the most nebulous of the four elements. Fire as the embodiment of an elemental energy is not a "thing" but a process. You can't hold fire as you can hold a stone, cup water in your hands, or even hold your breath. You can hold what is burning, but you can't hold burning itself.

The four elements are embodied, according to magicians, in four special "L" words. Earth is law, for the structure of the material universe. Water is love, for love is the highest form of flowing emotion. Air is life, for the breath grants life. And fire is light. The light of elemental fire embodies our will, and gets to the core of magick. Magick is the art and science of expressing your will. Magicians distinguish your desires and wants from your True Will. In Greek, Will is referred to as Thelema, and that is the name magician Aleister Crowley used for his own tradition, focused upon True Will. While we all need all elements in balance to live our lives, magicians and Witches are particularly concerned about will, so fire plays a strong role in their lives.

Some think of True Will as destiny, and I have a hard time with that idea, as many people assume terms like destiny and fate mean things are automatically going to happen, with no effort on their part. I disagree when it comes to True Will. There is great effort expended to learn your True Will, but once you are in tune with it, regardless of the effort, there is nothing else you can do. But it's a process of purifying and self-illumination to understand what our

True Will is, and the challenge to express it in every moment. That is the work of a magickal adept.

The Light Within

A teaching found in magickal traditions across the world is the concept of the three-part soul. Not a popular teaching among the masses who have been indoctrinated on the one body, one soul and one life paradigm prevalent in the West. Nevertheless, it speaks to our understanding of inner light not just from the luminous body of light but in our core identity. Previously we referenced it as the three essential substances of the alchemists: sulfur, mercury and salt. Sulfur can burn, rather noxiously despite being a mineral, and liquid mercury and solid salt can both reflect light. Like the four elements of the ancients, these three substances are also symbolic, embodying deeper principles unseen by most. In early Christianity they could be called soul, spirit, and body. Various traditions have different names for them. They could also be called energy, information and structure, or the part of us that is unique, the part of us that is universal, and the part of us that is the matrix holding the two together. In the most simple language, they are often referred to as the higher self, the lower self, and the middle self, though some disagree on those names in reference to which of the alchemical terms apply to which self. Personally, I believe our understanding of the three selves changes as we evolve and initiate deeper into the mysteries.

One of the irreverent images of these three selves used in my tradition of Witchcraft harkens back to the excommunication rites of the Catholic Church. The three souls are named for the bell, book and candle, popularized by movies and television. When removing someone from the body of the Church, a Bishop would ring a bell twelve times, for the death of the individual spiritually to the Church, close the holy book to mark the separation between the individual and the Church, and extinguish a candle, extinguishing the soul from the light of the Christian god.

The middle self, also called the Namer in our Temple tradition, is like the book. It collects information and ideas, cataloguing details, thoughts and judgements. While it might seem counter-intuitive, we associate it with the salt. Think of the salt as like the material human part of you, and like the quartz in a piece of electronics keeps it running, and devices can record information; this part of us can record what happens to us.

The lower self, the Shaper, is the bell. It resonates. It is emotional. It is musical and artistic. It responds immediately and instinctively, like we respond with attention to the ringing of a bell. The lower self relates to the mercury, as it's the same primal response, the same basic informational pattern, in each of us. It's universal.

The higher self, the Watcher, is like the candle. It radiates light by which it watches and we associate it with the sulfur. It is generally silent until personally engaged, and offers the opportunity to illuminate when used properly. The aware higher self is like the halo of light around the head. Again, the image of the candle flame takes such importance in our spiritual development, but it's important to realize that one cannot reach the light of the higher self without being in tune with the lower and middle selves in harmony and balance.

While the three selves are equated with salt, mercury, and sulfur in other traditions and models, they are all flames and, when in harmony, are conjoined as a triple flame or a three-colored flame in the heart. I was first exposed to this teaching in a more Theosophically-influenced New Age tradition. The triple flame of the heart was aligned with the deep concepts of love, will, and wisdom. This was really about holding unconditional love; what modern Witches call Perfect Love, and others might call Agape; the True Will of the magicians, and the Deep Wisdom, the true Sophia. I was then exposed to a similar triple heart and triple soul flame meditation in the work of author and faery seer Orion Foxwood.

Exercise: Triple Flame Alignment

Stand up. Center yourself with your feet flat on the floor. Breathe deeply in. Hold your breath for a moment. Exhale out deeply. Repeat for a total of three deep breaths. Imagine that at your heart level, both sternum and the center of your back, is an opening like a mouth that will inhale and exhale from the chest. Likewise, imagine similar openings at the soles of your feet and at the top of your head.

Breathe in, and breathe in through the heart space. Think of the middle self, the personal self who is walking in this world, the person you identify. Think of the wisdom you wish to activate in this self. Breathe from the heart space one to three breaths until you feel the heart area energized with life force forming a little flame, colored yellow or gold.

Breathe in, and breathe in from the soles of your feet. Reflect on the lower self, the primal self who is connected to the ancestors and animals instinctually. Think of the love connecting all of nature and activate that love within you. Breathe up from the feet into the body and up to the heart, one to three breaths, or until you feel this energy take on the form of a blue flame in the heart.

Breathe in, and breathe in from the crown of your head. Reflect on the higher self, the divine spark, as if you are drawing more of that divinity down into your body. Think of the will, the sense of true purpose this higher self has, and seek to activate that will within you. Breathe this energy down into the heart for one to

The Lighting of Candles

three breaths, or until you feel this energy take the form of a red flame in the heart.

Breathe through all three centers together and fill the heart. You might find the red and yellow flames transpose, and the three merge into one tricolored flame with blue on the bottom, red in the middle and yellow on the top. As you exhale, you radiate out light like a star from the heart in all directions. The light fills all the cells of your body and radiates through your pores. It fills your entire aura and shines past your personal space out into the universe. Continue breathing until you stabilize this alignment.

In the Temple of Witchcraft, we have a prayer we recite internally to kindle the flame in the alignment of the three selves:

I am the Namer
I am the Shaper
I am the Watcher
The three in one
The one in three
As it was, as it is, as it always shall be.

The Inner Flame

One of the deeper mysteries of the magician is the alignment between the inner world spiritual work and the outer world ritual. You start to perceive how you are working on both planes at the same time, even when doing something as seemingly small as lighting a candle, which we now understand can have a huge effect in our life. Your words, gestures, and actions reverberate on all planes. They always have, but now you are becoming conscious of it, and that conscious awareness brings both a new level of power and a deeper spiritual dimension to all that you do. The simple act of moving a stick or rock can change things on the inner world, even if they have no discernible difference in our human world.

They can change the reality of the spiritual beings that reside in other realms and dimensions adjacent to ours, so we need to be as consciously united with our actions as possible when growing as magicians. By uniting the act of operative magick with our inner forces, our actions can bring vital and long-lasting changes.

One ritual action that is quite powerful is to use our aligned flame within the heart to mediate the physical flame of our magickal candles. When doing any magickal work, even just lighting a candle to meditate, first align the three flames within your heart and focus on your love, will, and wisdom. When you hold the match, lighter, or taper candle in your hand, envision and intend the light of your heart flowing down your arm and filling the vessel. The flame struck is also home to part of the flame of your heart. As in the wisdom of James Keller, you have shared your candle flame, but nothing within you has been diminished. When you light the candle, know that you are sharing a bit of your inner light, and that flame before you is burning on the inner planes as well as the outer physical world of observation.

Temple Keepers

The process of keeping that inner light going strong can be helped by tending to an outer flame. This flame isn't to fulfill our needs, hopes, and desires, as with our candle spells in the previous chapters, though they are important, have no doubt. Like following the steps in the pyramid of Maslow's Hierarchy of Needs, rooted in the indigenous wisdom of the Blackfoot Nation, we often require our basic needs and wants met before we start the work of self-actualization and true purpose. That's why many magickal traditions, rather than focus on renunciation of the world to focus on spiritual matters, build themselves up with practical spiritual practices. We learn more about how to be in the world, doing magick for health, protection, prosperity, and relationships. With an understanding of the connective force between all things, we can then direct our attention to less tangible things.

I am trained in a temple tradition of Witchcraft, meaning we look to rural cunning ones and folk healers, as well as to the Pagan Priestesses and Priests of the ancient world's temples as our spiritual ancestors. In such practices, the idea of keeping a sacred fire is continued from our spiritual ancestors.

While figures such as Hecate, Prometheus, and Lucifer did not have popular temple traditions, Hecate's devotees most often gathered in the crossroads. She actually did have a temple we know of in Turkey. We find flame keepers in the ancient world in the cults of the Greek Hestia and Roman Vesta. Hestia had both a private form of worship and a public form of worship. Her officially recognized sanctuary was in the community hearth, which held the community's sacred fire. This hearth was called the Prytaneum. The fire of the Prytaneum was the living embodiment of the community blessing, vitality, and unity. Such fire hearths were found at all levels of community, state, city, and village. The flame was tended by the Prytanis, the chief or ruler of the community, along with his family, and they often made their residence in or near the Prytaneum. While a sanctuary to Hestia as the goddess of hearth and home, and the Prytaneum being the hearth of the community, it became the center of activity for the rulers and politicians. It was the home for all. Many important public actions and rituals were taken at the hearth, including the entertaining of foreign guests and diplomats. When a new colony was founded, a flame from the public hearth of the mother community would be carried into the newly established settlement to kindle the flame in the Prytaneum of the new community. At times, community flames would be doused and relit in rituals of purification and rekindling.

Vesta held a similar role in Roman society, and her worship and veneration led to the popular order of full-time priestesses known as the Vestal Virgins. The flame of Vesta was considered paramount to the continuation, success and security of Rome, so they maintained one of the few full-time Roman priesthoods, dedicating themselves to tending this eternal flame.

In private, each home, each hearth within the home, was a sanctuary to the household goddess of Hestia or Vesta. She cared not only for the community of rulers and politicians looking over everyone, but she could be found in the home where the family kept warm, made food, and gathered together. Hestia/Vesta worship in Greece and Rome was a part of the household aspect of religion. Unlike religion for many of us today, religious practice was not reserved for the temples on holy days, but found in everyday actions. The first offering of every meal was made to Hestia. Usually, the first and last offerings of wine libations at any feast were made to her. While she was attended to by the family, the lady of the household was her primary caretaker.

The Celtic Brid holds a similar role as fire tender. As a goddess of healing through the sacred power of wells, poetic inspiration, and smith-craft, she held a similar role in the Irish Celtic society, and her worship has been reinvigorated by modern Pagans and Witches today. Bridget's feast day, absorbed into the Neopagan Wheel of the Year, Imbolc, is a festival about returning light, celebrated with candles. She was so beloved by the Irish people that Christianity syncretized her with the Christian saint Bridget, absorbing her attributes and stories into one figure, creating whom we know today as St. Bridget of Kildare, Ireland. In Kildare, a sacred flame was maintained perpetually by nineteen nuns. This

The Lighting of Candles

has been compared to the tradition of the Roman Vestal Virgins and appears to be a continuation of an ancient Indo-European tradition.

Likewise, the Irish Celts had a similar tradition of ritually dousing their hearth fires, usually on the "new year" of Samhain, or today celebrated as Halloween. The community, or king's fire, would be ceremonially relit and then shared with each household, passing the flame to relight the hearth flames.

Today with modern ovens and electric stoves, we don't understand the constant tending of the hearth fire and the importance of keeping the fire going in the household for comfort, food, and warmth. Our convenience disconnects us from the vitality of the living flame in the home and the central role of the household goddess.

Indigenous people in many lands keep their own hearth traditions alive. I am particularly struck by the teachings of the Mayans, who keep their heart as a central part of the home and community. In the teachings of healer Beatrice Torres Waight, it's called a heart flame. Traditionally the Mayan hearth has a triangle of three stones in the center of it. In their cosmology, the cosmic hearth is where the World Tree rose. In a past age, the "people of wood" were destroyed by flood and their hearthstones were scattered. To reorder the world, the hearthstones had to be restored. The three stars in Orion's belt are often equated with the three hearthstones. Though others say, since it's a "triangle" that the three stars in Orion that are the hearthstones are the lower left belt star Alnitak, along with Rigel and Saiph below. The Orion Nebula is the fire and smoke of the cosmic hearth. Placing the hearthstones in the home "orders" the home in accordance with the universe. Modern New Age interpretations talk about how the simple triangle, and the three-dimensional Platonic solid, the tetrahedron, are the basic alchemical symbols of fire.

You can find the concept of the fire temple again in the complex development of Zoroastrian traditions. The Zoroastrians honor three "grades" of fire, referring to their consecration and ritual purity. The image of the fire itself is the divinity, rather than anthropomorphized images of deity. Large temples are built to hold and maintain the Zoroastrian fires to this day. Despite being a lesser-known religion in comparison to the mainstream traditions, these fire temples are still alive.

And, of course, the mainstream religions also have their sanctuary lights. Jewish synagogues have the Ner Tamid, the eternal light or eternal flame of the temple. It hangs over the ark in the temple. In the Jewish faith, it's a symbol of God's eternal presence in the temple, the community, and in the members' individual lives. Traditionally it is an oil lamp associated with both the menorah and an incense altar burning before the ark. Modern temples use gas or an electric bulb. Some are even solar-powered.

In a similar fashion, Christian churches also keep an altar or sanctuary lamp. While candles might abound in a service, at least one lamp, oil or wax, is left burning before the tabernacle as a sign of the presence of Christ. The lamp is referred to as a chancel lamp when the consecrated sacramental wafers are present in the tabernacle. Various traditions of the lamp are found in Roman Catholic, Eastern Orthodox, Anglican, Lutheran, and Methodist churches. Other Christian traditions without the same rites of Holy Communion will still have a lamp. The lamp is often colored red, but not required to be, to simply distinguish it from the white votives in the church. Like the Ner Tamid, it may be suspended by a chain over the tabernacle, but can also appear on a stand, affixed to the wall or on a ledge beside the tabernacle. Candles and oil lamps are preferred over modern sources of light.

While we might not be temple fire keepers in the Zoroastrian temple or any other worldwide tradition, and are seemingly disconnected from the hearth-fire cults of the Indo-Europeans with our modern kitchens, we can reclaim these traditions in our homes on a deep and personal level, even if the hearth fire is not the main focus of our lives and homes. Magick should teach us one does not need to be a renunciate of the world, a cloistered clergy member to maintain a home temple. To the ancients, every home was a sacred space, and we should reclaim that concept. Even in a sacred home, there might be a particular place for meditation, prayer, and ritual. From this space, whether it's the kitchen stove, bedroom nightstand, the family room hearth, or the intricate working altar of a magician, we can keep the light.

One of the traditions among modern Witches, Magicians, and other magickal priestesses and priests is the tending of a sacred flame, as we do hearken to these deities who are bearers of light on all levels. Many of us keep a consecrated candle flame going on our home altars whenever we are in residence. For many years my mother and I tended a home temple where a white seven-day jar candle would be tended to first thing in the morning. When everyone was leaving the home it would be ritually snuffed with a blessing, and when one of us returned, it would be relit. We tended not to keep it going all night, but would again snuff it when the last person at home went to bed. It was our focus for meditation and ritual, and all flames on our altar were lit from it as a Master Candle. This central pillar was the candle of the Great Spirit, and we held it in an iron cauldron in the center of the altar. This light kept a cycle of blessing and illumination in our corner of the world, benefiting not only our own lives and home, but, we believe, many others all around us. The effects of sacred work in temples resonates outward into their environment and communities.

If you belong to a specific tradition, people in the tradition might keep a consecrated flame perpetually burning in a physical shrine or temple. I know a Druid tradition that does, and our own Temple of Witchcraft maintains a similar seven-day candle in a metal lantern, in our main hearth shrine. The candle is dressed with our consecration oil blend and shared with initiates of our first degree, to light their own altar candles. The light was drawn from our inner vision temple and physically lit with a candle from a Kildare Bridget flame. When the flame cannot be continuously passed from old flame to new, usually due to travel concerns with the keepers of the flame, a vision of it is kept in the tradition's inner temple, and a new flame is lit from a blessed taper candle holding the spirit of the flame. At Samhain, it is ritually snuffed and relit. The intention is to illuminate the members of our temple, guide us to connect with the spirits of the temple, guide new members, guide away those who might fit someplace else better, heal, protect and illuminate us, and radiate the magick and healing out into the world.

You don't even have to identify as a priestess or priest to be a keeper of the flame and to tend the light. While ancient Greece had the ruling Prytanis for the community flame, they also had the household kitchen shrines. I highly recommend keeping a sacred flame as a part of your own magickal and spiritual development. Simply obtain a long-lasting candle. I recommend the seven-day jar candles. To consecrate it ritually when you are not aligned with a specific magickal tradition that tends a flame, you can simply cleanse the candle in purifying incense smoke and water. Anoint it with a simple oil you consider holy. No carving or decorating is needed, though if you want to put something on it to designate it as special, you are welcome to do so. In our earliest temple candles, my mother wove a rainbow bundle of threads around the top of the glass jar, tying it with a ritual knot of intention for peace and healing in the world.

Align your three selves in the heart flame. Then light the altar temple candle from your heart flame with any prayer that seems appropriate for you, or modify this one:

I light this candle in honor of the Divine Powers
May you offer healing, blessing, and protection to all who may need
them
And to the world
For the Highest Good
So mote it be.

As a Witch, I might replace Divine Powers with Goddess and God, and from this point perform my altar devotionals, starting with something like "Please guide me on the crooked path with Love, Will, and Wisdom. Blessed be." Depending on your own traditions, beliefs, and experiences, your own version of the candle blessing will be different.

For those who are temple keepers, the prayer can be expanded for the specific community it serves to illuminate. Here is mine:

We light this candle in honor of the Gods and Spirits of our Temple
In the name of the Great Mother, The Weaver and the Web, the Soul of
the Cosmos
In the name of the Great Father, the Singer and the Song, the Keeper of
the Gates
In the name of the Child of Light filled with Love, Will and Wisdom
In the name of the Faery Courts, the Angels, the Creatures, Ancestors
and Mighty Dead,

May this flame offer light to all our members, granting blessings,
  healing and protection as needed.
May this flame guide those to us in harmony with our Work.
May this flame guide those away from us who are not in harmony, to
  find what they need.
So mote it be.

I keep my seven-day glass altar candle in an iron cauldron upon my main working altar, and light it when I rise in the morning and for as long as I'm home, and snuff it when I'm leaving or going to bed. Others like to use an oil lamp, where the flame is shielded by glass.

Our temple community keeps a perpetual candle in a glass and metal lantern, in the actual hearth of the temple. We tend to light a new candle from the flame of the old before it extinguishes itself. In both cases, we use these temple candles as the Master Candle for our other candle working.

In traditional Witchcraft and Wiccan lore, an elder maintaining traditions and passing them on is considered a "Keeper of the Flame" showing the metaphoric solidarity with the ancient hearth keepers. A beloved Craft elder, Lady Circe, who was a true Keeper of the Flame, known today because of beloved famous students such as Orion Foxwood keeping her name and teachings alive, is credited with teaching her students this deep wisdom on the light:

"We Witches are to lead mankind back to the light to save them from
  themselves. We are the guardians of humanity."

It's a grand notion and some would think it's arrogant. Most think of Witches as the outcasts of society, having no role within the greater whole, but she taught us that our purpose is grand. Outsiders are the regenerating principle within a system. Only those who have been cast out, destroyed, and reborn can bring that same revitalization and outside perspective to the whole. And worshipers of light-bearing gods, Lucifers, we are here to lead mankind back to the light. Think about this every time you light your sacred flame upon your altar. Think about it every time you light a candle in need or desire for yourself or another. Be a tender of the sacred flame, a keeper of the flame, and lead all the people of the world back to the light.

BIBLIOGRAPHY

Alvarado, Denise. *Voodoo Hoodoo Spell Book*. San Francisco, CA: Weiser Books, 2011.

Biasi, Jean-Louis de. *Rediscover the Magick of the Gods and Goddesses*. Woodbury, MN: Llewellyn Publications, 2014.

Buckland, Raymond. *The Fortune-Telling Book: the Encyclopedia of Divination and Soothsaying*. Canton, MI: Visible Ink Press, 2004.

Buckland, Raymond. *Practical Candleburning Rituals*. St. Paul, MN: Llewellyn Publications, 1970.

Cunningham, Scott. *Divination for Beginners: Reading the Past, Present & Future*. St. Paul, MN: Llewellyn Worldwide, 2003.

Crowther, Patricia. *Lid Off the Cauldron: A Wicca Handbook*. Capall Bann, Chieveley, Berks, 1981, 1998.

Grant, Ember. *Magical Candle Crafting*. Woodbury, MN: Llewellyn Publications, 2011.

Hey, Charmaine. *The Magic Candle*. Old Bethpage, NY: Original Publications, 1982.

Nema. *Maat Magick: A Guide to Self Initiation*. York Beach, ME: Weiser Books, 1995.

Pajeon, Kala & Ketz. *The Candle Magick Handbook*. New York, NY: Citadel Press Books, 1991.

Renee, Manina. *By Candlelight*. St. Paul, MN: Llewellyn Publications, 2014.

Silva, Katherine. *Fire Heart: The Life and Teachings of Maya Medicine Woman Miss Beatrice Torres Waight*. Self-Published, 2011.

Sir James George Frazer (1854–1941). *The Golden Bough*. New York, NY: Oxford Press, 1994.

Smith, Jacki. *Coventry Magic*. San Francisco, CA: Red Wheel/Weiser, 2011.

Swings-Christian, Curt R. *Candlemaking for Ritual Use*. Parsippany, NJ: Croc Press, 1997.

Vinci, Leo. *The Book of Practical Candle Magic.* Newburyport, MA: Red Wheel/Weiser, 1981 (Aquarian Press), 2005 (RWW).

Webster, Richard. *Candle Magic for Beginners.* St. Paul, MN: Llewellyn Publications, 2004.

Yronwode, Catherine and Mikhail Strabo. *The Art of Hoodoo Candle Magic.* Forestville, CA: Missionary Independent Spiritual Church, 2013.

Online Resources

Grimassi, Raven. *http://www.witchvox.com/va/dt_va.html? a=uscae&c=wordse&id=8522:* June 28th. 2004

Llewellyn.com. Rev Ray T. Malbrough *https://www.llewellyn.com/ author.php?author_id=2536:* June 26, 2017

http://candles.org/history/: January 13, 2017.

http://conjuredoctor.blogspot.com/2012/03/truth-about-road-opener-abre-camino.html: July 13, 2017

https://en.wikipedia.org/wiki/Altar_lamp: January 3, 2017

https://en.wikipedia.org/wiki/History_of_candle_making: January 13, 2017

https://en.wikipedia.org/wiki/Novena_to_Saint_Michael: Feb 8, 2017.

https://en.wikipedia.org/wiki/Prayer_to_Saint_Michael: Feb 8, 2017.

https://en.wikipedia.org/wiki/Pyromancy: June 27, 2017

https://en.wikipedia.org/wiki/Saint_Michael_in_the_Catholic_Church: Feb 8, 2017.

https://en.wikipedia.org/wiki/Sanctuary_lamp: January 3, 2017

http://hoodoorootworkconjure.yuku.com/topic/292/The-Holy-Guardian-Angel-and-the-Master-Candle.WJylrneZNE4: Feb 7, 2017.

http://realpagan.net/m/group/discussion?id=6330711%3ATopic%3A21644: Feb 7, 2017.

http://www.alleghenycandles.com/real-bayberry-candle.html: July 8, 2017

http://www.artofmanliness.com/2015/11/24/diy-chandlery-how-to-make-your-own-candles/: January 13, 2017.

http://www.buyacandle.com/shop_bayberrycandle.html: July 8, 2017

http://www.candlecauldron.com/burntimes.html: Feb 8, 2017.

https://www.creolemoon.com/road-opener.html: July 13, 2017

http://www.energymuse.com/blog/bayberry-candles/: July 8, 2017

ABOUT THE AUTHOR

Christopher Penczak is an award winning author, teacher and healing practitioner. As an advocate for the timeless perennial wisdom of the ages, he is rooted firmly in the traditions of modern witchcraft and Earth based religions, but draws from a wide range of spiritual traditions including shamanism, alchemy, herbalism, Theosophy and Hermetic Qabalah to forge his own magickal traditions. His many books include *Magick of Reiki, Spirit Allies, The Mystic Foundation* and *The Inner Temple of Witchcraft.* He is the co-founder of the Temple of Witchcraft tradition and not for profit religious organization to advance the spiritual traditions of witchcraft, as well as the co-founder of Copper Cauldron Publishing, a company dedicated to producing books, recordings and tools for magickal inspiration and evolution. He has been a faculty member of the North Eastern Institute of Whole Health and a founding member of The Gifts of Grace, an interfaith foundation dedicated to acts of community service, both based in New Hampshire. He maintains a teaching and healing practice in New England, but travels extensively lecturing. More information can be found at *www.christopherpenczak.com* and *www.templeofwitchcraft.org.*

The Temple of Witchcraft
MYSTERY SCHOOL AND SEMINARY

Witchcraft is a tradition of experience, and the best way to experience the path of the Witch is to actively train in its magickal and spiritual lessons. The Temple of Witchcraft provides a complete system of training and tradition, with four degrees found in the Mystery School for personal and magickal development and a fifth degree in the Seminary for the training of High Priestesses and High Priests interested in serving the gods, spirits, and community as ministers. Teachings are divided by degree into the Oracular, Fertility, Ecstatic, Gnostic, and Resurrection Mysteries. Training emphasizes the ability to look within, awaken your own gifts and abilities, and perform both lesser and greater magicks for your own evolution and the betterment of the world around you. The Temple of Witchcraft offers both in-person and online courses with direct teaching and mentorship. Classes use the *Temple of Witchcraft* series of books and CD Companions as primary texts, supplemented monthly with information from the Temple's Book of Shadows, MP3 recordings of lectures and meditations from our founders, social support through group discussion with classmates, and direct individual feedback from a mentor. For more information and current schedules, please visit: *www.templeofwitchcraft.org.*

The Lighting of Candles

CPSIA information can be obtained
at www.ICGtesting.com
Printed in the USA
LVHW061221250922
729163LV00014B/603

9 781940 755513